Lesbian Rule

I0129186

NEXT WAVE:

NEW DIRECTIONS

IN WOMEN'S STUDIES

A series edited by Inderpal

Grewal, Caren Kaplan,

and Robyn Wiegman

Lesbian Rule

CULTURAL CRITICISM AND

THE VALUE OF DESIRE

Amy Villarejo

Duke University Press

Durham and London

2003

Designed by Amy Ruth Buchanan
Typeset in Scala by Tseng
Information Systems, Inc.
Library of Congress Cataloging-
in-Publication Data appear on
the last printed page of this book.

*Publication of this book was made
possible by a subvention granted by the
Hull Memorial Publication Fund of
Cornell University.*

Contents

Acknowledgments

Though the faults of this book are my own, I owe thanks and give it with pleasure to a number of organizations, thinkers, makers, friends, and family members for their inspiration, support, advice, confidence, and care. Begun as a dissertation at the University of Pittsburgh, this project was supported there by a Mellon Foundation grant. Paul Bové read the dissertation carefully and remains a strong interlocutor in the book's implicit address; Colin MacCabe provided dual inspiration as an academic member of my committee but also as a resource for the issues of independent media and media education that are central to the present incarnation. Gayatri Chakravorty Spivak graciously agreed to remain on my committee from a distance; her care in reading closely instructs my own efforts constantly, and I depend on her thought in what follows.

Marcia Landy, who directed the dissertation from which this book springs, has been more than a teacher, an intellectual mentor, and a comrade. I hope what lies between these pages bears some trace of her questioning and relentless intellectual work. I remain simply grateful for her presence in my life.

While at Cornell, I have received generous grants from the President's Council on Cornell Women and from the Society for the Humanities. Production of this book was supported by the Hull Memorial Publication Fund of Cornell University. Faculty, staff, and student members of the newly named Program in Feminist, Gender and Sexuality Studies, the Lesbian Gay Bisexual Studies Program, and the Department of Theatre, Film, and Dance nurtured the project as well, and I am grateful to belong to these wonderfully different communities. Graduate and undergraduate students in all three areas have challenged me, but I owe particular thanks to my successive waves of undergraduates in my course on the history and theory of documentary and experimental film; they helped me enormously to redraw the context for this book.

I am also especially thankful to those makers and organizations who made their resources and time available to me: to Peggy Gilpin; to the offices of Ulrike Ottinger for gracious permission to reprint the images from *Exile Shanghai;* to the San Francisco Jewish Film Festival and Atara Releasing; to Frameline; to Women Make Movies; to the Lesbian Herstory Archives; to David Johnson for *Chained Girls* and *The Lavender Lens;* to Barbara Hammer for an encouraging word at the Persistent Vision conference; to Lynn Fernie for making *Forbidden Love* and for, with Ellen Flanders, organizing that conference; and to Ann Bannon for her reading and recollections. Thanks to Ellis Hanson and Duke University Press for publishing an earlier version of chapter 5 in *Out Takes*. Thanks also to Erik Rentschler, David Bathrick, and *New German Critique* for accepting a version of chapter three for publication.

From Pittsburgh onward, I have been submerged in a group of friends with whom thinking, hoisting beers, talking, playing, reading, and publishing have been indistinct activities, not only due to the beers but to the seamlessness of the knit. The group's boundaries remain permanently unclear, but here's a start: Joy Van Fuqua, Sally Meckling, Madhava Prasad, Anna McCarthy, Rich Cante, Angelo Restivo, Mary Beth Haralovich, Steven Cohan, Ina Rae Hark, Alex Doty, Cathy Davidson, Mimi White, Ann Cvetkovich, Tara McPherson, José Muñoz, Lynn Spigel, Patty White, Jody Greene, Debbie Zimmerman, Ruby Rich, Diana Reed, Kara Keeling, Jackie Byars, Eric Zinner, Tom Waugh, Vanessa Domico . . . In Ithaca, the overlapping set of my coconspirators includes Rebecca Schneider, David Bathrick, Patty Zimmermann, Gina Marchetti, Byron Suber, Tim Murray, Vincent Grenier, Biddy Martin, Ellis Hanson, and Mary Fessenden. Matthew Tinkcom belongs in the intersecting arcs of this Venn diagram; he alone knows how much I've leaned upon him, and I'd like him to know how much fun I have with him. Marcia and Stanley Shostak, are friends, and friends who ask all the hard questions. I thank them for that, for countless evenings around the plexiglass table and for their companionship.

Ken Wissoker showed interest in this project early on, and his faith in its growth sustained me during the revision process. As I have come to know him as an editor, I have also been honored by his friendship and have come to rely on his judgment and insight. The anonymous readers of the manuscript while in still in dissertation form gave me the gifts of serious consideration and rigorous criticism; I could not have had better readers and better suggestions. Also at Duke, Christine Dahlin and Leigh Anne Couch guided me through the production process with care and grace.

My parents, Don and Merna Villarejo, are also models of being-in-the-world for me; their commitment to change, their sense of responsibility in thinking, and their skills at playing hard set the bar high. I thank them for the figurative and real fuel over the past ten years especially. Finally, there is no way to describe my gratitude and love for Andrea Hammer, with whom I am accumulating years in the forward as well as the backward direction, who made of a house on an unfamiliar spit of land a home in which to finish this book, who daily makes life a joy, and who makes *being* an activity for two. (Or five—thanks to all the critters, Slash, Taag, and the late Quince for additional cuddles.)

Lesbian rule: a mason's rule made of lead, which could be bent to fit the curves of a molding (Aristotle, *Eth. Nic.* v. x. 7); hence, *fig.*, a principle of judgment that is pliant and accommodating. — *Oxford English Dictionary*

In college and in the years just after, I frequented a lesbian bar called Hepburn's. Named obviously after Katharine, the bar was decorated with production-still enlargements of Hepburn's face. Teeny pads of lavender paper, with a discreet *Hepburn's* across the top, sat in old-fashioned glasses alongside miniature pencils, ready for the exchange of phone numbers and note-taking. (On reflection it appears that I did more of the latter than the former.) On one of those pads, about ten years ago, I wrote "Sylvia Scarlett. Why lesbian?"

Most of the photographs in that bar featured Hepburn in her famous cross-dressing role in the 1935 film *Sylvia Scarlett*, directed by the gay and extraordinary George Cukor. With hair slicked back and shirt collar framing her young patrician face, Hepburn's image as a dashing boy clearly excited a lesbian reading, set *lesbian* somehow reverberating. Hepburn's — the bar — borrowed the image and also those excitations, that indeterminate allure, for its own. In some ways, it made perfect sense: the bar was in Philadelphia, a city identified with Hepburn not only through a later George Cukor film in which she starred, *The Philadelphia Story* (1940), but also through Hepburn's time spent near Philadelphia at Bryn Mawr College, as I was. Like other Cukor films and indeed like other films in which women disguised themselves as boys or men, *Sylvia Scarlett* offered a beautiful orchestration of inversion, a playful romp along the lines of gender and sexual difference, with the bonus attractions of chiseled stars and high production values. *Sylvia Scarlett*, like the bar itself, nestles into what Judith Mayne reminds us is a liminal space, oscillating between visibility and invisibility, wherein we find ourselves secretly knowing that to which others remain oblivious.[1]

Figure 1. Katharine Hepburn, dressed as a young boy for her role in *Sylvia Scarlett*, is caught by a mirror next to costar Cary Grant. Gay director George Cukor leans in. Courtesy of Photofest.

Call it what you will, "gaydar," recognition, or identification remains one of the most elusive, and therefore provocative, procedures of modern queer life. Founded on vision, but suggesting, through the reference to radar, something that flies beneath the visible or the screen, this procedure nonetheless falters before the demands of visual evidence. There is, in other words, no final ground upon which one can determine why that photograph of Katharine Hepburn signifies lesbian, why a cross-dressing Hollywood fantasy such as *Sylvia Scarlett,* or more famously in lesbian theory, Garbo's *Queen Christina,* edges into a collective consciousness as a "lesbian" narrative.[2] While an image or a film may rely on historical cues or, defying the heavy hands of film censors, hint at what some might call a lesbian subtext, there remains no ultimate certainty with which one can pronounce the content of that image or film lesbian. Instead, something in a context allows viewers to produce a ground for their readings, to make an image or narrative work as "lesbian" even, sometimes, against the will of those who created it. The lesbian bar called Hepburn's, in fact, took a name that quite literally belongs to someone else and someone quite singular, borrowing her image and setting into motion a set of vibrations. About this I then had one question that pressed ultimately into priority: what did Katharine Hepburn *herself* think of the fact that a bunch of Philadelphia lesbians had made her proper name into a sustaining configuration of lesbian life, all based on a wacky film role a half-century earlier? Had she some insight, from within the belly of the beast that is moviemaking, into her own image, persona, allure? How did she understand her own name as a commodity, now pirated by a lesbian bar?

I asked her. In a carefully worded but altogether too long letter, I asked her whether she was interested in the mobility of that role, these processes of detachment and appropriation in the name and cause of lesbian visibility and community. Her response, characteristically Hepburn, is the impetus for this book. I quote it in full and thank her for the kindness of a reply:

Dear Amy Villarejo,
I'm sorry—I can't answer those questions—I'm really too busy to understand why anyone would want them answered—Good Luck—

A double dismissal: not only is *she* too busy to answer my questions, but she's too busy to understand why *anyone* (read, in her right mind) would want them answered! The central terms of the argument of *Lesbian Rule* take precisely this "anyone" as my interlocutor. I hope to begin to con-

Figure 2. Boyish Katharine Hepburn, in a promotional
still for *Sylvia Scarlett*. Courtesy of Photofest.

vince such an "anyone" by the end of this book that the first question
we should ask about visibility, about making lesbians appear, is this: at
what cost?

Lesbian Rule

This book takes *lesbian* as a modifier, not as a noun but as an adjective,
examining three conceivably lesbian modifications of a noun's province:
lesbian people, lesbian places, and lesbian things. I like that dimension
of rote involved in the grammatical breakdown of a noun, the commonplace and commonsensical repetition of people, place, and thing modi-
fied with a lesbian inflection or provenance; for that reason, my emphasis
is less on other categories that would be equally descriptive of the book's
focus: lesbian texts, for example, or lesbian scenes, or lesbian commodi-

ties. The book is, throughout, centrally concerned with the politics of lesbian appearance; it takes as its predominant objects of analysis non-fiction, rather than narrative, films. As a study of the politics of lesbian appearance, it sits at the intersection of queer theory, feminist theory, cinema studies, and cultural studies, but it likely straddles these domains uncomfortably, insofar as each brings its own history, questions, and paradigms.

As the epigraph indicates, the phrase *lesbian rule* appears in Aristotle's *Nicomachean Ethics* to describe, by figuration, an ethical principle, a principle of pliancy in judgment. Between the thing itself, the mason's rule, and the figurative meaning, elasticity in judgment, there is a material connection: the malleable nature of lead, which can be bent. By contrast, the noun *lesbian* is currently used to reference two states of being between which there is no material connection, except, of course, that being who is the referent of the term. The word attempts to manage two meanings: both the ontological state of simply being a lesbian, whatever that might come to mean, and an ethicopolitical state wherein lesbian designates something like a progressive, emancipatory, or liberatory politics. It cannot manage them both entirely successfully. When lesbian becomes (an) image, it fares even less well at containing the slippages between meanings.

Even when two words exist to designate the ontological domain and the related ethicopolitical one, such as *woman* and *feminist,* there are no firm grounds for deriving the latter from the former. In two examples from different idioms with significantly consonant aims, both Denise Riley and Judith Butler have urged us to reconsider the priority of ontology, opening *woman* to an expressive, expansive, and permanently unbounded collectivity and thereby understanding *feminist* as an itinerary determined genealogically rather than programmatically.[3] In the wake of their work, scholars have come to think that there is no confident way of predicting *how* gender will be consolidated in the service of regulatory mechanisms in any given place or moment. What is certain is that it *will,* and, further, that it will do so vociferously to uphold the force of compulsory heterosexuality. Enmeshed in the social relations produced and reproduced through capitalist exploitation, themselves racialized and split according to the international division of labor, gender is a lived experience understood only by cleaving it from a larger matrix. Severing gender from that matrix allows for the possibility of understanding its particularity, and yet the context—what a poststructuralist might call the text in the general sense—makes the abstraction possible. To understand the relationship between *woman* and *feminist,* therefore, is to grapple with the contradictory and uneven, material and psychic, deployment of gender binarism in the service of heteronormativity, and in the perpetuation of distinct social relations.

Despite the imbrication of the name *woman* with the ethicopolitical projects—for there are many—of feminism, feminist theory relies on the rigorous separation of these two categories, even if that separation suspends or displaces the ontological question of what a woman is. For one of the central and necessary preoccupations of feminist inquiry is, of course, the disjunction between woman and feminist: why are all women *not* feminists? Why do some women not endorse the very political program that would seek to redress or undo their own repression? The measure of that distance between woman and feminist propels, for example, Marxist feminist inquiry into material, historical, and ideological explanations for the disjunction, and psychoanalytic feminist inquiry into the mechanisms of desire and power that would explain the reproduction of subordination to a patriarchal law. The noncoincidence of the category and the political program similarly acts as the motor for the radical deconstruction, decentering, historicization, or suspension of both terms, *woman* and *feminist.*

Notwithstanding the very real question—set in motion by Monique Wittig—of whether lesbians are women, and the further question of what might or ought to be the relationship between the study of gender and the study of sexuality, I here am isolating a relationship of analogy: how are we to mark, much less measure, a disjunction between ontology and politics in the case of *lesbian,* in the absence of a separate word for each position? When or why do we need to do so? The bulk of this book is devoted to the argument that when lesbian appears, her appearance functions as a substitute or as a cover for the very distinction I think we need collectively to make between who or what we *are* (into what we are inserted) and what we want to *become* (how we may change that which we confront). Far from functioning simply as a liberating symbol, a positive image, or an object of desire, I argue that lesbian appearance simultaneously conceals the very relationship between sexual difference and social relations that would allow us to generate a politics *of* that difference. The demand to make lesbians visible, whether as ammunition for anti-homophobic campaigns or as figures for identification, renders lesbian static, makes lesbian into (an) image, and forestalls any examination of lesbian within context.

Lesbian Rule, therefore, seeks to restore that context. I seek to understand what happens in the production and circulation of lesbian — not to claim that lesbian encodes some other master narrative but to open lesbian to a dense and uneven complex of perception and expression, labor and production, consumption and reception, bodily and sexual practices, habits of mind and reading, class differentiations and racialized positions, industrial effects, national locations, movement and stasis, and hence organizations of time and space. In order to show how such an opening takes place, and in order to explain what kinds of texts best facilitate such an opening, I turn to several initial definitional, contextual, and methodological issues raised by such a study: first, the significance of the terms I have chosen for my title — lesbian, cultural criticism, value, and desire — then two larger paradoxes on which the study of lesbian here turns.

Terminology: Lesbian, Value, Desire

If the term *lesbian* is in its final hours, slowly to be overtaken by the term *queer,* let this book then stand as an elegy to it. But I suspect for several reasons that its days, even perhaps its years, are not yet numbered. First, it has crept into national culture and commodity culture. Lesbian murderers, lesbian chic, lesbian books, lesbian videos, lesbian cruises, lesbian s/m, lesbian erotica, lesbian comedians, lesbian athletes, lesbian photographs, and lesbian jewelry: all of these sustain existences beyond the confines of subcultural definition and most certainly beyond the restricted borders of academic scrutiny. They are available, and they circulate, as Lisa Duggan has shown beautifully by way of example in her historical investigation of the lesbian love-murder story.[4] While *lesbian* is sometimes subsumed by the term *queer* or coupled with the term *gay,* within the logic of commodity culture it functions more powerfully to describe a niche market and therefore enjoys a quasi-autonomous status.[5] This status is, in fact, enjoined by the specific practices of cinema. To pay attention to commodity culture is certainly not to accept its terms uncritically, but when even Martha Stewart knows that "space is a commodity" (as she told me in a recent e-mail from Martha Stewart Omnimedia), it becomes all the more imperative to know the terms and the logics of one's objects of study, not to assume that they are naive or altogether removed from the critical languages of the academy.

Second, and more theoretically significant, *lesbian* stands as reminder of the dense and richly complicated site that sexuality is and has been. To the extent that sexuality has a history, *lesbian* as a name for a particular pathology certainly partakes of that nineteenth-century "banal" invention that Michel Foucault began to elaborate and that is at the center of much of queer theory.[6] *Lesbian* names a set of inheritances from more recent moments, as well, including the legacies of the lesbian-feminist movements, with which I came of age, of the past quarter century. In the name of *lesbian* inherited from those movements, a vibrant sphere of cultural and artistic production flourishes despite the extent to which that sphere has morphed from its original incarnations. What used to be called "women's music," for example, thrives now under the banner of the singer-songwriter. At the same time, lesbianism remains subject to violent erasure and abjection by cultures driven by homophobia and misogyny, including nominally progressive and queer ones. In this regard, I echo Biddy Martin's concern that plain old-fashioned misogyny and queer vanguardism alike can share an implicit disdain for femininity "played straight," whereby "something called femininity becomes the tacit ground in relation to which other positions become figural and mobile."[7] Against the force of its erasure, I want to mark *lesbian*'s resonance, history, and richness.

The third reason to retain the term *lesbian* is to subject it to the kind of rigorous treatment it deserves, pushing at the extent to which we can work its specificity and limits from within. I am taken, toward these ends, by Peggy Phelan's provocative reading of *Silverlake Life*, wherein she is after what may be a "specific form of lesbian interpellation, a way of addressing both implicitly and explicitly those who don't appear in the visual field of the cultural imaginary."[8] While Phelan's angle of inquiry into cinema through psychoanalysis differs from my own (as I discuss briefly below regarding the term *desire*), and while her performative intimacy inhabits an idiom distinct from my own perhaps more sober style, I am drawn to explore what might be undertaken in the name of the exclusion she notices and to probe the exceptions to that exclusion, those lesbians who only appear as rigorously as possible within the name *lesbian*.

Phelan's essay, like all the best writing on culture, does not take gay life as an object for reflection without interrogating the proximate and urgent stakes of such reflection. It is, in other words, engaged intellectual work, linking the self to the process of study, linking one's own political and intellectual investments to the writing-work of cultural criticism. While I happen to be of the opinion that very few authors of academic monographs successfully sustain that fragile balance between autobiography and critical argument, I do find useful those deictic gestures that disclose the production of the value of a given work. Why study *this* film, or *that* concept? Why frame the question *that* way? What is the function of *this* critical lineage? The more clearly one lays out the stakes of a given inquiry—the value of the study undertaken—the more one might avoid the twin dangers of taking the self as an adequate measure of the readership and, more perilously, of the topic at hand. Sometimes, too, it makes a potential political difference to use the terms *we* or *our*, rather than lurk consistently behind the ostensible objectivity of *one*. When I want to foreground an idea of belonging, then, I use *we*, although I recognize that such prescriptive collectivities might immediately arouse readerly suspicion.

As many cultural critics confront the stakes of their own work, I have not resolved the tension between the modernist hope for engaged criticism and poststructuralist protocols of reading. To live within this tension is to place emphasis on the *transformations* of key terms and ideas as they move, to uncover lineages but also to leave open the destinations. The concept of value partakes of a modernist lineage through Marxism, a tie I want to retain. Seeking to avoid mechanistic understandings of modernity and postmodernism, I emphasize instead transformations in the culture industry, its strategies for consolidating hegemony, postwar shifts in the contours of the family involving new sites of social control, and changes in the very modes of thinking about representation and its limits. In the face of these shifts, it nonetheless remains important, to my mind, to summon the language of a Marxist lineage against idealism, against linear rather than dialectical thinking, against anti-intellectualism, and against the twin foes of liberalism and conservatism. In addition to a long line of writers and thinkers including Marx and Engels, Antonio Gramsci, and Raymond Williams, Marxism invokes a history of struggle that I don't want to forfeit by distancing myself from it for reasons of its actual failure in the collapse of the Soviet Union and Eastern European Communism, or its latent or even fully obvious theoretical and historical stumbling blocks. If Marxism can be embraced without the baggage of unquestioned fidelity, the bashing or poststructuralism or the pious invocation of realpolitik, I seek to embrace it, and not simply when I examine documentaries about China and Cuba.[9]

All of these qualifiers, notwithstanding proliferating debates regarding neo- and post-Marxism, signal the perils of retaining a paradigm, program, or model out of fidelity, but the conceptual and political power of Marxism and the abstraction that is "value" remain for me undiminished. For Marx, of course, value is that "contentless and simple" abstraction that makes possible his analysis of the system, beginning with an analysis of the commodity form. Through "value," Marx finds his way to use and to exchange, and to the fundamental ruse of capitalist exploitation: the extraction of surplus value through the exchange of wages for labor power. While *value* is not the sole privileged term or master term of all of the analyses in the present book, it does inform this study of the politics of lesbian appearance in several ways.

First, value is everywhere operative, if almost everywhere concealed. Cinema, an industrial art of the highest order, requires the labor of a massive number of individuals whose contributions hide beneath the singular authorial, directorial signature and whose labors are, moreover, naturalized through the conventions of the narrative cinema. One of the preconditions of stardom, for example that of Katharine Hepburn, is that the labors of makeup artists and hairstylists, acting coaches and speech therapists, appear to be organic features of the star's glamorous persona. The organization and division of labor necessary to the production of commercial cinema are staggering barriers to the analysis of cinema as anything other than text, and few critics surmount them. Production files, union regulations, intellectual property laws, merchandising agreements, much less the labyrinthine circuits of distribution and exhibition — all of these can yield knowledge about the specific form of commodity-production that is the commercial cinema, and scholars who do take on the challenges of contextual analysis are slowly chipping away at the limits of textual and formal analysis, given the youth of the discipline of film studies. And while a few scholars tackle the production of lesbians in narrative cinema, popular cultural historians writing for a wider readership have mined the rich terrain of gossip and innuendo central to Hollywood in search of the backstories of lesbian lives, as Diana McLellan has done, for example, in her saucy book, *The Girls: Sappho Goes to Hollywood*.[10] On both scholarly and more popular registers, historians of cinematic lesbians confront complicated questions inherent to the commercial narrative cinema.

Rather than take as my object the dominant cinema shorthanded as Hollywood, I am here predominantly interested in documentary, or nonfiction, film, and specifically lesbian documentary of the past forty-odd years.[11] Not only are documentary film's channels of production, distribution, and exhibition more available to exploration than those of the commercial narrative cinema, but its raison d'être is not, ultimately, profit. Historically, then, the films I examine are more tied to the European art cinema, the feminist counter-cinema of the past quarter century, and the recent queer cinema than to commercial narrative cinema; the institutions thereby associated with these films tend to be dinosaurs of alternative public cultures such as the museum, the film festival, the not-for-profit distributor, the women's bookstore, and the Unitarian church basement. Underfunded and under attack, these institutions should not, however, be seen as severed from the apparatuses of the film industry. Like these institutions, lesbian documentary serves distinct social and rhetorical purposes within the context of dominant cinema: to express lesbian's autonomous forms, to record lesbian's history, to promote lesbian's visibility.[12]

Visibility most of all, for it seems that it is on the terrain of the visible that gender binarism is most strictly enforced. At the same time, one tends to rely most heavily on visual cues to extrapolate sexual difference from gender presentation, so that one can read Hepburn or Garbo in trousers as lesbian. Although many have long marked the tyrannical companionship between gender and sexuality, gay and lesbian and queer peoples have not fought hard politically to delink gender codes and sexual orientation, although queer and transgender politics have incipient potential and the right to insist upon such a cleavage. Rather, it has been crucial to gay and lesbian history to solidify a certain guarantee: that the visual evidence of cross-dressing in the past, say, means that there were gays and lesbians "just like us" then, or enough like "us" to ensure that we, too, will survive.[13] In gay humor, in art, in rituals, and in everyday lives, there is a certain common-sense knowingness about appearance. While documentary cinema depends upon this common sense, it also has the potential to challenge it.

Narrative cinema also does much to conceal the intersubjective nature of the right to look—the fact that one is always looking from somewhere and that one has received some prior authorization to look. This constellation is social and individual, scripted by the determinations of collective life and the vagaries of conscious and unconscious structures.

Figure 3. Garbo in drag, with costar John Gilbert in *Queen Christina*. Courtesy of Photofest.

Made invisible by the darkness of the theater, or rendered part of a mass by the trajectory of the commodity, the spectator and the consumer, respectively, become instead empty generalized subject-positions or placeholders for what one might want to term "actual viewers." Rather than attempt from the opposite direction to begin with the actual viewer, as an ethnographer might, I turn to documentary cinema in the spirit of Roland Barthes' observation that the image and the actual are, in fact, co-constituted: if not one and the same, then the one an "emanation" of the other. For it is photography's essence, claims Barthes in *Camera Lucida*, that the referent of the photograph adheres to it.[14] To call something a documentary is to make an appeal, however mediated and contingent, to a pre-filmic referent, the real, not necessarily in terms opposed entirely to fiction but instead in terms that displace that facile opposition. As Linda Williams puts it:

> Truth is "not guaranteed" and cannot be transparently reflected by a mirror with a memory, yet some kinds of partial and contingent truths are nevertheless the always receding goal of the documentary

Figure 4. The queen of queer Hollywood: Greta Garbo in *Queen Christina*. Courtesy of Photofest.

tradition. Instead of careening between idealistic faith in documentary truth and cynical recourse to fiction, we do better to define documentary not as an essence of truth but as a set of truths. The advantage, and the difficulty, of the definition is that it holds to the concept of the real—indeed, of a "real" at all—even in the face of tendencies to assimilate documentary entirely into the rules and norms of fiction.[15]

As Barthes notes similarly with regard to the shock photo, the horror derives not from the representation of the calamity but instead from "the fact that *we are looking at it* from inside our freedom."[16] Like the genre of the shock photo, documentary cinema confronts the paradox whereby the filmmaker runs the risk of overconstructing the scene before its spectators, substituting himself for the spectator, as Barthes says, in the formation of his subject, dispossessing him thereby of his judgment. And like the genre of the shock photo, documentary cinema derives much of its power precisely from the intersubjective encounter it structures and seeks not to overcode. In many ways, I think, documentary work has less in common with popular narrative cinema and more in common with the gazes one permits or denies oneself in daily encounters with people and their bodies: at extremes of size or ornamentation, at the differently figured or at the indeterminately gendered. Looking at the other from inside one's normativeness or from the outside as solidarity: either gesture relies upon the authorization to look *and* to narrate, to assume something about the other based upon what one knows of oneself. This is inevitable, perhaps even mundane, but rarely explored, as this book seeks to do, in terms of what cinema itself makes possible of such actions and knowledge.

Value, then, also involves the value of desire: the deployment from *within* a point of view of the cinematic lesbian *toward* some goal of social inclusion, justice, political representation, or historical project. Partaking of a felicitous slide between two senses of the word representation (the sense of portrait and the sense of proxy), the common sense of visibility is that it does both: by appearing, so it would go, we belong. To promote portraits of lesbian lives is to promote representational presence in public culture and therefore heightened public authority. And yet, I argue, to present lesbian as image is to arrest the dynamism such a signifier can trigger, as well as to require some conception of politics, or the social, on behalf of which lesbian is thought to intervene as image. What visibility misses, in other words, is mobility: not mechanistic assimilation to the status quo but complex systems of judgment, intervention, the exchange of services and bodies, uncritical as well as critical adherence to tradition, stylizations of self and surroundings and the like that constitute being lesbian and appearing as lesbian. Surely it is true that the production of cultural intelligibility and legitimacy requires the making-visible of political subjects, and just as surely it is true that visibility does not function as the theoretical subject's predication. Competing determinations structure the visible *and* invisible traces of descent deposited in subjects, and sexuality or lesbian identity may or may not be the signs under which one finds oneself emerging as social actor or consigned to abjection. As I suggested above, and it bears repeating, I am after the *slide* between the two senses of representation in this book, and I am stunned by the mobility I see at work in the lesbian cinema.

Documentary film provides the most congenial ground for investigating the politics of lesbian appearance simply because its apparatus is more available to contextual analysis and its representation codes yield their rhetorical stakes more clearly. Documentary cinema also, however, makes the most straightforward claims about the value of desire: lesbian needn't be derived from a reading "against the grain" of the film or by "decoding" a film's subtext, and the critic needn't legitimate or defend such knotted reading practices. Lesbian is right there, staring at you, haranguing you, imploring you, or telling you stories. The politics are, as a professor once said to a student eager to "read" politics in recent British film, *in the films*. As I will however suggest in analysis of documentary films, what distinguishes exciting lesbian work on cinema is its ecumenical treatment of form. Most of the academic books on lesbian reading or spectatorship (such as those by Judith Mayne and Patricia White) move necessarily and comfortably from Hollywood to the European art cinema to experimental film in order to develop flexible paradigms for the analysis of lesbian appearance. While my studies of documentary films pay close attention to the conventions of that form, draw upon critical work in documentary cinema, and examine the particular circumstances of documentary production, distribution, and exhibition, my readings nonetheless are located within the traffic in other forms not even cinematic and otherwise. If value sets things moving, one needs to be critically agile rather than restricted to sometimes constraining disciplinary divisions. (My sense of the value of examining documentary alongside, for example, experimental film comes most palpably from teaching European and Soviet cinema of the twenties and thirties, where the terms fail to capture the connections between Eisenstein and Vigo, or Ruttmann and Ivens, or Leger and Delluc.) Documentary cinema has also been most agile in its own treatment of lesbian lives, as well as lesbian desire.

Sex, sexuality, the erotic, the amorous, affect, emotion, desire: all of these are or could be condensed in the term *lesbian,* and while it would be foolish, if not churlish, to insist on their separation from one another or from *lesbian,* it would be equally mistaken to allow them to function as they often do as equivalent terms. As Butler argues, if sex (the designation of male/female) is an effect rather than the ground of gender, gender is not itself a substantive noun but an effect constrained by a grammar of regulated modification: gender is the effect of repetition within constraint, performatively produced. The regulatory apparatus follows a binary logic (masculine/feminine) that would also appear to produce sexuality along binary poles (heterosexuality/homosexuality), but both gender and sexuality appear as binary *because* they are produced within constraint. Following Butler's *Gender Trouble* and readings of it, I take gender to designate an apparatus of production, the means by which sex is established as a neutral, prediscursive, or natural ground for cultural inscription. Sexuality can be seen as an apparatus of the production of naturalized identity: one's "own" sexuality. Through the machine processing of mobile desire into fixed, binary positions, sexuality also conceals the extent to which one achieves such a subject-position through subjection to the very law of regulation. If gender and sexuality, then, can be seen as grammatical effects rather than as substantive nouns—and I do take it as my starting point that this is a convincing theoretical frame—it becomes even more difficult to situate them in relation to those domains of feeling and experience that seem grounded in bodies and desires such as emotion and affect, sex, and the erotic. I understand Butler's work and much of what has followed *Gender Trouble* to elaborate these fragile and necessary connections.[17]

Indeed, it seems important, given the mutual interdependence and reference of these domains indexed by the term *lesbian,* to signal whenever possible how and why one privileges one sense of it above or below another. In my own critical inventory, the term *lesbian* remains permanently open and insubstantial, modifying rather than designating. Affect, emotion, and desire, on the other hand, function rather differently. Affect used in the general sense, as opposed to isolating specific affects such as shame, opposes itself to reason by designating a disposition or feeling that eludes reason's grasp. In this sense, affect becomes a useful way of designating that which is in excess of a rational deliberative scheme and can function as a synonym for desire, insofar as that term involves the feeling of longing, inchoate and propulsive. If emotion domesticates affect, it also carries with it a responsive, intersubjective sense that any single affect does not: shame might be an effect of the process of queer subjection, identity construction, while anger is an emotional response to acts of hatred directed toward queers. Both affect and emotion find systematization in hegemonic discourses such as romantic love. Both affect and emotion are coded clearly in dominant narrative cinema, which system is, of course, a fine vehicle but not a seamless one for hegemonic values. The close-up, as Deleuze has noted, produces faciality as the surface for affectivity's disclosure and exploration, while melodrama is a privileged idiom for transcoding social conflict into emotional binarism.[18] In documentary cinema, the role of the close-up remains crucial in disclosing affect. Narration, in the general sense of a film's mode of organizing its story as well as in the more narrow sense of a spoken guide, helps us locate a film's emotional tones. While the syntax differs from the conventions of narrative cinema, documentary is no less agile in its invocation and manipulation of feeling than its narrative counterpart.

Desire is, finally, that term which returns me to psychoanalysis. My treatment of Freud and Lacan is neither systematic nor comprehensive, but that warning should not be taken to mean that these figures are nowhere important. It is, I think, impossible *not* to follow psychoanalysis into, say, the gaze, the fetish, and forms of prohibition more generally. I am, moreover, particularly galvanized by that rare work that puts psychoanalytic theory and clinical practice into conversation with one another, and with work that sees psychoanalytic theory as explosive, generative, expansive.[19] In the context of examining the relationship between psychoanalysis and race, Hortense Spillers condenses a list of eight topics psychoanalysis crucially raises, a list I find sharp and suggestive.

> (1) self-division; (2) the mimetic and transitive character of desire; (3) the economies of displacement—associative and disjunctive; (4) the paradox of the life-death pull; (5) the tragic elements couched in the transfer of social powers from one generation of historical actors to another; (6) the preeminent distinctions that attach to the "Twin Towers" of human social being—"Mama" and "Papa" . . . ; (7) the "paradox of the negative," or the sign's power to designate by negation; and (8) the special relationship that adheres between exile and writing.[20]

What prompts me, above all, to emphasize the term *desire* above some other possibilities is a social transcoding of the fourth term in Spillers's list, that vexing question with which I began this discussion of the idea of lesbian rule: why is it that some women do not become feminists? That is, what leads some to act against their own interests, to long for their own destruction? One version of that question is that with which Eve Sedgwick begins her essay, "How to Bring Your Kids Up Gay," by invoking the haunting knowledge of gay teen suicide.[21] She asks, why pursue a life in which one is sure to meet with shame and with hatred, with abjection and with stinging solitude? Another version: what are the dangers of assuming that lesbians desire differently? Or that there is such a thing as lesbian desire? Desire in this sense is another name for distinction: for being special, chosen, or worthy in a lineage of fierce survivors. Like many queer people, I turn to the movies for their fantasies and for escape as much as for realist portraits of survivors and kin; I turn to documentaries to confirm that I *can* know and *can* be in the face of much evidence to the contrary. The life-death pull, as Spillers describes it, designates that propulsive force of desire, that which compels us toward the other and also toward life itself. While it can seem to have some specific content or shape—as in lesbian desire—it remains elusive, unpredictable, and capricious.

As a result of its elusiveness, one cannot speak easily or accurately about lesbian desire, even as cinema depends on representing it. *Desire,* as one name for what the term *lesbian* can suggest, nonetheless has no determinate value even as it propels us. What is the value of desire? It has no particular value, it cannot be assigned a definite value, and yet I shall argue that we nonetheless move with it. At the same time, the majority of scholarly projects undertaken under the sign of lesbian assume an emancipatory or liberatory effect, regardless of the extent to which they are able to specify in what particular way or definite mode they contribute to an emancipatory itinerary, however designated. To offer a comparison, when not saturated in the attempt to be incendiary, Paul Gilroy starts to work the cracks of a similar paradox in his book *Against Race,* in which he begins to notice, for example, the complicity between some versions of black nationalism and fascism. In his case, such recognition requires him no longer to assume in advance the emancipatory value of projects undertaken under the sign of blackness, but *at the same time* not to assume that the sign of blackness will disclose emancipatory projects in the forms we expect (i.e., desire can torque them into new formations such as gangsta rap) or in the forms we, as it were, desire (our own longings may be retrograde or historically outmoded).[22] He is thus caught arguing "against race" by taking it up incessantly, as I, too, will do with the sign lesbian.

The second paradox I discuss is more properly a contradiction. I lend the name *lesbian rule* to a provisional politics of the difference "lesbian" might make, even while I shall argue in subsequent chapters that *lesbian* is best understood as a "catachresis," a metaphor without an adequate referent. With an always inadequate referent, *lesbian* by definition disappears, or will in advance be an evanescent ethical subject of politics. My definitional stance, as it is elaborated especially in the first two chapters, precludes the task of the following chapters: tracing lesbian visibility as an object that can be known.[23]

The first paradox, that the value of desire cannot be calculated, and the second contradiction, the impossible derivation of a politics from a catachrestical name, structure the readings that follow. I try to make the sense of being caught productive by tracing context carefully; the alternative is to finesse the contradiction in order to make it disappear temporarily. Here is a familiar example using a "based-on-a-true-story" documentary nexus that illustrates in a mini-reading the cost of lesbian visibility, even while we cannot *not* work with or embrace its possibilities: the story of Brandon Teena.

Brandon Teena: An Example

The film *Boys Don't Cry* (Peirce 1999) is not the only text to tackle the Brandon Teena story, a story that goes something like this: "Brandon Teena was born Teena Brandon in Lincoln, Nebraska. When she decides that she is really a male, she changes her name and, at age twenty, moves to nearby Falls City. As Brandon, he begins dating several girls who find him thoughtful and charming, but when word gets out that he is a she, Brandon is brutally raped and, a week later, on New Year's Eve, is murdered." That synopsis comes from the publicity materials from the 1998 feature-length documentary *The Brandon Teena Story*, made with $350,000 by Susan Muska and Gréta Ólafsdottir. Made before *The Brandon Teena Story*, Alisa Lebow's short, low-budget/no-budget documentary on transgender activist and author Leslie Feinberg, *Outlaw*, mourns the death of Brandon Teena alongside that of the infamous Greenwich Village drag queen and Stonewaller, Marcia Johnston. These texts all belong, in important ways, to the queer cinema; remarkably, all of the filmmakers are out lesbians, and they participate in a politicized queer media culture in New York City. In other words, one could rightly imagine that these films resemble one another more in tone and in their stakes than they resemble the daytime television talk shows that have addressed the Brandon Teena murder, or the nineteen-page *New Yorker* story in 1997 on the Brandon Teena case, or Shu Lea Chang's interactive installation on Brandon Teena at the Guggenheim Museum.

To ask a very limited question of these films, then—how do these projects, in ways associated both with lesbian and queer nominations, think about the place or the scene of Brandon Teena's story, the American heartland? The *New York Times,* in Stephen Holden's review of the *Brandon Teena Story*, refers to the case "that encapsulates the deep-seated fears about gender and sexuality harbored by millions of Americans, especially those living in the heartland."[24] One might chalk up such a displacement—from sophisticated city folk to heartland bigots, from the

blue-for-Gore to red-for-Bush on those election maps—to *Times* paro-
chialism. But here are the filmmakers themselves: "[The people involved
in the Brandon Teena case] are coming from an area that is not cutting-
edge, postmodern. We're an informed audience as far as transgender and
gender issues, but most people in America are not."[25]

Such rhetoric amplifies the distinction between us and them. It marks
the place of the film's enunciation as theoretically sophisticated by ap-
propriating the buzzwords of the academic humanities to shore up authority. By contrast, the American people are understood to be naive and
uninformed, against spectators' assumptions that it may be the job of
the documentary to educate them. It is not. The visual language of the
film confirms rather than disturbs the division between insider and out-
sider, the knowing and the clueless. The filmmakers' car window constantly frames the bleak Nebraska landscape and enforces their point of
view, while the various interviewees fidget nervously in the filmmakers'
presence. The reverse shots of the two urban women filmmakers further underscore their difference in appearance from the awkward Mid-
western participants in the life-world of Brandon Teena. Finally, when
a group of activists from the political group Transsexual Menace appear at the local courthouse, the cleavage between the urban outsiders
and the incredulous townies becomes unmanageable, bursting from the
film's seams and dampening whatever pedagogical force the documentary might have sought in its earlier moments, or whatever education
Transsexual Menace may actually have effected in its activities. In whose
name does the film thus condescend? In the name of what emancipatory
project does it paint the radicals against the dummies?

Boys Don't Cry departs from the condescension many have noticed in
the *Brandon Teena Story* in several ways: in its derealization of the landscape, in its nocturnal prowl, in Peirce's control over character in her
careful script and stunning direction of Hilary Swank in the role of Brandon Teena, and, most importantly, in the proximity *Boys Don't Cry* takes
to Brandon's obvious glee at passing and at courtship. The film also aligns
itself with his terror in their failure, through conventions that the narrative—as opposed to documentary—form allows. And yet a reading of
the film cannot help but notice how *Boys Don't Cry* represents the very
gesture it condemns: requiring Brandon to speak the pathology of transgender, to confess to a "sexual identity crisis," even as the film knowingly
stages the confession as an act of heteronormative discipline.

The sequence in which Brandon must proffer his confession contributes to a contradictory view of Brandon. On the one hand, the film makes Brandon in the image of a lesbian aesthetic, an alluring butch figured through rhetoric familiar to lesbian history and mise-en-scène. On the other hand, Peirce acknowledges through the narrative and dialogue that Brandon is not drawn to an urban scene, postmodern or otherwise; Brandon does not want to go to New York or to Los Angeles in order to become part of a sophisticated subculture in regard to gender and sexuality; Brandon instead wants to be a boy who is adored by girls in Falls City, Nebraska. It is not simply that Brandon's confession to the sheriff that he is suffering a "sexual identity crisis" is coerced, is a performative instance in which Brandon is made to inhabit the very discourse that will pathologize her/him as "a girl who likes to run around pretending she's a boy," in the stinging and dismissive words of the law. To notice this is only half the point. For the spectator is meant to make sense of this moment from within the knowledge that she has read Foucault, or, at the very least, the spectator is presumed to have some access to the coercive dimensions of Brandon's confession, not from outside but from, as it were, the inside/out. This place of enunciation, this vantage point of theoretical sophistication and knowingness, is the ethical epicenter of the Brandon Teena story as it has been told in this set of films: it is "true" insofar as recorded on tapes of Brandon's interview after the rape, and these tapes figure powerfully in Muska and Ólafsdottir's film. They figured powerfully in the subsequent indictment of the sheriffs for their harassment of Brandon and failure to protect him adequately from his eventual murderers.

If one were to inhabit the judging truth of this place of confession, one would be confident that "those people" just didn't understand transgender, rather than permitting the possibility that the common sense of gay, lesbian, or queer understanding also needs to be put into play. If one were instead to put the value of desire up for grabs, one might notice that the Brandon Teena story in all of its manifestations is less about identity than about forgery: the passing of bad gender, the enactment of a kind of karaoke masculinity, the pursuit of an elusive or reversed signature. One might probe the ways in which the Brandon Teena story, as disseminated in the films I have mentioned, circulates a domesticated and normative version of queerness itself that nonetheless provokes an authenticating effect, at the expense, I would argue, of the very constituency whose interests it seeks and claims to represent. Boys Don't Cry made its way to HBO, and queer people are paying for it in both senses, a complicated loop that provokes further questions about the film's status as a commodity, a thing.

A Roadmap to *Lesbian Rule*

What kind of text, then, is the Brandon Teena story? It includes very different types of films, books, articles, and art; it expands and changes shape according to information and interest. *Lesbian Rule* proceeds by trying to focus on these types of expansive texts, enunciative contexts, and discursive locations simultaneously, and from within the tensions (paradox, contradiction) I described above. The division of the chapters of the book is in some measure merely a mimicry of the common sense or rote recitations of the noun in order to dislodge the noun's authority: let me look not at The Lesbian, but at lesbian people, lesbian places, lesbian things. In so modifying the generic noun, *lesbian* opens to a range of objects.

The first two chapters, "Lesbian Rule" and "*Droits de regards/Right of Inspection,*" situate my project theoretically through close readings of several texts. Because this book bears the traces of several large arenas of thought, I have not attempted a standard review of the available literature; it is simply too massive and disjunctive. Instead, in "Lesbian Rule" I focus very tightly on a few ideas that have staying power over the course of the book's explorations: affective value as elaborated in an essay by Gayatri Spivak and other mediations between the psychic and the social, such as that which come in the idea of the fetish and in affectivity more generally. I treat several studies that might appear to bear a similarity to the present undertaking (the work of William Pietz, Teresa de Lauretis, and Elizabeth Grosz), demonstrating how it is that I read and begin a conversation. The central task of the first chapter is, above all, to name some of the stakes of lesbian appearance through different languages of abstraction.

It is that strategy I develop further in the second chapter, where I turn from ideas in words to ideas in images: the cover photograph from Butler's book, *Gender Trouble,* and a photographic project and essay by Marie-Françoise Plissart and Jacques Derrida. Through this pairing of image and text, I hone in on these pressing questions: how do we read images as lesbian? What and who makes a lesbian image? Are photographs "in" language, "in" specific languages? What is the act of translation between image and language? In addressing these questions, I want to take the images seriously, to treat them with care and rigor, and to develop—in the sense of the photographic process—a language of my own that does not merely describe but responds to them. The impetus for this kind of close contextual reading comes from noticing how frequently films, videos, television programs, and photographs function illustratively in theoretical or critical arguments that themselves refuse to see them *as* films, videos, television programs, or photographs. Insofar as lesbian increasingly appears as image, I contend that it is an urgent task to probe the dimensions and effects of that appearance as precisely and strictly as possible. If one can see lesbian people as and in images, and if such image-making may take us out of the realm of talking about lesbian people as such, then it is imperative to see that operation as complicatedly pleasurable, tyrannical, reductive, phantasmic, and conventional, to name a few possibilities. The first two chapters try to enlarge the list.

The next two chapters, "Archiving the Diaspora" and "Absolut Queer," turn more explicitly to places or to scenes of lesbian appearance: to China and to Cuba, respectively. Deploying the model for contextual analysis I develop in the first two chapters, I seek in "Archiving the Diaspora" to discover a lesbian impression in Ulrike Ottinger's documentary, *Exile Shanghai*, on the exiled Jews who resided in Shanghai during the Second World War. That is, taking a documentary film by a lesbian filmmaker that appears to have nothing whatsoever to do with lesbians, I ask of it to what extent Ottinger's lesbianism matters, whether and how it might be seen to contribute to her understandings of exile, of cross-cultural encounter, of place. Item number eight on Spillers's list of productive dimensions of psychoanalysis acquires significance in this chapter, since exile becomes for Ottinger an idealized place of lesbian enunciation. If, as I have suggested, the value of desire is dynamic and mobile, it also moves through the circuits of a changing set of social relations, among them the effects of de-industrialization, globalization, or planetarization, and the international division of labor upon which they depend. Among them also are challenges to the logic of the market and capitalist democracy in China and in Cuba, whatever one might think about how these two experiments have fared. In one sense, then, I try to find in Ottinger's film on the Shanghai exiles a direct confrontation with and meditation on value understood as the ground for social organization. Her film thus can be read as an essay on fetishism *and* on affective value-coding through a lesbian impression. In another sense, Ottinger—a German Jewish lesbian—provides another way into a lesbian sense of place insofar as her film beckons toward histories of the Holocaust, of scenes and archives of persecution and survival. I am interested in how gay men and lesbians enjoin that archive as targets of Nazi genocide but also as frequently unacknowledged victims in the memory and study of the Shoah. I contend that queer witness and queer diaspora function obliquely as a lesbian impression in *Exile Shanghai*.

The fourth chapter, "Absolut Queer," is similarly preoccupied with exile, not with its romanticization as a privileged trope or point of view for the displacements effected by late capitalism but instead as a lived experience that produces the bulk of our understanding of Cuba. In the chapter's title, readers may recognize the form of a series of print advertisements for Absolut Vodka. I use its reference as a way to mark (1) an obvious pun in the association of Fidel Castro's rule with absolute authority, (2) the extent to which our knowledge of Cuba comes frequently through the circuits of American capitalist culture, and (3) the fact that many gay and lesbian film festivals, where queer people might have their few encounters with works on or about Cuba, are subsidized by corporate sponsors such as Absolut. The circuits in which independent documentaries travel are, in other words, not pure but contradictory routes for public cultures. By analyzing a group of films that collectively offer a prehistory for Julian Schnabel's film, *Before Night Falls* (2000), about the gay Cuban writer Reinaldo Arenas, I try to follow the perverse logic whereby discussions of Cuba's persecution of gay men and lesbians seem to form the ground for anti-Revolutionary and more general denunciations of the Cuban struggle from the place of exile in the United States. Ramifications of place have seldom been more critical or central in this time of displacement, exile, extraterritoriality, banishment, and territorial dispute. But place also offers me a way to think about knowledge production itself, about what one knows of Cuba from exposure to it through queer film and film festivals, and about what one can know from documentary more generally. Finally, the Cuban documentaries prompt me to think about the ethical knots in the relationship between power and knowledge: "One could dream about what would be the lesson of someone who didn't have the keys to his own knowledge, who didn't arrogate it to himself. He would give place to the place, leaving the keys with the other to unlock the words from their enclosure."[26]

From place, I turn in the fifth chapter and the conclusion to commodities, or things, specifically to lesbian pulp novels and to lesbian videos. While the study of things has become more prominent and exciting in the university, through the work of Bill Brown, for example, it remains nonetheless difficult to ask after the sexuality of things. To brand a commodity with a destination—videos "meant" for lesbians— is a usual enough practice, although one should remember that a commodity may not reach its intended destination, nor might it end its journey there. Althusser's model of interpellation acknowledges the former but not the latter possibilities for subject-formation. In a more colloquial sense, however, I live with stuff and am interested in stuff, where value hangs out and especially how it mutates when the determination of value involves affective dimensions, including and beyond what Danae Clark has described as "commodity lesbianism."[27] Displacements involve the time of things, the travel of commodities beyond their usual circuits of exchange and into surprising and new relationships; the popularity of *Antiques Roadshow* perhaps attests to the mutations of which capitalism is capable in times of scarcity and fear. And I find no single word or idea pliant enough to manage these mutations and schemes of value-determination: camp, kitsch, schlock, nostalgia, thrift, shopping, recycling, misuse, and absolutely earnest pleasure and recognition are all in play with lesbian things. In the fifth chapter, then, I begin with the documentary film *Forbidden Love* and leap from it to the work of lesbian pulp novels that the film itself uses as a springboard for memory and as a framing device. I argue that the pulp paperback's cover—the site of enough anxiety in the 1950s to prompt a senate investigation into the possibilities for their regulation—conceals the movement of affective value, both in terms of lesbian readers' investment in the realist dimensions of the worlds the novels explore, but also in terms of what the paperback cover purports to manage but cannot: the illicit contents of the book itself. The representational ruse of the cover ultimately provides a figure for how lesbian appearance might be seen to function in a wider sense: simultaneously revealing and concealing, rendering apparently visible but also covering over the workings of value that make that appearance possible.

From the pulps I move, finally, to that other commodity staple of representation: the videotape, or, on the cusp of the video's outmodedness, the DVD. Like the paperback, the videotape mediates isolated consumption with community-formation. One can read or watch at home alone, and through such atomized consumption, one is stitched to others like atoms, learning about one another through displaced documents of community. The conclusion relishes a few videotape documentaries in order to acknowledge the increasing complexity of media circuits and queer communities in the age in which the world picture is emerging on the plasma screens of the home theater. The gesture is meant as an opening rather than as a final word; I hope the reader will rent a few tapes or DVDs and engage them.

Chapter 1

Lesbian Rule

The task of this book is mirrored in its structure—modification, displacement, not jettisoning or replacing. It is not a book about "the lesbian" but about a lesbian modification, not the noun, but the adjective. It is not an argument that seeks to take the place of another but instead to modify, reshape, redraw. Were there not a critical literature and an effulgent cultural sphere of the lesbian self, this book would not have been possible to conceive. Similarly, were there not a sustained conversation about the limits of the self, the borders of representation and the displacements constitutive of that very domain called sexuality, this book would have no interlocutors.

Lesbian Rule is a sustained exercise in reading sexual rhetoric, particularly the rhetorical construction of the lesbian in documentary cinema. Queer theory has gravitated toward visual culture in its metaphors, in its examples, in its central tropes, and in its offhand figures. By noticing the ways in which visual reference preoccupies philosophical or theoretical reflection, I seek to develop a more nuanced and supple mode of reading "the lesbian" wherever it is that she may appear, whatever she may conceal. Reading *lesbian* as a catachresis allows me to examine the slippery movement that lesbian appearance reveals and conceals between sexual difference and social relations; next, I examine several influential and provocative conceptions of fetishism, providing as that discourse does one model of understanding what happens when meaning is produced from a clash in value-codings, and fixed on an object. Fetish discourse, understood as a theory of affective value, explains why *lesbian* works as a catachresis: it is a discourse that has attempted to manage the very slippage a catachresis names, and fetish discourse—influential as it has been in lesbian theory—can thus be read as a cover story itself. The politics of fetish discourse require investigation for their historical underpinnings and for their ramifications for queer politics today. My goal is to develop the beginning of a model, elaborated in the second chapter as well, for understanding how *lesbian* might also name that clash: the visualization of a possibility of something else.

Lesbian Morphology I: Catachresis

What does it mean to treat the name *lesbian* as a catachresis? The term *catachresis* is central to Gayatri Spivak's deconstructive Marxist feminism, much of which has derived from a reading of Jacques Derrida that I follow in order to gloss the term, although not to restrict it. In the most general way, then, words used as metaphors shimmer with history. The empirical, everyday, and idiomatic meanings entailed in the history of language constitute the narrow sense of any given word; these haunt the general sense, the register of the conceptual and metaphorical within which a privileged word is meant to function discursively, within a philosophic, literary, scientific, anthropological, sociological, or psychoanalytic system. This haunting, the spectrality wherein the general sense cannot escape the ghosts of the narrow sense, is what Derrida calls the burden of paleonymy. As Spivak has noted, nowhere in his writings does Derrida offer a systematic explanation of this divide, the extent to which the narrow and general senses always blend into one another, "cracked and barred" in language generally as in his own writings in particular.[1]

For Spivak's reading of Derrida, more important is the way in which the divided relationship between the narrow and general senses "makes for the necessary lack of fit between discourse and example, the necessary crisis between theory and practice that marks deconstruction."[2] One can exploit, in other words, the slide from the general sense to the narrow sense. To notice the disjunction and to move within it is to acknowledge the requisite gap between discursive registers, the ways in which theory and practice (or whichever names one wants to bestow upon the registers) modify one another. What Derrida stages through his own use of the words which carry this divided charge in his writing is movement within disjunction, the necessity of risking decision in the face of the impossibility of deciding, and the limits of determination and therefore of representation as an effect-structure.

Reading and writing (as well as trace, *différance, parergon*) function as two such concept-metaphors in Derrida's early writing, and they are densely imbricated with the double bind that founds deconstruction. Spivak glosses them to problematize transparent claims to epistemological power on ethnic or cultural bases, not to dismiss the embrace of limited or practical identity claims but to trouble the efficacy of collective validation by invoking the discontinuity between the subject of epistemology and that of ethicopolitics.

> Writing and reading in such general senses mark two different positions in relation to the uneven many-strandedness of "being." Writing is a position where the *absence* of the weaver from the web is structurally necessary. Reading is a position where I (or a group of us with whom I share an identificatory label) make this anonymous web my own, even as I find in it a guarantee of my existence as me, one of us. Between the two positions, there are displacements and consolidations, a disjunction in order to conjugate a representative self.[3]

Noticing the quotation marks around "being" in this passage, one sees a kind of translation at work, a movement that discloses the enabling lack of fit between the narrow sense and the general sense. The philosophical significance of Being (ontology) is both referenced and displaced by the lower case (being), signaling in its wake the importance of the distinction between the ontological and the ontic for Derrida's reading of Heidegger; the narrow sense, the ontic (the intimate and inaccessible) sense, of being is thereby summoned in the general sense. The necessary disjunction between reading and writing—what Derrida calls the graphematic structure—is further necessarily situated within the very possibility of thought: the mechanics of starting assumptions, a structure of repetition posited as self-evidence, finessed or suppressed in order to get anything going.

In Spivak's reading of Derrida, this catachrestical movement between the narrow and the general sense is precisely what is enabling about deconstruction, the recognition, in other words, that the subject is always centered.

> Deconstruction persistently notices that this centering is an effect-structure with indeterminable boundaries that can only be deciphered as determining. No politics can occupy itself with only this enabling epistemological double bind. But when a political analysis or a program forgets this it runs the risk of declaring ruptures where there is also a repetition—a risk that can result in varieties of fundamentalism, of which the onto/epistemo/ethicopolitical confusion is a characteristic symptom.[4]

Such confusion, I think, marks writing on lesbian, precisely because the name *lesbian* seeks to encompass each of these valences; unlike the relationship between *women* and *feminism,* there is no ethicopolitical counterpart *name* for lesbian, although *queer* is beginning to do that work of designation. I seek to establish specifically the specular morphology of *lesbian* in contradistinction to the claims of ontological self-evidence and representational priority which characterize postwar politics of sexuality, particular in their demands for visibility. Reading *lesbian* as a catachresis, as both figurative and literal, produces a disjunctive field traced by the name *lesbian* as a value-coding of the differential produced by gender and sexual indeterminacy, which differential can only be deciphered as determining. To modify my initial claim, it is therefore not only a task of reading "the lesbian" wherever it is that she may appear, but, perhaps more pressingly, to interrogate the operation at work in making the lesbian visible, to examine those specific conditions of legibility or recognition that underwrite lesbian as image. Between the narrow sense of *lesbian* and its general sense deployment as a name for a political program, there is movement, disjunction, slippage; to read *lesbian* as a catachresis is to begin to generate a sense of the value of desire, of affective value.

Affective Value

To say that the name *lesbian* traces a field produced through value-coding is to allege a point of contact or convergence between the interior and the exterior, between affect and economy, between the psychic and the social. The more powerful attempts theoretically to locate such crucial mediators have come, to my mind, in readings of performativity and fetishism, both alternatives to models of false consciousness, both preserving a sense of agency, both capable of functioning as theories of affective value. The following chapter will take up the idea of mediation and translation in more detail in an extended discussion of Derrida's *Droits de regards.* Here, however, I turn to an essay that similarly contributes to such an undertaking of stitching the psychic to the social, one to which I return regularly in order to pick at the abstraction it ultimately produces: "affective value." What is it, and might it provide an alternate or companion name for the type of value-coding produced through the name *lesbian?*

Affective value arises in Spivak's essay, "Scattered Speculations on the Question of Value," an essay that begins to treat the question of value through the predication of the subject.[5] The essay proceeds from the assumption that subject-predication is methodologically necessary, a starting point that functions as an implicit (or occasionally explicit) jab at theoretical enterprises that betray "metaphysical longing" (154) or tacit traces of idealist subject-predication. The idealist subject-predication is consciousness, "not thought" but rather the subject's irreducible "intendedness" (154) toward the object. Her real focus in the essay is, however, the materialist predication of the subject such as Marx's. The materialist subject-predication is labor power, "not work (labor) but rather the irreducible possibility that the subject be more than adequate— super-adequate—to itself, labor-*power*" (154). If the issue of subject-predication is a generalized theoretical task, Spivak uses, as a practical context for its exploration, the issue of canon-formation and contestation. Such a context provides for her an opportunity to distinguish domination (a designation for power relations in a general sense) and exploitation (a specific maneuver of capitalism in extracting surplus value from labor power), as well as stages her incessant attention to the discontinuous opposition between theory and practice we saw above.

Spivak's project in "Scattered Speculations" is to challenge continuist inscriptions of Marx's work, with a reading emphasizing instead the textualization of the chain of value, rendering the materialist predication of the subject on labor-power indeterminate. Her reading of the first sixty pages of *Capital,* volume one of the *Grundisse,* along with "The Chapter on Money" and "The Chapter on Capital," goes something like this: Marx sought to examine the "concept-phenomenon" money (a seemingly unified concept) and lifted the lid (Spivak's metaphor of cooking) on a boiling mess. The name for that mess is value, a "contentless and simple" (*inhaltslos und einfach*) thing which makes possible everything: exchange, communication, sociality. Value escapes the onto-phenomenological question, "What is it?" To investigate value is instead to map a chain of relationships. The chain is this: Value (representation)—Money (transformation)—Capital. There are many carefully crafted steps in between, but what is cooking in Spivak's essay, among other things, is a calculated counterargument to the vestiges of continuist reading in Jean-Joseph Goux's structuralist domestication of Marx, through which he wrenches an isomorphic relationship between the development of the money-form and the Lacanian account of the emergence of genital sexuality: gold equals the phallus. Goux's argument, in Spivak's reading, is an instance of the structuralist desire to translate morphological similarities in discontinuous sign systems into isomor-phic identities. By so doing, in Spivak's view, it becomes however neces-sary "to exclude the fields of force that make them heterogeneous, indeed discontinuous" (156).

My interest in Spivak's textualization of the chain of value, to which I turn in a moment, lies in her ability to generate a category—affec-tive value—that can address the relations between these discontinuous sign systems (economy, psyche), not rigidly mapped sexual identities, through the production, circulation, and coding of value. Affective value preserves the discontinuity of sign systems while at the same time fore-grounding their interdependence, the extent to which they are severed from the general text at a cost. "Sexuality" might not, as a result of her understanding, be preserved on the side of social reproduction (birth-family-home-growth) and/or interiority (as it is for psychoanalysis), but rather thought of as a complicated strand of sociality not easily cut.

Let me rehearse briefly Spivak's argument as I understand it. The continuous reading of Marx's scheme of value (whereby one em-phasizes the uni-linear progressive account of the emergence of the money-form) betrays indeterminacy through its inability to answer the onto-phenomenological question, "what is value?" Its consideration of use-value and exchange-value excludes modes of thinking (dialectical and deconstructive among them) other than analogy or isomorphism, in order to elide problematic discontinuities and in order to emphasize a distinct beginning, middle, and end of an argument. Continuist and structuralist versions of Marx's scheme of value, while they read through the "straining logic of Marx's metaphors" (157), tend nonetheless to es-cape the onto-phenomenological question through a reliance on the idea of excess. Through the example of the emergence of exchange, Spivak shows that Goux's reading collapses the intricate differences between use-value, exchange-value, surplus-value, and money by seeing the ex-clusion of money from the commodity form as due to being-in-excess rather than as due precisely to the requirement that the money-form not operate on two registers at once, "measuring and carrying Value" (157). A deconstructive reading, rather than emphasizing linear or analogical relationships in the concept-phenomenon value, posits its textuality.

In order for something to be textual, it must be open at both ends. Spivak shows that the continuist attempt to insert labor at the begin-ning of the chain of value, to posit its origin as labor-power, seals off the movement of the dialectic and thus the indeterminacy of value that

opens other possibilities for thinking labor's relation to other social determinations (such as Gayle Rubin and others have taken up in regard to
the complicity between patriarchy and capitalism). This is Spivak's way
of saying that the designation of "representation" involves a differential
rather than self-adequation. By tracing each step of Marx's materialist
dialectical analysis of value, Spivak reveals indeterminacies in the chain.
Position: the money commodity is defined in its separation from itself,
in its doubleness, on the one hand, "as a specific product whose natural
form of existence ideally contains (latently contains) its exchange value,
and in the other aspect as manifest exchange value (money) in which all
connection with the natural form of the product is stripped away again—
this double, *differentiated* existence must develop into a *difference*" (Marx,
cited in Spivak, 159).

This difference is also an indifference. The money-commodity's differentiated existence renders issues of difference among individuals
(who *seem* distinguished one from the other by virtue of education, personal dependence, etc.) illusory, "indifferent" (*Gleichgültkeit–im Sinne
der indifferenez*). Negation: money, which facilitates exchange, is a vanishing point; outside of exchange, it would not be money. Also, in this
moment of its "positive" appearance, a more subtle negation is possible,
in that fake money can do its job as well as the real article (a slippage
Derrida explores further in *Given Time, I: Counterfeit Money*). As Spivak
puts it, in more philosophical language, "the self-adequation of the idea,
itself contingent upon a negative relationship, here between the idea of
money and circulation as totality, works in the service of a functional
in-adequation (fake = real)" (159–60). Negation of the negation: realization, the movement of money in the moment of capital accumulation,
but also the release of the commodity from the circuit of production into
consumption, or the dissolution of the thing acquired in accumulation.
For Spivak, this movement marks not only a contradiction but a rupture
which "leads off into the open-endedness of textuality" (160).

Having demonstrated indeterminacy in the first links of the chain,
Spivak turns to transformation between money and capital, the second
relation designated between the second two links. In the passage Spivak
cites, Marx displaces the question of the *origins* of capitalist accumulation, postulated through the concept of primitive accumulation, to a
question of *process*, reinforcing Spivak's critique of the continuist assumption of value's origin in labor—primitive accumulation is nothing
but "the historical process of divorcing the producer from the means of

production" (Marx, cited in Spivak, 161). The next step is crucial. The birth of capital logic is the moment of its historical possibility; it does not emerge through coercion or the accumulation of interest-capital or merchant's capital. By historical possibility, Marx means the historical possibility of the predication of the subject through labor-power, the social possibility, therefore, of this predication. Because the subject can be predicated as structurally superadequate to itself, productive of surplus labor over necessary labor, Marx suggests that "Capital consumes the use-value of labor-power" (Marx, cited in Spivak, 161). This reading, then, makes visible the force of capital logic, a force which importantly precludes a nostalgic return to use-value; indeed, Spivak cites the range of circumstances this desire for a return can accommodate. Insofar as it is Spivak's contention that revolutionary practice involves the insertion of illogic into good use-value fit, it therefore carries no theological-teleological justification. There is thereby a certain consonance between Spivak's reading of Marx and Foucault's reading of Nietzsche. The open-endedness of the role of use-value puts the entire chain of value into play; this is precisely what Spivak means by an "insertion" into textuality.

Spivak understands use-value, therefore, as both outside and inside the system of value-determinations—outside because it is outside the circuit of exchange, inside because it is a superfluity or parasite of use-value, which dominates production as a whole. She thus uses it as a deconstructive lever (that is, something one can pull in order to disclose determinacy as an effect) and as an instance of invagination (where the part-whole relationship is turned inside-out). The special case is what renders indeterminate the materialist predication of the subject. "One case of use-value can be that of the worker wishing to consume the (affect of the) work itself . . . The question of *affectively* necessary labor brings in the attendant question of desire and thus questions in another way the mere philosophical justice of capital logic [the good use-value fit between capital and free labor] without necessarily shifting into utopian idealism" (162).

Spivak's last move is the expansion of the textuality of value following the introduction of this category of affectively necessary labor. Affectively necessary labor requires a reformulation of the concept of socially necessary labor, labor required in order for the worker to reproduce himself as useful for capital. Spivak's remark is suggestive, and represents the starting point for my own elaboration of the affective value traced by the name *lesbian:* "if the dynamics of birth-growth-family-life reproduction is given as much attention as, let us say, the relationship between fixed and variable capitals in their several moments, the 'materialist' predication of the subject as labor-power is rendered indeterminate in yet another way, without therefore being 'refuted' by varieties of utopianism and 'idealism' " (163). The indeterminacy need not be closed off by establishing an opposition between, say, Marxism and feminism, or by inscribing the family simply as a unit through which the worker is (re)produced, or by legitimizing domestic labor within capital logic ("wages for housework"). What the category of affectively necessary labor introduces is the complexity of the value-form across the registers commonly called the economic and the cultural, the "irreducible complicity" (164), not the isomorphism, between cultural and economic value-systems.

The rather significant point, then, is *not* to close off the indeterminacy of the "materialist" subject predication as labor-power, to denounce it as gender-exclusive and then move on to "women," or for that matter, "sexuality," "the private," "melodrama," or other realms to which the other is consigned by the demand of power to code a differential as a division. Nor can we isolate what Spivak dubs the "dynamics of birth-growth-family-life reproduction" (the domain of the cultural? Privacy? Sexuality?) as our object of analysis in a manner that simply analogizes it to capital logic. My initial presupposition is that the production and appropriation of value apply to affective and social codings as well as (not "merely") economic codings. If the social domain is understood to be an affectively coded site of exchange and surplus, the moment of value "as it is gender-coded has historically led to the appropriation of the sexual differential, subtracted from, but represented as, the theoretical fiction of sexual identity."[6] No doubt, sexual identity has its effects, but this arithmetic suggests that we concentrate on the historical coding of affective value in analysis, or on what Miranda Joseph describes as the "embodiment" of value in critique.[7]

Keep the lesbian in mind even when she is not in sight. The central consequence of Spivak's reading involves understanding how affect and desire are not banished from considerations of economy, nor are they relegated to the sphere of women's work or considerations of reproduction. Instead, she provides a model for recognizing a relationship between sexuality and capitalism that is nuanced, not reductive, and that preserves these different registers of what Spivak describes in my earlier citation as "positions in relation to the uneven many-strandedness of 'being'."

Affective value describes the difference lesbian might make, even while leaving open the horizons transformed by the value of her desire. Other theoretical models similarly stitch the sociohistorical register to the affective domain. The fetish is one such theory that has provided fertile discursive ground upon which the lesbian has been made visible. Under the cover of the fetish—that object of dubious significance invested with curiously strong currents of value—lesbian appears, yet fetish theory is not, to my mind, primarily a theory of false consciousness, even within the Marxist tradition. It has become influential as a theoretical mediator between the psychic and the social primarily because it is a theory of affective value that explains how *lesbian* works as a catachresis.

Fetish Discourse

The bibliography on fetishism has outgrown the modest resources of Freud's essay and Marx's dependence on the term in his analysis of commodity relations. That these two men should have taken up the term, however, requires explanation, and no better history of the concept exists beyond William Pietz's articles that initially appeared in the journal *Res*. In my discussion, I rely on Pietz's guidance in his initial work and examine how his position seems to have shifted in more recent writing as a reaction against poststructuralism, closing off the very potential for an understanding of value that he opened in the earlier articles. His initial thesis is that the fetish, both as an idea and a problem, originated "in the cross-cultural spaces of the coast of West Africa during the sixteenth and seventeenth centuries."[8] This origin is not absolute but marks the descent of what he calls a theoretical materialism that emerged out of a cross-cultural encounter. This descent might be traced as against the attribution of the term to authentic "native" contexts or against false universalism which subsumes fetishism "to an allegedly universal tendency toward privileging phallic symbolism" (5). Instead, Pietz argues that the term arose out of the spaces along the West African coastline that were necessarily intercultural, requiring a scheme in which to transcode and translate objects between "radically different social systems"

(6). His method of analysis views the fetish, therefore, as radically historical, used in a number of exemplary instances which constitute the archive of its history with nothing standing outside of that archive. Insofar as these usages are embedded within a "total historical reality" (7), however, Pietz argues that the historical specificity of the model of the fetish can provide criteria for a *theoretical* model of the fetish, traced through the coding of value. Such a theoretical model bears a structural resemblance to the idea of affective value, seeking as both do to describe a dynamic process of socially determined value-coding within which *lesbian* as catachresis moves.

The fetish, as it arises in its specific context, further embeds two characteristics which linger in its various more recent conceptual formulations—the irreducible materiality of the fetish, and the ordering of singularity and repetition in the structure of the fetish. These structural emphases give rise to a number of themes basic to the problematic of the fetish, the most evident of which is the idea of "generating a social order out of a chaotic principle of contingency" (8). The idea of the fetish as creating a unity from heterogeneity obtains in its three most famous appropriations: (1) in Marx's attraction to the idea of the fetish, which fixes personal consciousness in objective illusion; (2) in nineteenth-century psychology and later in Freud's psychoanalytic formulations, which emphasize the power of a singular personal event to structure desire; and (3) in modernist art's emphasis on the "singular chance encounter of heterogeneous elements" (9). These conceptions, in Pietz's reading, can be understood through the coding of value, the relation of social value to personhood or individuality, the dependence of social value on specific institutional systems for marking the value of material things, and "the idea of certain material objects as the loci of fixed structures of the inscription, displacement, reversal and overestimation of value" (9). The final idea that emerges in fetish discourse is the theme of the embodied individual, the "subjection of the human body (as the material locus of action and desire) to the influence of certain significant material objects that, although cut off from the body, function as its controlling organs at certain moments" (10).

A general theory of the fetish, articulated through the abstraction of value, can provide a framework for understanding the coding of affective value and articulating the relation of the individual to the social through specific intensities, investments, perceptions, and codings. Pietz reads

Marx against his structuralist domesticators, as does Spivak, to move away from an idea of the fetish as false consciousness toward the idea of the fetish as a theory of value. Because the fetish-concept emerges in a cross-cultural encounter of value codes of radically differentiated social orders, the "truth" of the fetish (insofar as it may disclose such a thing) is revealed in its ability to fix value *comparatively*. Marx's reading of the fetishism of bourgeois economy thus requires, for example, that circulation and the capitalist mode of production be understood historically. "The whole mystery of commodities, all the magic and necromancy that surrounds the products of labor on the basis of commodity production, vanishes therefore as soon as we come to other forms of production."[9] What Pietz, too, is at pains to theorize is the specific form of the mediation of a particular conception of the individual and the social, which can be understood as a process of value-coding cued by this passage. To condense his "general theory of the fetish," Pietz posits fundamental characteristics in a lengthy passage that is, to my mind, the best statement of the stakes of his argument.

> The fetish is always a meaningful fixation of a singular event; it is above all a "historical" object, the enduring material form and force of an unrepeatable event. This object is "territorialized" in material space (an earthly matrix), whether in the form of a geographical locality, a marked site on the surface of the human body, or a medium of inscription or configuration defined by some portable or wearable thing. The historical object is territorialized in the form of a "reification": some thing or shape (*meuble*) whose status is that of a self-contained entity identifiable within the territory. It is recognizable as a discrete thing (a *res*) because of its status as a significant object within the value codes proper to the productive and ideological systems of a given society. This reified, territorialized historical object is also "personalized" in the sense that beyond its status as a collective social object it evokes an intensely personal response from individuals. This intense relation to the individual's experience of his or her own living self through an impassioned response to the fetish object is always incommensurable with (whether in a way that reinforces or undercuts) the social value codes within which the fetish holds the status of a material signifier. It is in those "disavowals" and "perspectives of flight" whose possibility is opened by the clash of this incommensurable difference that the fetish might be identified as the site of both

the formation and the revelation of ideology and value-consciousness.
(12–13)

It seems clear that Pietz is here proposing, in strikingly Deleuzian language, the fetish as a generalized theory of the collective material object, of value, of history. His comments are admittedly preliminary, but they seem to me extraordinarily suggestive insofar as they orchestrate a number of movements: the coding of affect and the body (not strictly within the categories of the conscious and the unconscious, or within a set of enumerated affects) in a rhetoric of identification and disavowal (not merely in their psychoanalytic valences); the articulation of that ensemble (not simply the individual) with value-codings that solidify connections with "territorialized" social things or material objects which themselves embody socially significant values; and the situation of the encounter with a "series of singular historical fixations" (14). The fetish as *tout object historique* may then be the site of ideological reification as well as "impassioned spontaneous criticism" (14). Pietz elaborates on the historical field of the fetish in the remainder of his essay and points toward future work in subsequent essays; it is of crucial significance to remember that the fetish *as a specific historical matrix* arose out of the cross-cultural encounter. To reduce it to its most familiar contexts in Marx and in psychoanalysis is to evade its specific origins and, therefore, its function as a mediator of the colonial encounter "gathering an otherwise unconnected multiplicity into the unity of its enduring singularity" (15).

More recently, however, Pietz has seemed to renege on the potential I see in this early essay to understand the mediation between the individual and the social as dense and indeterminate. He tightens his focus on Marx, replacing his earlier conception of territorialization and reification with a loosely metaphysical conception of species-being as direct apprehension. This move deserves closer analysis for the ways in which it limits the dynamism of the earlier model. In "Fetishism and Materialism: The Limits of Theory in Marx," Pietz attacks a lineage of "semiological" misreadings of Marx, a chain from Lévi-Strauss, Barthes, and Althusser to Baudrillard, Derrida, Lacan, and Žižek. Fetishism serves as a nodal point for an intellectual history of recent Marxist debate, and Pietz is justified in his criticism of the disservice done by structuralists in yoking the fetish to ideology, on the one hand, and to alienation, on the other. His venom appears to be directed more toward the theoretical implications of the semiological reading whereby, first, fetishism becomes a kind of formalist passion when the use/exchange relation is analogized to the syntagmatic and paradigmatic axes of the signifier/signified relation (through Levi-Strauss) and to the combinatory and rhetorical logic of Freud's conceptions of dream-work. The result, seen most clearly in Barthes' essay "Myth Today," but also in Baudrillard's fascination with commodified meaning resulting from similar analogizing, is a particularly flattering conception of critical activity, where the "poststructuralist critic of culture could then conceive a politics as a sort of radical analysis of these cultural logics analogous to Freud's psychoanalysis of individuals."[10] Whether one takes issue with Pietz's straw poststructuralist man, his cautions against the perversion of a critical intellectual function provide a timely counterpoint to the more familiar criticisms of Althusserian or even Gramscian vanguardism, given the overblown claims for "subversion" in recent cultural analysis.[11] Pietz is critical of celebrations of radical indeterminacy and contingency that he sees in Laclau and Mouffe's work, and he is similarly troubled by a return to the very Hegelianism of the left variety Marx sought initially to criticize. What might a critical materialist reading of the fetish have to offer by comparison?

While Pietz in this essay reiterates much of what he had considered earlier in the *Res* essays, his focus shifts slightly to trace the critique of religion at the center of the early Marx's reading of the fetish. It is in this shift that he believes that he discloses the critical potential of a certain reorientation of fetish discourse. Among his central and complicatedly layered propositions is that the language of fetishism in Marx is "a way of evoking the materialist imaginary proper to a communist mode of apprehending capitalist reality" (129). One can see here the beginning of a displacement of the binarisms that dominate ideology critique through a resolutely materialist methodology. The dual critique of religion and political economy that Marx developed in the twenty years preceding the three volumes of *Capital*, Pietz argues, gives rise to a concept of fetishism which embeds not a simple binary of essence/appearance, truth/illusion, but a way of producing a subject capable of contemplating the reality of the illusion that is capital in its essence, a subject founded on the historical and material convergence of the savage fetishist and the worker. The fetish(ist) thus could be seen as a supplement to the materialist predication of the subject Spivak investigates, introducing affect in a different coding and on a different plane, and it is toward this supplementary relation that I want to work — seeing fetishism not as a mechanism of false consciousness but as a theory of affective value that explains how lesbian functions as catachresis.

As in his earlier work, Pietz emphasizes the conflicts between the contradictory, clashing value orders of religion and money that exemplify early (1760–1830s) conceptions of fetishism, but he also now investigates Marx's preliminary (1842) equation of fetishism with a "religion of sensuous desire" (133) in all of that phrase's resonances. "Sensuous desire" reverberates with myriad untheorized historical forces grounded in lived experience and personal suffering, expressed in desire-driven delusions about the animate status of natural objects directly apprehended. Religion, Marx emphasizes, "is the general theory of this world, its encyclopedic compendium, its logic in popular form" (Marx, cited in Pietz, 142). The "pure condition of un-enlightenment" (136), fetishism as the nontranscendental religion of sensuous desire, offers a crucial ground, argues Pietz, in post-Enlightenment philosophy for a displacement of theology in favor of anticlerical activities and the emergent human sciences, a ground that establishes, as Marx suggested in his own dissertation, the predication of all religious beliefs in primitive causal reasoning, not Enlightenment reason but desire and credulity, again, directly apprehended. The investment of animate power called "sensuous desire" cannot be allegorized or transubstantiated into a signifier of the concept or ideal even in Kant's apparent philosophic aesthetic "solution" to the problem of purposive intentionality. Fetishism therefore continues to escape the compulsion to function as a categorical principle in the epistemic orders of physical nature and human action. Associated with the savage, "primitive" mode of reasoning as well as with "primitive accumulation," the fetishist appears to provide a radical ground, indeed a limit, for a critique of monotheism also in Hegel's dialectizing of religion in relation to the state.

Likewise, Pietz suggests, fetishism comes to function in Marx's reading of Hegel as a materialist point of unthinkability in civil society. Since, in *The Philosophy of Right,* Hegel establishes the universal principle of civil society *outside* itself (in the family and in the state), Marx, of course, attempts to locate *within* civil society a universal class and principle of identity. This class and principle, however, is not dissociated from the ethical and spiritual (social) apprehension of real pain and suffering, and thus acquires a dual character. Pietz's language is consistent with

Antonio Gramsci's understanding of common sense, until it ultimately is domesticated in the world historical finale of Pietz's essay.

> The truth of religion is found in its potently fantastic theorization of the pain and degradation of oppressed people as a form of spiritual resistance to conditions that, in radically threatening people's very humanity, reveal the specific values that constitute our identity as human. Human experience of material poverty and social oppression is here viewed as the source of a spiritually powerful moral authority that is the concrete subjective ground of a radically democratic emancipatory politics. The materialist subject of this radically human ground is twice located by Marx: in the maximally alienated perspective of the primitive fetishist, a cultural other for whom material conditions are themselves spiritual values, who judges civil society from outside all civilization, and in the maximally degraded viewpoint of the proletarian, bourgeois society's other, forced to the physical margin of subsistence, whose value judgments express the most fundamental needs of human life. (143)

The force of this dual predication cannot be overestimated, claims Pietz, in terms of its impact on the formulation of fetishism in *Capital*, for the very viewpoint from which the proletarian perceives the essence of capital is expressed through the language of fetishism. That is, rather than preserving the language of fetishism on the side of the spiritual, religion's other, Marx comes to express the whole ruse of capital's appearance as a real illusion in that same language. Thus, "after the critiques of Hegel and Feuerbach, the discourse about fetishism marks the question of the material articulation between the embodied individual of 'sensuous desire' and historically specific divisions of labor" (144).

In Pietz's reading of the first chapter of *Capital*, the various transformations effected by money are first regarded as fetishistic. In this reading he is not far at all from Spivak's "poststructuralist" textualization of the chain of value upon which the money form's emergence depends. It is too easy to forget that Marx, in insisting upon the physical immateriality of value, develops an account of the emergence of the general equivalent as a three-fold fetishistic operation. When a material object (gold or silver) is endowed with a new quality, that of a general form, it expresses a general relation (of exchange): "it *is* this relation realized as a sensuous object" (146). *Fetishism* comes to name these translations on the side of bourgeois economy, reading the text of circulation, not production: from the apprehension of a general form to a universal form, from the apprehension of possibility to necessity, and from the terrain of common practice to law. The fetishistic inversion of bourgeois economy therefore perceives the means (monetarized productive capital with the capacity to fulfill needs and desires external to its logic and origins) as an end in itself, where capital becomes an instrumentalized power of command and rule expressed in the state. While Marx expresses the systemic layers of fetishism as a repeating process among the three divisions in his "Trinity Formula" (land/rent, labor/wages, capital/profits), he locates capitalism's most objectified form in interest-bearing capital, but not as a subjective illusion where money "simply" appears to generate more money through interest. The moment, then, of revelation of capital's political truth as social government is, as Pietz sees it, in the full development of financial fetishism in the credit-debt system; the "political-economic reality of capitalist society appears in public culture as fetishistic (as an alien and perversely unnatural reality)" (149). The perception, however, of the fetish-character of capital's political truth relies not only on a collective proletarian class produced through embodied action but also on the materialist subject's second perverse ground, the fetish-underside, where the direct apprehension and expression of sensuous desire produces a clashing or competing intensity, a memory-repetition that contests necessity as contingency not in idealist terms but historically, leading to the world historical crescendo of capitalism's collapse.

Pietz's more recent essay is a curious attempt to rewrite poststructuralism as antimaterialism and thus to safeguard a sanctified critical practice against perversion. The most worrisome turn of the essay, however, forsakes incommensurability for decidability. Where the fetishist earlier recodes impassioned response in a manner that reinforces or undercuts socially sanctioned value-coding (through disavowal, an at-the-same-time logic), now fetishism as a direct apprehension of sensuous desire is located as a *necessarily* emancipatory perspective. In his verve to displace constricting readings of essence/appearance and truth/illusion binarisms in *Capital*, Pietz installs a Möbius model of the fetish whereby reality appears as false to anything other than the exteriorized perspective of truth as emancipation. This logic permits a different form of analogizing, of the savage primitive with the embodied prole, and the materialist, i.e., historically specific, mode of critique does not create an identity but an equivalence that restabilizes what had earlier appeared as undecidable. We lose the force of Pietz's earlier essay that proposes the fetish as *one name* for a process involving the coding of value, a materialist mediation between the personal and social. Those formulations offered a model for investigating the attribution of affective value not as a singular or originary moment but as inserted into history. History is thus understood not as linear or progressive (the force of world-historical teleology) but *retrospective,* based on repetition within social codes and normative practices that lend the process historical meaning. In this retrospection, moreover, history and morality (affect, intensive investment in sensuous desire) are co-constituted through the metaphor of the fetish. Pietz's earlier essay suggests ways to theorize affective investment (fandom, for example, or intensive responses to images as well as things) as a flow of territorialized material things with socially coded bodies, their surfaces and their sexualized inscriptions, again as constantly remapped through and within social codings of value. As a general theory, Pietz proposed that the fetish name an operation of valuation rather than a specific moment of value in relation to a master signifier. That general theory allows for the catachrestical movement that I argue happens under the name *lesbian.* The psychoanalytic variation on the concept of the fetish, on the other hand, places primary importance on the originary glimpse of the mother's lack, as Derrida puts it, "all this proceeding from the spectacle of the woman's two legs, seen from below, with, in the center of two erect members, between the two, the fleece of hair (*la toison*)."[12] In Freud's essay and its traditional interpretations, the fetish is directly associated with male homosexuality, functioning sometimes as a substitute with which the homosexual can make do in order to function as a heterosexual, feigning a closure of the ostensible problem. Might the fetish function, then, as a lever to disrupt the containment of the binarism homosexual/heterosexual, indeed to probe the apparent commodification of affect more generally? Must sexuality and its gender binarisms be fixed within the determinate schemes of value-coding, or might the crisis Pietz traces as the fetish open the question of gender?

Female Fetishism/Lesbian Fetishism

Departing more from Freud than from Marx, a companion literature has emerged around the ostensibly critical potential of female fetishism in literary criticism, in art history, and in cultural studies in America and Britain. In the volume titled *Female Fetishism: A New Look,* Lorraine Gamman and Merja Makinen survey what they understand as the three types of fetishism (commodity, anthropological, and psychiatric) in order to paste together a conception of the female fetishist who is articulated with bodily perversions and rebellions such as bulimia, the politics of food, and also with an emancipatory queer politics.[13] The book is generally a culturalist, semiologically driven demonstration of what Pietz characterizes as the flattering conception of critical theory now holding sway, speaking in the name of female agency and queer visibility in pastiche mode. While Gamman and Makinen do engage psychoanalytic readings, their debts to Baudrillard are acknowledged in tame conclusions about simulacra. In a much more rigorous vein, Teresa de Lauretis and Elizabeth Grosz have read the concept of the fetish in Freud as associated with lesbianism, and de Lauretis uses the concept of the fetish through her "eccentric reading" as the basis for a general theory of lesbian desire.[14] Something in the structure of the fetish has made it congenial, then, to investigations of both gender and homosexuality, but these examinations have tended to rely upon the psychoanalytic account of fetishism rather than its historical emergence or meanings acquired through other discourses such as materialism or colonialism. In the remainder of this chapter, I read de Lauretis' book and Grosz's essay with the specific task of understanding how their reliance on the psychoanalytic version of the fetish limits conceptions of lesbian appearance by cleaving one form of value-coding, in sociality, from another, in sexuality, precisely when the concept of the fetish might reveal the extent to which they are co-constituted. Rather than valorize Marx and Pietz over Freud and de Lauretis and Grosz, I seek in what follows to reunite precisely what the concept fetish brings together: the social coding of desire within clashing schemes of value.

The argument of de Lauretis's *The Practice of Love* involves a number of layers that require attention in order to pinpoint the moments at which the cleavage is most palpable. First, de Lauretis focuses on Freud's negative theory of sexuality, wherein "the 'normal' is conceived only by approximation, is more a projection than an actual state of being, while perversion and neurosis (the repressed form of perversion) are the actual forms and contents of sexuality" (xii). De Lauretis proposes that this reading of Freud is particularly useful for lesbians "whose self-definition, self-representation, and personal and political identity are not only grounded in the sphere of the sexual, but actually constituted in relation to a *sexual* difference from socially dominant, institutionalized heterosexual forms" (xii). (The way of specifying the difference between the sexual and social here might return us to Hennessey's well-earned impatience with such confusion.) This conception of "sexual difference" grounds de Lauretis's argument and, to her mind, underscores the central role that sexuality plays in "subjectivity" and in all sociosymbolic forms, including racialized and gendered structures to which I will return (xiii). Sexual difference is also counterposed to sexual indifference, a charge leveled against feminist and other theoretical enterprises that fail to distinguish between straight women and lesbians, or that rest on concepts of indeterminacy or undecidability by metaphorizing lesbianism. De Lauretis seems particularly hostile to what she understands as deconstruction for this reason. Sexual difference, then, can be usefully explored through psychoanalysis for two reasons: (1) through Freud's theory of perversion, lesbian sexuality would no longer be anchored to an ahistorical understanding of the masculinity complex, and (2) that theory also offers a model of perverse desire (nonheterosexual, nonreproductive). The first problematic, the coding of lesbianism as tied to the masculinity *complex*, does allow de Lauretis to think of lesbian sexuality apart from its most conventional psychoanalytic formulations, as I will endeavor to show, despite the extent to which she retains a butch/femme matrix of lesbian identity. The second, the production of a model of perverse desire through Freud, fails in its precise lack of attention to sexuality as value-coded *within* and *throughout* social relations.

The second layer of de Lauretis's argument involves method, that is, her understanding of theory as producing, on the model of Freud, "passionate fictions" (*The Practice of Love*, xiv). By this phrase de Lauretis marks the insertion of a socially and historically situated "I" into a particular kind of writing practice, a methodological assumption that licenses the revelation of de Lauretis's experiences "as a lesbian" and her reactions to lesbian representations in *The Practice of Love*. And more important, passionate fictions also produce "resonances" rather than readings; if an account or theoretical formulation "resonates" with de Lauretis's own thinking or experience, she validates it on that basis. I mention this aspect of her book to signal a potential problem I mentioned in the introduction—taking the self as an unquestioned and self-evident reference point for the usefulness/validity of intellectual work. This ground becomes especially significant in de Lauretis's attraction to the nonmasculine woman, a distinction that seems to solidify an ahistorical binarism between butches and femmes that might be more powerfully summoned by developing an inventory of the traces deposited in the "I" who is Teresa de Lauretis.

What resonates, in any event, is fetishism. Through an elaborate and persuasive reading of Freud through Laplanche and Pontalis and through Bersani and Dutoit, de Lauretis realigns fetishism with lesbian sexuality. To do so, she insists on the tremendous significance of originary experience, the threat of castration, in the formation of sexuality. Her application (metaphorization?) of fetishism to lesbians redirects attention from the recognition of the paternal phallus as such to the role of the fantasy in fetishism, from the phallus to the fantasy-phallus.

> If the term *castration* designates the paternal (patriarchal) prohibition of access to the mother's and/or female body, with its fantasy of unity and plenitude, and if the term *phallus* designates the sign that signifies the subject's desire to recapture that plenitude through (hetero)sexual union, then that notion of castration and *some* notion of phallus— some notion of signifier of desire—are necessary to understand the process and forms of subjectivity. However, while psychoanalysis insists that the signifier of desire is the paternal phallus alone, presuming that sexuality is normatively heterosexual and reproductive, Bersani and Dutoit say it is a fantasy-phallus, "an inappropriate object precariously attached to a desiring fantasy, unsupported by any perceptual memory." (231)

The fetish, then, as signifier of perverse desire within the economy of heteronormativity, serves as a sign of prohibition, difference, and desire necessary to a theory of lesbian sexuality in a nonheteronormative system: "through the mechanism of disavowal, the female subject of perverse desire displaces the wish for the missing female body [the lack of a libidinally invested body-image produced by the double loss of the maternal body and the threatened loss of the female body itself] and the (non)perception of its absence onto a series of fetish objects or signs that signify at once the wish and the absence (loss), and re-present the absent (lost, denied) and wished-for female body" (263).

De Lauretis's account of the fetish exhibits these formal characteristics: the fetish denotes a relation of substitution, not for the phallus as master-signifier but for the double loss of the maternal body and a lack of being in her body-ego ("not having the phallus" as a psychic process of disavowal); it is constituted retroactively, not in a single instance of subjective development (264); and it is historically constituted insofar as the fetish-object and the subject of perverse desire are understood to be constituted within socio-historical determinations. With regard to the latter point, de Lauretis argues that fetish-objects for lesbians have historically been objects or signs with masculine connotations not because they "stand in" for the missing penis but because they "convey . . . the cultural meaning of sexual (genital) activity and yearning toward other women" (263). In a provocative moment, de Lauretis speculates that this process of signification of prohibition provides a translation into psychic terms of Foucault's insight that the discourses of homosexuality, inversion, and the like made possible not only the construction and regulation of perversion but also "the formation of a 'reverse' discourse: homosexuality began to speak in its own behalf, to demand that its legitimacy or 'naturality' be acknowledged, often in the same vocabulary, using the same categories by which it was medically disqualified."[15] De Lauretis follows this connection with the following translation of the process she has been describing.

> The disavowal of castration is a force that propels the drive *away* from the originally lost object (the mother) and toward the objects/signs that *both acknowledge and deny* a second, more consequential, narcissistic loss (the subject's own libidinally lost body-image), thus keeping at bay the lack of being that threatens the ego. This "displacement of value" [SE 23:277] or transfer of affect onto the fetish allows the subject to reinvest libidinally in the female body, in other women, through its fantasmatic or intrapsychic image, of which the fetish is a metonymic sign. (265)

What is significant for my purposes in this reformulation is the simultaneous acknowledgement that the fetish marks the clash of different schemes of value and that it is coded through the bestowal, or transfer, or investment of affect. One could take the route offered by Freud's use of displacement (*Entstellung*) to probe the lurking presence of the proper, of the phallogocentric economy within the formulation de Lauretis is offering as a perverse theory of desire. In broader strokes, however, de Lauretis effectively accomplishes a mystification of the lesbian by assigning to her a specific, perverse role in relation to value/affect, much as Pietz contains the movement of value in relation to a master signifier. The fetish is a substitute for an answer to the onto-phenomenological question, what is a lesbian? But as a process specific to lesbian desire, the fetish is reduced to its psycho-sexual dimension, shedding its sociohistorical context, and de Lauretis's invocation of semiosis in her final chapter as an analogous coding of the social is reminiscent of what Spivak calls Goux's last-ditch analogizing of the psychic to the social, an argument with which de Lauretis is not unfamiliar.[16] If the fetish can name a general theory of value-coding, it must be able to account for the clash in schemes of value that the fetish mediates. In my reading, the two poles between which the fetish mediates in de Lauretis are not "the lesbian" and "heteronormativity" but the "the lesbian" and "another lesbian" (she is adamant that it takes two to do the dance of perverse desire). The social, more specifically the masculine/feminine binary, becomes the dance floor for this encounter. De Lauretis thus operates on a register whereon the lesbian is assumed to be, recognizable in films and books, but, despite a familiar disclaimer, the fetish ultimately functions in her account to isolate "the sexual" from the very "symbolic and material effects of other cultural, and most significantly racial, differences in the constitution of the social subject" (xiii).

De Lauretis is a careful and nuanced thinker, whose formal characterization of the fetish also bears remarkable similarity to Pietz's general theory. I read *The Practice of Love,* therefore, as providing a complementary understanding of how to work the possibilities of the fetish from within psychoanalytic horizons toward a pliant understanding of lesbian sexuality and toward a nimble understanding of lesbian appearance. Elizabeth Grosz is less careful about what "politics" might mean in relation to the fetish, despite her able reading of Freud in "Lesbian Fetishism?" I turn briefly to that essay before concluding this consideration of how fetish discourse might contribute to an understanding of value-coding in relation to sexuality.

Grosz begins with what she calls a disavowal: she knows that lesbians cannot be fetishists strictly speaking, but she argues that perhaps in a "more strategic and political sense . . . there can be a form of female fetishism . . . [and] that lesbianism provides its most manifest and tangible expression."[17] That is, Grosz claims that both " 'normal' (i.e., heterosexual) femininity and female homosexuality can be seen—in sociopolitical terms—to be in excess of their psychoanalytic descriptions as a form of fetishism (in the same way that . . . feminism can be seen as a form of mass or collective psychosis, a political disavowal of women's social reality as oppressed)" (102). Fetishism is equated, then, with excess, aligned to the interests of feminist theory in "its struggles" (ibid.) whatever they might be, and disavowal (which predates the unconscious in psychoanalytic language) appears to have a corollary in "sociopolitical" feminist theory. This slippage between the psychic and the political is much less controlled than it is in de Lauretis's text, and it determines the conclusions Grosz draws at the end of her essay. Grosz knows, however, what disavowal is and emphasizes its importance to the male fetishist in her recitation of Freud's writing on fetishism. As Freud positions the fetishist between neurosis and psychosis, between hallucination and substitution (to use Grosz's language), he affirms that the fetishist "did not simply contradict his perceptions and hallucinate a penis where there was none to be seen, he effected no more than a displacement of value — he transferred the importance of the penis to another part of the body."[18] In Grosz's view, this displacement of value can be read in relation to the female disavowal of castration, the third type of which, "the masculinity complex," might be understood to have a possible connection to lesbian fetishism.

The logic runs this way: on Freud's account (and Lacan's, for that matter), female fetishism is an impossibility because fetishism is a disavowal of the mother's castration, and "the girl" has no need for that disavowal. She may, however, disavow her own castration, leading her on one of three unhappy paths — to heterosexual narcissism, hysteria, or the masculinity complex. In the former, the feminine subject (taken quickly as "the girl" by Grosz) develops a narcissistic investment in her own body by way of compensation for its perceived inferiority; she becomes the phallus, the object of desire, by displacing the value of the phallus onto her entire body (through regimes of self-regulation and -stylization). "She paints/shaves/plucks/dyes/diets/exercises her body, and clearly derives pleasure from compliments about her looks. Her whole body becomes the phallus to compensate for her genital deficiency, which she is able to disavow through her narcissistic self-investment" (111). In hysteria, the second neurotic path resulting from female disavowal, it is rather a part of the body that becomes phallicized, a hysterogenic zone that expresses the disavowal of castration by embodying the hysteric's eschewal of masculine desire; this preserves pre-Oedipal attachment to the mother or mother-substitutes. The relation, as Grosz argues, between narcissism and hysteria may be seen as one of degree rather than one of kind.

> Whereas the narcissist's whole body is the phallus (and thus she requires an external love object to bestow on her the status of the object of desire, thus accounting for her reliance on an anaclitic

lover, whether heterosexual or homosexual), the hysteric gains a self-defined status as phallic. A part of her own body takes on the function of the phallus (confirming her own object-like status in patriarchy) while her subjectivity remains in an active position (one which takes her own body as its object). (112)

The third possible effect of "the girl's" disavowal of her castration is the masculinity complex, often but not always associated with the perversion of female homosexuality. In this case, "the girl" refuses to accept her secondary and subordinate status. She styles herself as the object of the same treatment as men, and she refuses to act differently as well. Retaining the active clitoris rather than "moving on" to the passive vagina as her leading sexual organ, "the girl" who "suffers" from the masculinity complex may also retain "the maternal figure as the model on which to base her later object attachments, in which case she will continue to love a female mother substitute" (ibid.). Such is one version of female homosexuality, the one that produces the masculinity complex; the other involves an acceptance of castration, the temporary taking on of the father as the appropriate love object but then a detour where, instead of finding a father-substitute, the female homosexual seeks out a phallic woman ("a woman, one may suspect, with a masculinity complex" [113]).

In the woman with the masculinity complex, Grosz finds points of convergence with fetishism. Like the fetishist, she takes on a substitute for the phallus outside her own body (not the case with both the narcissist and the hysteric, who phallicize their own bodies), in her case another woman, and she is therefore able to function as if she has the phallus rather than is the phallus. But while the fetishist is content, the masculine woman is dissatisfied, both because her phallic object is another subject, a woman socially devalued through the fear of femininity, and because she is reminded always of the disparity between her equality with men in fantasy and the opposing social reality (compounded, too, by the dangers of homophobia). This dissatisfaction implies a splitting of the ego, and this splitting, claims Grosz, "inclines the masculine woman to feminism itself, insofar as feminism, or any oppositional political movement, involves a disavowal of social reality so that change becomes conceivable and possible" (114).

Grosz is not simply misreading Freud. Her reading has serious theoretical consequences, foremost among which is a model of lesbian relations that architecturally disintegrates under slippages between neurosis and perversion, incommensurate fetish-objects, psychic mechanisms, and social activism, disavowal and denial. Lesbian fetishism, if it exists, would explain nothing other than a meeting of two perverts defined at opposite ends of the pathological spectrum—one "suffering" from the masculinity complex and the other seeking her out by way of a detour of displacement. Grosz qualifies this universalized coupling through an appeal to what she claims are actually existing social arrangements between lesbians (vaguely alluding to the butch/femme paradigm), confirming Freud.

> In the case of an unnamed female homosexual, [Freud] describes her as behaving like a chivalrous male lover, displaying many of the characteristics attributed to the anaclitic or male type. She loves "like a man." Although we may dispute the appropriateness of this description to all kinds of lesbian love relations, it seems clear that it certainly describes at least one kind of lesbian relationship, that in which there is a form of reproduction of typical heterosexually coded relations between narcissistic (feminine) and anaclitic (masculine) lovers. (113)

What does it mean to love "like a man" when one "is" a woman? What do *masculine* and *feminine* designate here? Where do we find "typical heterosexually coded relations" in lesbian relations? What, in other words, might be gained by lending the name "fetishist" to this butch/femme couple? To Grosz, "it is not entirely clear, and it is for this reason that my answer must remain strategic" (114). With the declared aim of preserving an account of the unconscious and the psyche for feminism, she seems to have accomplished the installation of a vexingly static entity called the lesbian, condemned to isolation and ostracism from which the lesbian escapes to feminism. Not de Lauretis's dance floor of lesbian desire but an unhappy wallflower on the margins of heteronormative privilege—it is this wallflower who becomes the subject of feminism when her *denial* of social reality spurs her toward activist change. The model of lesbian fetishism Grosz proposes thus shares with the one developed by de Lauretis a paradoxical understanding of the specular economy of the fetish. On the one hand, both are underwritten by visual apprehension and confirmation of the gender binary, and, on the other, both seem blind to contextualizing the psychoanalytic valences of fetishism within social and historical parameters as a route toward apprehending that which clashes with our own schemes of value-coding. These three examples of fetish-discourse (Pietz, de Lauretis, Grosz) nonetheless provide several routes toward a reading of *lesbian* as catachresis.

Value, contentless and simple, is also dynamic. Fetish-discourse, as long as it refuses to domesticate the fetish for pragmatic utility, provides one but only one way to trace what *lesbian* marks as a catachresis.[19] Fetish-discourse consolidates relations among modernity, the visual and sexual difference, and *lesbian* could be seen to name a similar constellation of modern identity, appearance, and sexuality. Reading *lesbian* in fetishistic terms in the least restrictive way possible allows *lesbian* the dynamism and mobility produced by *lesbian* as catachresis.

Chapter 2

Droits de Regards/Right of Inspection:
For Agnes and Inez Albright

Throughout this book I have argued, along with others, that looking, the right to look, to interpret that look, and, if one wishes, to employ that look to facilitate visual plea-sure, can also be appropriated as a subcultural strategy that I have sought here to mark as lesbian.—Clare Whatling, *Screen Dreams: Fantasizing Lesbians in Film*

While this study obviously privileges the intersection between the category "lesbian" and deconstruction, it does not do so on the basis of any natural affinity or hostility between the two. Like the category "lesbian" the strategies of deconstruction are not credited with any inherent politics, either radical or reactionary, anti-homophobic or homophobic. —Annamarie Jagose, *Lesbian Utopics*

I take the first part of this chapter's title from a joint project by Jacques Derrida and Marie-Françoise Plissart, published in 1985 in France but not reprinted in its entirety in the United States until 1998.[1] For many of Derrida's anglophone readers, the book is a relatively new treat, and it introduces us to Plissart's photography, as Derrida is aware. As with many of Derrida's texts, the French title resists translation, suggesting at once the right to look, the right to the gaze, or the laws of looking, as well as the right to control, the acts of overseeing or supervising. Those readers steeped in film-theory debates will, of course, recognize instantly the constellation of gendered spectatorship, power, and legal-istic control in the title's resonances, and these elements are, in fact, ex-plored both in Plissart's photographic series and Derrida's comments, themselves arranged and printed as a sort of mock dialogue or conver-sation among several parties. Beyond the thematic level, however, Plis-sart's photographs and Derrida's reading of them stage—rather than cite or discuss—a number of scenes that are central to this book's concern with the specular morphology of the lesbian: with the mise-en-scène of her appearance, its significance, its stakes, its props (in both senses), its fetishes, and its games.

What does it mean to assert a "specular morphology" of *lesbian,* or lesbian *as* image? It means to suggest that lesbian has a privileged relation to sight, not as essence but as effect. I am not saying that lesbian is merely appearance, but that it is in appearance that lesbian frequently is. This is not to exclude or continue to denigrate touch, smell, sound, or taste (for surely at least some of us, save Queen Victoria, have felt, smelled, heard, and tasted lesbians), but it is to suggest that lesbian is most commonly *seen.* Why, and in what ways? What does it mean to see a lesbian, and what do we think when we think we have seen a lesbian? What are the politics of the look?

Droits de regards, in the spirit of the second of my epigraphs, which insists on no *necessary* kinship between deconstruction and "antihomophobic" politics, directly challenges the assumptions of the first epigraph, as I, too, will seek to do in what follows. I argue that Plissart's photos and Derrida's reading of them refuse the a priori "subcultural" status of the lesbian, the language of voluntaristic appropriation, and the narcissistic pursuit of pleasure in looking understood merely as identification. Instead, the "right of inspection" presses as a question and as a pressing determination any time one reads an image, or a series of images or movements, in cinema as in photography.

In *Droits de regards/Right of Inspection,* Plissart and Derrida appear, furthermore, to present *both* lesbians *and* photography; for that combination alone, the project would appear congenial, if not seductive, to any study devoted to the appearance of lesbian and the value of sexual difference, especially one such as this, undertaken through a framework inherited from the past twenty-odd years of critical works often collected under the rubric of poststructuralism. Despite the significant differences between photography and cinematography, there are profound and frequently ignored kinships between them; despite the variety of projects undertaken in the name of poststructuralism, few indeed present themselves *as* what one might provisionally call image(s). As one might expect, however, both of the project's authors, or the artist and her commentator, or the novelist and her critic (any choice restricts or programs the generic treatment of the text) bestow upon the reader/spectator something rather more enigmatic, more latent, than this combination might suggest. It remains for the reader/spectator to use the language of photography's chemistry, to develop its tones further. To do so, I turn to a more familiar photograph in order to set the stage for the more extended reading of Plissart and Derrida's project to which this chapter is devoted.

Reading Photographs

I read the cover image of Agnes and Inez Albright from Judith Butler's *Gender Trouble* as an invitation to work further on the relation between lesbian and image. First published in 1989 and reprinted with the same cover photograph in what Routledge proudly calls a "10th Anniversary Edition," *Gender Trouble* requires nothing of the introduction that Plissart and Derrida's project does for a United States academic readership. The book was simply transformative, as much for its dazzling intellectual work as its committed queer understanding. It galvanized many scholars, philosophers, queer theorists, feminists; indeed, Butler's work continues to do so because it was an expansive undertaking with a broad horizon. Questions thankfully remain regarding *Gender Trouble*'s project, among them the proliferation Butler sought to address in her subsequent volume, *Bodies That Matter.* In a kind of doubled rhetorical voice, Butler seems to channel in her own voice the questions put to her by others.

> If there is no such subject who decides on its gender, and if, on the contrary, gender is part of what decides the subject, how might one formulate a project that preserves gender practices as sites of critical agency? If gender is constructed through relations of power and, specifically, normative constraints that not only produce but also regulate various bodily beings, how might agency be derived from this notion of gender as the effect of productive constraint? If gender is not an artifice to be taken on or taken off at will and, hence, not an effect of choice, how are we to understand the constitutive and compelling status of gender norms without falling into the trap of cultural determinism? How precisely are we to understand the ritualized repetition by which such norms produce and stabilize not only the effects of gender but the materiality of sex? And can this repetition, this rearticulation, also constitute the occasion for a critical reworking of apparently constitutive gender norms?[2]

I would add the further question, and I do so with the proposition that Plissart's photographic series and Derrida's commentary will address what is at stake in those above: can we *see* gender trouble? In Agnes (and not Inez?) Albright?

The photograph of the two women, presumably sisters, would seem in fact to function as a cover illustration of the gender trouble that will follow inside the pages of Butler's book, a ruse of representational fidelity that follows the conventions and protocols of paperback publishing. In brief, the cover attracts our attention and signals, even if obliquely, the content to follow. To recall the uncredited photograph, as it appears on the Routledge volume: the tone is sepia; Agnes and Inez stand head to toe before the camera in a studio with canvas backdrop, Agnes (presumably) on the left, with hand on (presumably) Inez's shoulder. Agnes gazes directly, seemingly confidently into the lens, perhaps an effect of the focus, which is pulled tightest on Agnes' face, Inez slightly to the left; both are dressed in what one might be tempted to call frocks, for the style appears to belong to something like "late Victorian/early frontier," long-sleeved and adorned with frills around the arms and chest. Agnes's hair is short, cropped; Inez's is parted in the middle and gathered at her neck, Emily Dickinson-style.

The book cover is meant, the potential buyer supposes, to provide a condensation, substitute, or metonymy for the interior content, here understood to be the double sense of "trouble" Butler imparts to the couplet "gender trouble." For trouble is both rebellion and reprimand.

> To make trouble was, within the reigning discourse of my childhood, something one should never do precisely because that would get one *in* trouble. The rebellion and its reprimand seemed to be caught up in the same terms, a phenomenon that gave rise to my first critical insight into the subtle ruse of power: the prevailing law threatened one with trouble, even put one in trouble, all to keep one out of trouble. Hence, I concluded that trouble is inevitable and the task, how best to make it, what best way to be in it.[3]

Let me generate some questions, then, about this photo and the work that it does on the cover of *Gender Trouble*, knowing that I would do equally well to put these to the cover's designer, Tara Klurman, as much as to the book's author and its many astute readers: Do Agnes and Inez Albright thus *represent* both senses of trouble's inevitability? Is gender trouble poignantly tied to the time of childhood, of Agnes and Inez Albright's, as well as Judith Butler's, pedagogical and disciplinary initiation into power's ruses? Does the gaze of the camera thereby become

Figure 5. Cover of the magazine *Sinister Wisdom*. This image was also used for the cover of Judith Butler's *Gender Trouble*. Lesbian Herstory Archives.

power itself, that prevailing law which is capable of threatening, putting one in jeopardy, as well as steering one clear of trouble's way? Who, then, has the right to look (at it, at them), or the right to control their image? Does Agnes embody, signal, or present the "subversion" or trouble that produces the gender norms that Inez obeys as retroactive effect? Is it Agnes who is perhaps a lesbian? Queer? Or is it Inez who passes as a result of Agnes's "visible" gender difference? How would we know? Is this photograph, fractured and torn or previously folded in half, shorn from its scene of inscription (who knows which?) *and* from its initial cover appearance on the lesbian-feminist journal *Sinister Wisdom,* an "instance," an "example," a "signifier," or an "iteration" of gender performativity, or does the latter indeed resist representation itself? And what is the affect produced by that tear (the rip), that tear (the drip) one could shed over the seam that divides Agnes from Inez?

Like the two other quasi-visual examples Butler invokes in *Gender Trouble,* Divine and Greta Garbo, the cover photograph of Agnes and Inez Albright stands as an unread paratext, sliding between the narrow sense of a performance before the camera and the general sense of performativity, derived from Austin through Derrida, that is at the core of *Gender Trouble*'s theoretical project. The photo would appear to stage gender trouble insofar as it confounds the neat alignment of masculine and feminine gender signifiers, but the films and photographs (like Jennie Livingston's film *Paris is Burning* in *Bodies That Matter*) remain generalized and unexamined *as films and photographs.* These, as I will show in this chapter, obey conventions, are produced through specific technologies, appear in contexts, from which they may be severed, reattached, recombined with different but significant effects. They can be read rhetorically, through genre, through their particular signifying systems, and they invite such readings.

In changing venue, the photograph that appears on the cover of *Gender Trouble* actually lost some contextual force which I seek to restore here. As a cover illustration for the lesbian journal *Sinister Wisdom* 21 (1982), edited by the luminous figures Michelle Cliff and Adrienne Rich, the caption is expanded: "two sisters: Agnes and Inez; Alamance Country, North Carolina, circa 1895; family collection of Catherine Nicholson." We can now begin to locate these sisters regionally; we can now posit and explore an affective connection between these family members and one of the journal's founding editors, Catherine Nicholson. We can locate the photograph in the context of studio photography of the turn of the century, and we can examine the photograph's role as reclamation within the context of cultural feminist or lesbian photography such as the pioneering work by JEB (who, incidentally, encouraged the early documentary work of Del LaGrace Volcano, whose photographs of drag kings extend our queer photographic archive in new directions). More significant even than these contexts, perhaps, is the use of other photographs in the same issue of *Sinister Wisdom*, for there is not a single image but several, and the others testify to a dominant illustrative role: the guarantee of historical continuity, of lesbians' presence in the past. The other photographs are "found" images of cross-dressing New England gals at play on a farm. They function to manage the slide of lesbian signification. By offering a visual guarantee of presence, they conjure continuity through a representational or illustrative self who finesses political origins and ends.

Such an illustrative function is not, however, understood simply or naively within the pages of *Sinister Wisdom*. In the 1982 journal's issue, the reclamation of history, the reconstruction of lesbian lives in the past, provides ground for discussion rather than certainty. What is, to my mind, most striking about reading the particular issue that follows under the cover of the Albright sisters today is the attention, the care it devotes to problems of history and representation, and in particular to the very status of feminist/lesbian discourse the journal seeks to forge. At the issue's end, for example, a collection of letters debates the ethical and political dimensions of anti-Semitism in feminist and lesbian communities, with a focus on what Adrienne Rich calls the "heart-work" that, in addition to mere words or facts, makes possible rigorous cross-cultural criticism from a feminist perspective.[4] Earlier and more centrally to the point, a review by Marian Roth of a then-new publication, *The Blatant Image: A Magazine of Feminist Photography*, considers the tension between photographs' illustrative, or literal, functions and their function as purely visual images, images that speak, as it were, on their own. Seeing the former as towing the line, acting to reinforce a "correct" or "relevant" position, Roth urges photographers, including herself, to trust in the capacity of the image to speak on its own, without commentary such as that required by *The Blatant Image* to accompany each submission. She concludes with an anecdote that zooms in on the vexing relationship between aesthetics and politics that have haunted photography.

> I lived in a political commune during the formative years of my art, and always felt the burden of the "right line." In fact, I did not dare

take a picture of a tree for three years, thinking it was frivolous and counter-revolutionary. One day at a workshop, I brought in a picture of a tree and confessed my fears. A fellow photographer told me that on the side of the tree, she could read the message, "free the Attica Brothers" (*Sinister Wisdom* 21 [1982]).

This chapter's task is to interrogate precisely *how* one reads visual images as lesbian, by insisting that when the lesbian appears as image, or cinematically, one reads the rhetoric of that appearance rigorously for its implications, philosophical and otherwise. I seek, in other words, to attend to the tyranny whereby lesbian is understood to appear *as* lesbian, that tautology through which we confirm the already known. If the "lesbian image" on the cover of Butler's book opens horizons of intelligibility having to do with cultural feminism and feminist art, so too do other apparently lesbian images provoke necessary contextual labors. By reading the photographs of Marie-Françoise Plissart along with Derrida, I seek to generate neither a model nor a method but a set of resources for the chapters that follow, chapters that move along the modifications of the noun *lesbian* I traced in the introduction. Keep the lesbian in mind: Plissart's photographs are "of" lesbians. While the context acquires density, the lesbian image becomes differently intelligible. I begin with the problematic of translation: of translating particular texts such as *Droits de regards*, of translating disciplines (philosophy to film scholarship), of translating systems (linguistic to imagistic or vice versa), of translation and its very possibility.

"What is a 'Relevant' Translation?"

David Wills, who translated Derrida's contribution to *Right of Inspection*, in his preface notes Derrida's characteristic "will to untranslatability" in defending his own textual choices in rendering the English version, informed as those choices are by Wills's sustained engagement with Derrida's works.[5] What Wills calls Derrida's will, perhaps dispersing his own signature as textual authority, may, however, be something more like a conspiracy, or an intention to muddy the scene of translation so that no culprit, no intending will, may be found. In "What is a 'Relevant' Translation?" Derrida addresses head-on the question of translation, specifically as organized by an economy that "relates the translatable to the untranslatable."[6] His essay prepares us for some of the translations at work and at play in *Droits de regards,* because it is an essay, as perhaps all of his are, on reading and writing. I take some time with it here to dwell with the reading practices the essay seems to me to display, since they are very different from the "method" of the reversal of binary terms many seem to associate with deconstruction or with Derrida's writings. Reading the lesbian image through these alternate protocols provides me with a more expansive repertoire for tracing the movements of *lesbian* as catachresis. Moreover, I follow the periodization offered by Spivak in the appendix to her *Critique of Postcolonial Reason* in referring to the essay to which we now turn as belonging to an "affirmative" mode.[7] (Although it is inconvenient and frequently precious to put quotation marks around everyday words, I do so here in order to denaturalize a routine gesture, all the while hoping that I do not overstep the reader's tolerance for the practice.)

At several points in the essay, Derrida returns us to several earlier texts in which he addresses specific translations or meditations on translation, such as Benjamin's essay, "The Task of the Translator," or the work of James Joyce. But another moment of translation drives the essay more generally and more forcefully, a moment when, in 1967, Derrida proposed to translate a crucial German word that "the entire world had until then agreed was untranslatable—or, if you prefer, a word for which no one had agreed with anyone on a stable, satisfying translation into any language" (196). That word, we know now, is none other than *Aufheben, Aufhebung,* Hegel's word for the dialectical movement simultaneously of suppression and elevation, "the double motif of the elevation and the replacement that preserves what it denies or destroys" (196). In English that word is frequently rendered as *supercession* or *sublation.* Derrida's proposal, in French, is the noun *relève,* the verb *relever,* the same word that gives us *relevant* and him his title.

In a monumental coup, Derrida has found a word, then, a translation, that the "entire world"—a marvelously trumped-up synonym for the world of philosophy—had "until then" been unable to find. It is, moreover, a translation for *the* word on which philosophy since Hegel hinges, "a word that Hegel says represents the speculative risk of the German language" (196). How should one read this gesture, this hubris? One may read it as boldly confident philosophizing, or as tongue-in-cheek, or as an opening, I think, upon the very set of issues and questions that ought to engage a reading of the essay.

What is monumental thinking, or writing? How does one demarcate (make a "cut" or decoupage) a field in addressing superlative figures, whether Hegel or Shakespeare, whose *Merchant of Venice* Derrida reads in the essay, whether of philosophy or literature or beyond the academic enclosure? How does one position oneself among the authors of the texts one reads, and among an audience that is specific, occasional? According to what economy, or determination of value? How do we decide, in short, whose text is best in any given field, itself marked only by exclusion, how do we address ourselves to it, and according to what principles or rules?

If an economy regulates the superlative text, so, too, might it regulate translation, wherein which operation the "relevant" translation is *the* translation; the best translation is translation itself. *Relevant* might thus be shown to be a name for translation itself, the Aufhebung is (a) translation. The economy of translation opens, therefore, onto what can and what cannot be translated: the "undecidable" words that have organized Derrida's writings in the past, as he adds in a parenthesis "*pharmakon,* supplément, différance, hymen, and so on" (196), as well as the homonyms or homophones that confound the economy of translation, insofar as its axiom is "word for word." If translation depends on the word, one must labor on the word itself.

By introducing the "economic" determination of translation (*economy* here signifying both "property," the proper, what is at home, as well as quantity), and of the Aufhebung, Derrida introduces the Marx who will read Hegel and speak to us of value, obliquely but clearly enough in Derrida's recurring invocation of the relationship between use- and exchange-value. The dialectical materialist cannot but shine behind the extension of a chain of value to meaning in this passage: "The measure of the *relève* or relevance, the price of a translation, is always what is called meaning, that is, value, preservation, truth as preservation (*Wahrheit, bewahren*) or the value of meaning, namely, what, in being freed from the body, is elevated above it, interiorizes it, spiritualizes it, preserves it in memory" (199). The encryption that is mourning, interiorization, returns us to the specter of Marx in Derrida's book of the same name, as much as to his reading there of another Shakespeare play, *Hamlet.* Moving backward to his earlier essays and enfolding his other works, Derrida reminds his own reader of context, of what is concealed by what is at hand, the textual equivalent of off-screen space, beyond the frame, or of what silence is to sound. This passage on mourning, then, also and equally importantly, signals a reading of that Freud who "has been mobilized and interrogated" (184 n.4) in his own accounts of "transfer, metaphor and translation" (ibid., in this note regarding the theme of the three caskets), as opposed, one surmises, to a Freud read faithfully and, indeed, monumentally. One cannot address everything, of course; Derrida's frequent self-citation and reference, however, reminds us that works are isolated only at a cost, through exclusion and frequently through sloppiness or anti-intellectual refusals to read and read carefully. If Derrida cites himself frequently, it is not necessary for us to decide whether the cause of the practice is reference to Freud's self-absorption, Derrida's own sense of monumentality, parody of the same, or the marking of a limit of one text that will, necessarily, invoke others.

As much, then, as Derrida moves through these issues, themes or preoccupations, he *stages* them, confounding, as he says, the "canonical distinction between *mention* and *use*" (175). One might risk the generalization that a hallmark of the affirmative mode is the indeterminate insistence on the performative dimensions of language, so that one does not simply "discuss" or "analyze" or "examine" or "interrogate" through a language presumed to be transparent, but one *works within* language itself. "The word" is in this way Derrida's theme in the essay ("the word will be my theme" [175]), but the "theme" is likewise caught in the distinction between mention and use. One speaks on one's theme, but Derrida will not only speak "of" the word—one cannot while using them. *Use* the noun, marks, therefore, one axis of the value of meaning. Insofar as there is a statement on method in this essay, it may be a single sentence: "The treasure trove amounts to a travail: it puts to work the languages, first of all, without adequation or transparency, here assuming the shape of a new writing or rewriting that is performative or poetic, not only in French, where a new use for the word emerges, but also in German and English" (198).

What is exciting about reading Derrida's essay and his work more generally has to do with the connections that collect, that recede and reappear as one rereads or remembers a move a few pages back. Not surprisingly, it is precisely this mobility that he, in turn, finds exciting in Plissart's photographs. When, for example, Derrida first introduces the idea of the word that would assume its coherence, he is working with the closeness, the at-homeness, we have with language that makes the idea of the bounded word incontestably familiar. We often forget, in this same familiarity, how the unity or identity, the independence of the word, remains a mysterious thing, precarious, not quite natural, that is to say historical, institutional, and conventional. There is no such thing as a word in nature (177). Derrida uses the abbreviation for translation (*tr.*) as the basis for a significant philosophical claim—insisting on the mark as the smallest possible iterative entity, as opposed to the word—in order to proliferate a number of words that will animate the essay, "to indicate that the motif of *labor* [*travail*], the *travail* of childbirth, but also the *transferential* and *transformational travail*, in all possible codes and not only that of psychoanalysis, will enter into competition with the apparently more neutral motif of *translation*, as *transaction* and as *transfer*" (176). In this sentence, then, we have already seen the iteration of the mark, the *tr* that makes possible a series that concatenates French and English (*travail* and travail), and that links several motifs, if not themes, of the essay. Moving between mention and use, claims and examples, Derrida "discusses" an economy of translation while translating.

While it would be possible to read each sentence of "What Is a 'Relevant' Translation?" for these iterations, I take the essay more generally as alerting his reader to the kinds of moves and concerns that ought to preoccupy her in reading Derrida's commentary on Plissart's photographic series. One needs to be aware, then, of the "will to untranslatability," the level of the mark (not the word) as the iterative entity, the positing of a system with its rules and also its chance dimensions, and the staging of an argument in performative or poetic writing. In turning to Plissart's photographs, the scene becomes further complicated by reading not another text (literary or philosophical) but another medium entirely, that of photography.

Right of Inspection

How would one discuss photographs photographically? Or images imagistically? Or cinema cinematically? How does one read, translate, render, or develop images in words? What is translatable? What is untranslatable?

In the beautifully designed Monacelli Press edition, Plissart's photographs have been reproduced in the series in which they originally appeared "in French." The first photograph in the English-language edition of *Right of Inspection* is, in fact, a photograph by Jeannine Govaers of the French-language book, *Droits de regards,* a placement *en abîme* that signals the abyssal structure one soon encounters through the photographic series itself: already, it is hard to tell what properly belongs to Plissart or to Derrida, to a signature or an eye. To confirm that structure, the second photograph, also by Govaers, is a photograph of the very book published by Monacelli, *Right of Inspection,* in English. Although it appears odd indeed to speak of a photograph being *in* a language, there is no doubt that the initial appearance of Plissart's photographs in a book published in France with a commentary, in the French language, by the eminent if not notorious Algerian-born French philosopher Jacques Derrida, at minimum locates the photographs within a linguistic context. Plissart, herself a Belgian, is also situated within language, or in the interstitial gap of two languages, at what Derrida will call a "linguistic frontier" between Flemish and French.[8] And, furthermore, elements of several different languages appear in some of the photographs themselves: a box of Marlboro cigarettes, fragments of graffiti, an injunction not to smoke, a page of words in Spanish, lettering on a bottle of mineral water. Sometimes the viewer can make out a word, its language and its role; at other times, the letters simply appear as marks, things among others. The photographs immerse their viewers in these chunks of many languages—as we are so immersed in our everyday mediatized lives—and yet photographs conventionally are thought to be outside of a linguistic community as "images."

Significantly, then, one of the tasks of Derrida's commentary seems to be to convince his reader (or the photographs' viewer) *not* to see these series of photographs as images but instead as something like textual occasions, or that which compels interpretive work, storytelling and theory-making, reading, exegesis, deciphering. Rather than refusing the language of the image, however, Derrida inhabits the world of its production as intimately as possible in his own commentary, taking up the specificity of photography as apparatus in order to conjugate a "photogrammar" (his word) appropriate to it and, furthermore, to ask who polices the line of that propriety. Rather than presume, moreover, that a "language of photography" exists at the level of the discrete image, Derrida summons its own language, the language *of* photography, in order to investigate its technologies or its modes of bringing itself into being.[9] To translate into philosophical language, his interest is as ontological as it is technological, or, better, attuned to photography as *techné*. He stays as close as he can in his language, that is, to what photography itself might be doing, taking his cue specifically from the 35-mm camera wielded by women that also appears in Plissart's photographs, insofar as his language is specific to single-lens reflex photography using negative film; he invokes and renders conceptual the language of emulsion, of the response of film to light, of developing (as chemistry develops), of the shot (including the command to be static, to demur), of the reflex and the mirror, and of the lens.

Plissart's photographs themselves resist reference in terms of "the image" for a number of reasons, many of which are apparent within the first few pages of her series. Most clearly, the photographs run serially; they are often laid out on the page in groups rather than individually, and they invite connections between themselves. When only one photograph occupies a page, it frequently will be in a graphic or other relation to several subsequent or previous right- or left-hand pages; when a series such as that develops, it will often function in relation to an opposite series, as a form of parallel editing, or shot/reverse shot. More frequently, however, several photographs over several pages will slowly make visible a shared interest, as though in a developer tray in the darkroom. On the first page, for example, two women's nude bodies lie amidst white sheets, one on her back with the other's hand in her crotch. We do not see their heads. Below on the same page, in two separate photographs, the woman initially on her back seems to have shifted onto the other woman, now lying on *her* back, and her hand, adorned with a ring, directs the other woman's hand from crotch to groin. On the next page, in a photograph arranged to occupy the vertical left length of the page, the two women (the same two?) are in the same position, but they are now framed waist-up, the one nuzzling the other's head (whose earring is visible). Next to this photograph, occupying the left length of the page, are three smaller ones: of an illuminated curtain blowing in a window, with an indistinct framed photograph in the corner of a grand room with elaborate molding, reflecting the outside light; of white booties, white pants, and a white shirt crumpled on a solid black surface, artificially lit and arranged as though in a still life; and finally, of the interior of the same room as in the top photo, cued by the presence of both the same molding and the same photograph, now seen, however, reflected on the surface of one of two French doors at the left of the frame, below a transom and beside a large mirror that also reflects a portion of the room. Formally, they all rely heavily on black and white contrast and balanced reflective surfaces. They also foreground their referential gestures, emphasizing frequently the photographing of photographs. Obeying the conventions of realism, they maintain their human subjects in relatively tight focus, naturalize the human body against its background, and retain the point of view of a third party or onlooker, especially in the medium distance (what in film

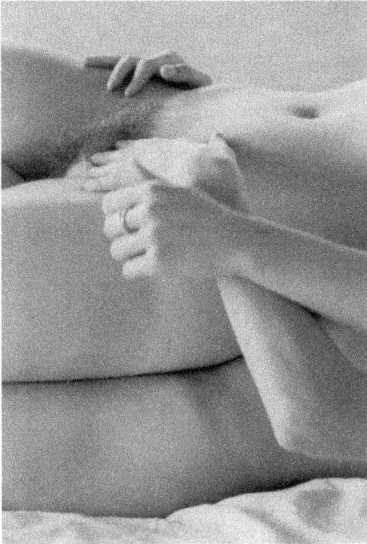

Figure 6. Photographs from *Droits de regards*. Courtesy of Editions de Minuit.

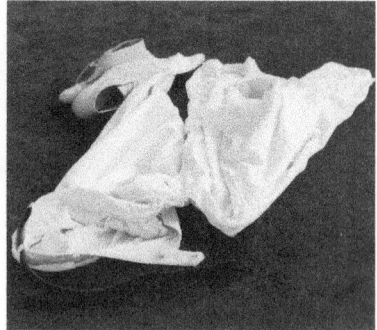

Figure 7. Photographs from *Droits de regards*. Courtesy of Editions de Minuit.

is called *plan américain*) shots on subsequent pages that return to the two women in bed.

As Derrida will remind his community of readers over and again, it is impossible *not* to tell ourselves stories the more we describe what we see; it is impossible *not* to make the causal connections that produce narrative. These women, these lesbians (they *are* making love), we tell ourselves, these are our characters. We differentiate them on the basis of small details: "the one with the ring," or the "the one with the boyish haircut." We give them nicknames, so that we can keep track of them throughout, as they change clothes, acquire new props. Perhaps, as our form of nicknaming, we lend them proper names, as one of Derrida's own characters does in his commentary: Dominique and Claude. Since we see these women in bed *next* to the two photographs of the room and the one of the shed clothing, we supply the connections upon which continuity editing depends. Like good Kuleshov subjects, we decide that they must be in *that* house in which this room is located; those must be *her* clothes on the floor, either woman's clothes, for there are two. This emphasis on linguistic shifters, or deictic indicators (*this* room, *those* clothes, *that* photograph) is significant, for it is the action through which those who encounter the photographs are positioned not merely as passive spectators but as narrators who occupy a relationship to the scene, as modernist detectives engaged in what Derrida will call police or psychoanalytic reconstruction.

There is, moreover, no *end* to the stories, in at least two senses: we can tell ourselves almost infinite stories about what has occurred or what will have taken place. If we qualify that claim with an "almost," we are thereby also bound to produce equally endless theoretical or exegetical speculations about what constitutes the limit, just as psychoanalysis must determine its own systemic limits, terminable and interminable. And the more we say, "no story," the more the *desire* for stories builds! But, in the second sense, we can move in several directions as we tell these stories: forward, backward, looping from the end or starting in the middle, departing and returning from elements that seem to inaugurate or conclude one series to elements in another, diagonally, as it were.

Whatever the direction, then, the series move or are set into motion, and for that reason, too, the comparatively static language of the image or of identity politics, for that matter, seems insufficient or ill-suited to this project. But if there are series seemingly without limit or end in the sense of a conclusion, it is not clear that we can name the genre of that which we encounter in these series' movement. If these are not images, what are they? In their movement, they invite comparisons to cinema. Since there are no words accompanying these photographs, we might modify the comparison to the silent cinema, but without its intertitles. Similarly, because they are not projected images, filmed to produce the illusion of motion as cinema requires, perhaps it is more appropriate to compare them to a photonovel, a genre in which Plissart has worked before. And yet, as is obvious but also bears a reminder, these photographs lack the text, balloons and captions that constitute the "novel" portion of photo*novel*. Neither quite cinema nor photonovel, the photographs nonetheless gesture toward both. If, in other words, Plissart's photographs are an innovation, a novel form or a new genre, one is witnessing the genesis or the generation of *a question regarding genre*. Those readers familiar with Derrida's work will not require the reminder that *genre* in French means both gender and genre. To raise the question of genre, of belonging to one or to another, is also to raise a question of gender, of belonging to one or *the* other, and both are central to reading or deciphering this quasi-photonovel about lesbians. To say that it is a question of *genre*, furthermore, is not to defer it indefinitely but to suspend an answer about how and where *genre* matters.

It may be important, however, to recall, as David Wills does in his translator's preface, the other iterative movements of *genre*, for they are imbricated in other untranslatable plays or moves upon which Derrida's commentary will depend. *Genre* also gives *générique*—in English, the word "generic" but also "film credits." As he did with *tr*. Derrida will take off from *gen-*, playing on generate, generation, generic, credits for creating (as in God or an author, the One or one who signs), creation, the fall, the Virgin, etc. In this concatenation, he creates and follows orders that are logical, analytical, rhetorical. As we have seen in the "translation" essay, however, he also disperses at the level not of the word but of the mark (the *gen-*), following performative iterations, declining, as by a grammar, tracing inversions, inhabiting yet "tampering with" the rhetorics this project develops.[10]

Two additional plays, then, can be added to that based on *genre;* Wills calls our attention to them in his notes, as well. The first I have already slipped in—that around *demeure*. The verb *to demur* means to remain or to stay (as in "stay put" for the shot), but as a noun refers to a sumptuous residence, the grand estate or *petit château* that is the mise-en-scène for most of these series (except for a few more noir-ish departures to the streets), and also has the legalistic sense of a command or an order in the phrase *mise en demeure*. The second stitches together some of what is gathered under the question of genre, in a play upon the *parties de dames*, the game of checkers that features prominently in some of the photographs, especially of the young women, but also may be understood as the game of women featured throughout the series. *Partie* easily suggests the fragments or parts (of people, of things, of stories, and the psychoanalytic sense of partial-objects, fragments, details, or fetishes), but it also functions in the sense of *partir*, or leaving (departures). As Wills notes, then, the "game that takes place from photograph to photograph is structured by women leaving the scene."[11] Also embedded in the partie de dames, then, are (1) diagonal movement: of a checkerboard and of these women leaving, down staircases, across rooms; (2) the equivalence in *dame* of woman and checker, later the whole and the piece; (3) the position of the woman who controls and the photographer who exercises her right of inspection over all the pieces/photographic subjects.

All these women, coming *and* going, all these series of women seem to entail a story that is concealed, a detective story, perhaps, involving a threat, or a primal scene that one cannot have seen but perhaps also will have imagined. As one enters into the system of diagonals, of the rules of composition, and the game determined by the apparatus, moreover, one depends upon a prior law that authorizes one's right to look, to enter in with the gaze.

> A text of images gives you, as much as it gives its "characters," a right to look, the simple right to look or to appropriate with the gaze, but it denies you that right at the same time: by means of its very apparatus it retains that authority by keeping for itself the right of inspection over whatever discourses you might like to put forth or whatever yarns you might spin about it, and that in fact come to mind before your eyes. They arise, they grow within you like desire itself, they invade you.[12]

By *the gaze* one assumes that Derrida means what Lacan means: not simply the look, not necessarily the eyes or the face of another, but "an *x*, the object when faced with which the subject becomes object."[13] The inversion of inside and outside ("they invade you") signals the prior authorization upon which the production of discourse—formal or colloquial, analysis or spinning yarns—depends; to make a reading presupposes that a right of inspection has been entrusted to it.

And so it is in this way that, finally, lesbian might be understood to be photographed, to become the subject of *or* for the right of inspection. What I seek, then, to emphasize is the way in which lesbian did not or will not appear as a self-evident entity, offered for recognition or identification. Like the shock photo, Plissart's photographic series function *intersubjectively,* even as they do so within a specific medium and genre, historically, and with a constrained image-repertoire. As Derrida suggests, this "genesis of sexual difference in effect *developed* like a genealogy of light and shade" (ix). To follow Lacan's understanding of the gaze, in the field of vision one is fundamentally in the world of subjectivity *and* subjectivation. "What determines me, at the most profound level, in the visible, is the gaze that is outside. It is through the gaze that I enter light and it is from the gaze that I receive its effects. Hence it comes about that the gaze is the instrument through which—if you will allow me to use a word, as I often do, in a fragmented form—I am *photo-graphed.*"[14] In this *partie de dames,* this game of checkers or of women, thus is inaugurated or put into play also an *imaginary* intersubjective relation which both Derrida and Lacan further understand to be uncertain, unstable, critical, as opposed to some blissed-out version of the imaginary as harmonious. Neither entirely in the domain of the symbolic nor that of the imaginary, one finds oneself traversing or oscillating in a photopsychoanalytic scene of inversion.

To render the connections between photography and psychoanalysis visible is not simply to develop something latent, as it were, in Derrida's text. He most explicitly links the two, frequently abbreviated as *P.* and *Ph.,* beginning with a quick reference to Walter Benjamin's observation that "the *invention* of photography and the *advent* of psychoanalysis *concur* [*convienment,* playing with the comings and goings]."[15] Both, he emphasizes, are sciences of the detail, arts of magnification. They instantiate new relationships between the part and the whole; they measure and calculate the importance of the detail in relation to the whole. Both photography and psychoanalysis, furthermore, install new temporalities, whether in the recalibration of time that is analysis, the eternality of the unconscious, or the instantaneity of the photograph: "It is perhaps an 'ahistory' that is being recounted here, such as photographic technique alone, through the invention of a new apparatus, can bring to mind and bring to pass; a different temporality, the so-called timelessness of the unconscious, the ring of the eternal return, the hymen and the affirmation of women."[16]

Opposing both photography and psychoanalysis to Foucault's use of Jeremy Bentham's figure of the panopticon in *Discipline and Punish*, Derrida alleges that neither photography nor psychoanalysis allows the right to *complete* inspection, despite the capacity of each to endow the detail with significance. Rather, he insists that the "silent liturgy of the fragment should remain discreet [also discrete] and not give rise to any dream of a *general theory* which is another name for the panoptical."[17] In part because the two domains, discourses or grammars remain discrete, they evade the whole gaze that would establish itself before the subject's eyes in its entirety. In Plissart's photographs as in the discourse of psychoanalysis, the whole as effect never remains distinct or discrete from the part into which it is reinserted or through which it appears. The whole, an idea of totality, the general theory, and the general economy may lurk as specters or phantoms, but they are neither promised nor given.

To summarize, the photographic series put into play, enter into, or authorize a right of inspection which they simultaneously withhold, by virtue of the fact that they reveal the very procedure through which a prior authorization allows the production of one's relation to them in discourse. Derrida reminds us through Giorgio Agamben, to whose work I turn briefly in the next chapter, that thinking itself originally meant "suspense."[18] To the extent to which these photographic series develop or reveal the limit between the inside and the outside ("they invade you"), we recognize that insofar as our "own" (proper, singular) desire compels discourse, that desire is in fact doubled or multiplied in the various trajectories of the right of inspection that appear to be presented or ordered "before" us. Such a limit has already been signaled in the doubling, or coupling, of checkerboard pieces or of women: in checkers, when a piece has reached the opponent's side of the board, that piece becomes, in French, a "queen," in English, a "king." (This is the same problem of naming that faced Queen Christina of Sweden made famous by Garbo, we might remember: the title *queen* is reserved for the wife of the king, but *king* is necessarily gendered masculine. Christina fit neither bill adequately or properly, yet she acted as sovereign under the name "queen.")

The undecidability of gender in translation thus yields to a larger conceptual problematic involving the relationship between doubling and coupling, turning and reversing, inverting. Perversion, after all, is always fragile, at the mercy of an inversion, a subversion; it is "this structure which gives it its value."[19] Insofar as there are two or more women, there is a question of doubling, of what makes a difference between one and two, of what difference two women make, of the difference between masculine and feminine and the (photo)grammar that develops this difference. Insofar as there are two or more women, there is also a question of coupling, of how coupling (inversion, perversion) comes to be developed but also of what coupling means when there are more than two—interrupting, with jealousy or with a threat, or what it means to be a third gazing upon two. In his commentary, Derrida seems both to play with and to confirm two genders and only two, exploring their shaky development and "tampering with" sexual difference. But he also hangs his most significant hopes on the possibilities of a third position, not a third gender, but a third gaze or alignment that reveals the limit of the photographic apparatus and a conceptual limit, as well. I turn to that third gaze to conclude this reading of *Right of Inspection*, before laying out its consequences for the subsequent chapters of *Lesbian Rule*.

In his reading of Plissart's photographs, Derrida obviously gestures toward ethical questions, and yet I have steered clear of that term thus far in my discussion of their joint projects, both because it holds within its history a philosophical specificity I am not prepared to address, but also because to use the word *ethics* appears in the minds of some to cast off the political or otherwise conceptual implications of a given discourse. Derrida repeatedly poses, yet never finally answers, the question, "What does it mean to play at checkers or women?"[20] Embedded in that question, as it has been embedded in all that I have been discussing, is the necessity of a relation that can be understood as an ethical relation as well as the revelation of a limit. As Derrida will put it, he seeks to open "the infinite uncertainty of a relation to the completely other, a relation without relations."[21] How is it possible to derive these questions from the diagonal comings and goings of women in Plissart's photographs?

Elles se regardent—they look at one another, which can mean, in French, three different things:

1. *Elles se regardent:* One looks at the other, looking at the other who doesn't *necessarily* look back at the moment she is seen. Here (in Plissart's photographic series) you have many examples of that.

2. *Elles se regardent:* Each one looks at *herself* in a mirror, without seeing the other. Here you have more than one example of that.

3. *Elles se regardent:* Both look at each other, their gazes intersecting, as one says, being exchanged, each watching the other watch her, right in her eyes, with infinite speculation (I see the other seeing me see her, I look at you at the instant you watch me watching you). Here you don't have a single example of that—for, like "I love you," it cannot but escape the camera lens (xxvii).

One is tempted to say that a general limit of representation is ultimately what *Droits de regards* reveals, as it reveals the limit of the first two grammars in the impossibility of the third. To the extent that photography cannot *record* this third sense, it is precisely what photography as apparatus reveals or develops. The third gaze, even if mythologized or idealized as love without possession, provides a glimpse of that which opens an ethical possibility: "the invention of the other."[22]

Plissart and Derrida spark reflection on what difference it might make that two women come together—sexually, ethically, and politically. They thus extend the idea of affective value in a realm most obstinately visual. Imbricated with the right and the effects of the gaze, *Right of Inspection* permits reflection precisely on the limits of lesbian *as* image, as much as the text prompts reconsideration of how an image may offer lesbian a vehicle for her presence.

Toward a Cinematic Reading

There is much in *Droits de regards,* both the photographic series and Derrida's commentary, I have not touched on or retouched. I have sought to visit only those foci which, in one way or another, program the readings in the following chapters. By way of summary, I light upon each element as it animates the places (Shanghai, Cuba) and things (pulp paperbacks, home videos) to which I soon turn.

First, these texts—from Butler's cover image of the Albright sisters, to a single issue of *Sinister Wisdom,* to Plissart's photographs, to two of Derrida's essays—demonstrate the *continuities* between cinema, photography, and other forms of visual culture. Just as Plissart's photographic series reveal that which eludes representation as its limit, they are also capable of bringing cinema into focus.[23] This is not to urge scholars to ignore the specificity of the motion picture, either "silent" (it rarely was) or sound, film or video, analog or digital; to the contrary, it is imperative to attend even more carefully to the medium and the scenes or sequences

Figures 8 and 9.
Photographs from
Droits de regards.
Courtesy of Editions
de Minuit.

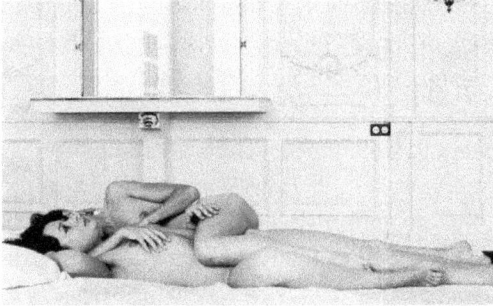

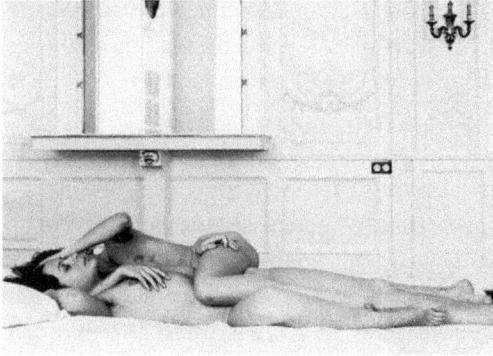

Figures 10 and 11.
Photographs from
Droits de regards.
Courtesy of Editions
de Minuit.

it makes available for analysis. Similarly, it is important to attend ever more widely to the horizons of its appearance, the strategies through which it makes meaning, the relations into which it places its spectators, and the discourses it authorizes. But one might do so by acknowledging simultaneously the extent to which media circulate and morph, as do artists; Ulrike Ottinger, to whose film *Exile Shanghai* I turn in the next chapter, is also a still photographer. It shows. And not only does documentary cinema share kin with documentary photography (historically and with regional and national variations), it also has the capacity to turn its lens on anyplace or anything at all: Belgium, Germany, Shanghai, Cuba, paperback book covers, maps of Lesbos, the making of movies, anything. Better to have a broad horizon of reference, then, to address its mobility.

Second, the goal of the readings of this chapter has been to challenge the usual practice of severing lesbian's appearance, rendering it *as* image, from the context of that appearance. When one sees something like the photograph of Agnes and Inez Albright, one might pose some of the questions Derrida's essay urges: who has the right of inspection, the right to look at this image, and by what processes are we those in whom that right is entrusted? To identify the Albrights or ourselves as those for whom gender trouble looms large in our psychobiographies or current practices—to say, in other words, that we *see* or recognize gender trouble as part of a struggle for visibility—is but a *start* in understanding the social dimensions of the photograph's (and therefore our) signification and is but a baby step in developing a nuanced and complex critical language of and for visuality. Context is almost infinite. In my readings of Butler's book, the journal *Sinister Wisdom*, and Plissart and Derrida's project, I omitted almost entirely any consideration of their lives as commodities and of the "right of inspection" that a title or a signature authorizes or lends in terms of rights, royalties, profit, publicity, or public life. A history of cultural and radical feminist media, along the lines of Rodger Streitmatter's history of the gay and lesbian press, has yet to be undertaken, but it would likely reveal much about the struggles not only of *Sinister Wisdom* but also *The Blatant Image* and its stable of contributors.[24] As queer film, video, photography, and digital work expand into new venues and occupy new relations to the circuits of production, distribution, and exhibition, it becomes more not less imperative to stand *in relation* to that work, not simply to applaud it. My understanding of contextual elaboration is thus tied, as I have suggested, to a politics of alliance that shatters claims for subversion based on the tautology of self-evidence.

Finally, then, the work of this chapter seeks to bring into conversation a number of disciplines and discourses that frequently remain unaware of one another. In the chapters on places and things to follow, such cross-fertilization is even more pronounced, since queer visual and mediatized life is uneven, brittle, and volatile. Keeping the lesbian in mind, seeing what happens when a lesbian *makes* an image, when a lesbian leaves an impression, I turn now to *Exile Shanghai* hoping to bring that vulnerability and mobility to the foreground.

Chapter 3

Archiving the Diaspora: A Lesbian Impression

M—,

I think this is excellent, although long and slow as you said. Interviews go on and on often repeating same information and many Shanghai shots seem pointless.

Still, it is an important and fascinating chapter in diaspora history. So *yes* [there is a box drawn around "yes"], show it. *No* [there is a box drawn around "no"], not as part of the main series. 4 hours of video day (?) also not certain — that's 1/3 of the day!

We should talk about how to use it.

D—

This note was tucked, I suppose accidentally, into my screening copy of Ulrike Ottinger's latest film in release in the United States, *Exile Shanghai* (1997). Its contents occasion, I want to argue, more than a programming decision for the 1997 San Francisco Jewish Film Festival; in fact, the note captures in fundamental fashion many of the preoccupations of much of the academic writing on Ottinger's work, including the frequent opacity of her images, the length of her films (particularly the documentaries, including *China–The Arts–Everyday Life* [1985], *Countdown* [1990], and *Taiga: A Journey to the Northern Land of the Mongols* [1991–2]), the "point of view" of her ethnographic practice, her fascination as indexed by the documentary titles with diaspora and with "the Orient," and, more generally, the sense of urgent debate that accompanies her work.[1] "We should talk about how to use it."

In short, Ottinger's films provoke spirited talk. Since Miriam Hansen's delightful feminist exploration, in *New German Critique*, of an "aesthetics of narcissism" in Ottinger's film *Bildnis einer Trinkerin/Ticket of No Return* (1979), the talk has circled pressingly around the relationship Hansen explores between Ottinger's aesthetics and her, or our, poli-

Figure 12. Ulrike Ottinger.
Courtesy of Women Make
Movies.

tics.[2] If, in fact, one is to judge from the predominantly feminist and lesbian reception of her films in the past two decades, it would appear that Ottinger's films audaciously rework central tropes of modernism (the dandy, the travelogue, the sideshow spectacle), furiously experiment with structures of narration (particularly through allegory), and daringly exploit new configurations of marginality and desire, yet all with varying effects. There is no dispute, however, that Ottinger is one of a handful of major lesbian filmmakers of the late century.

To chart those readings of her work briefly, especially for those of us who entered the discussion recently: Ottinger's early films were denigrated, especially in Germany in 1970s articles appearing in the journal *frauen und film,* whose writers rejected Ottinger's anti-illusionism, worlds of fantasy, and visual opulence as poor substitutes for social realism. A generation of scholars in the mid-eighties eloquently rescued Ottinger for a complex and critical feminism; these arguments, to my mind, remain powerful guides for reading Ottinger's films. But it remained for another generation, in the past decade especially, to comment from new angles; many wrestle with Ottinger's cultural politics and emphasize her ethnographic eye, even while they have galvanized fresh discussion regarding questions of sexuality and sexual difference. These debates, seen as a group, appear to stem just as much from Ottinger's rejection of realism and her refusal to tow the aesthetic line(s) of emancipatory movements (including feminist and lesbian/gay) as from her interest in ethnography and in "the Orient" in particular.[3] These elements of Ottinger's work intrigue me in *Exile Shanghai*, a film that might not otherwise "lend itself" to feminist or lesbian critical elaboration, since it does not focus explicitly on feminist or lesbian themes or issues. Readings as astute as those by feminist and lesbian scholars who redeemed Ottinger in the first go-round (Hansen, Hake, Bergstrom, Mayne, and others) have urged us to see in Ottinger's work a magnificently complicated challenge to orthodoxy (read as visual pleasure, as camp, as narcissism, as marginal lesbianism).[4] They also have forged a counterdiscourse to earlier ostensibly feminist dismissals of Ottinger's films, a set of tools that I use in facing the discourse of ethnography.

For it seems that the more recent assault on Ottinger's aesthetics, or more properly aestheticism, has come from those such as Katie Trumpener who see embedded in Ottinger's valorization of cultural spectacle yet another form of cultural imperialism, a mode of rendering other cultures (the Mongolians, for example, in *Johanna d'arc*) as static tableaux of Western fantasy. According to such a reading, in *China–die Kunste–der Alltag*, too, Ottinger's orientalism allows her, in the face of that which she does not or cannot comprehend, to make for a realm of pure freedom, without responsibility: "[the film] celebrates the *exoticisme pur* experienced by the aesthete who enters a deeply foreign culture for the first time and, unable to understand its verbal and visual languages, feels free to hear and see the culture as pure music or pure form" (96). That Ottinger has publicly expressed her indebtedness to ethnographers Victor Segalen and Michel Leiris may in fact fuel those charges of an expropriative documentary practice.[5] If Ottinger believes herself, in other words, to be raising "exoticism as a *question* of point of view," there appear to be at least a vocal few who believe that it has already been answered: Ottinger is thought variously to be a traditional ethnographer, a cultural imperialist, a Westerner fantasizing about the Orient, a false equalizer of real asymmetry, and the like. Does Ottinger now require a theoretical defense, a parry against these charges of ethnographic imperialism, a new discourse of redemption? Or might it be possible to read Ottinger's documentary differently, following the fissures of precisely the benevolent multiculturalism that produces such charges, and drawing from a different set of critical repertoires?

I want in this chapter to propose a bridge, a connection between these two domains—lesbian sexuality and Asia, particularly Shanghai, building on the insight Hake opens but treats very briefly wherein she seeks to "explore the significance of orientalism in *Madame X* and, even more importantly, to perceive it as part of the film's distinctly homosexual sensitivity (if one chooses to use that phrase)" (184). That is, I want to explore how *Exile Shanghai* may be understood as a lesbian's look at the Jewish diaspora in Asia. In what follows, I call these looks not a "homosexual sensitivity" but a "lesbian impression" (and remain, thereby, indebted to Hake's formulation), in the spirit of the larger project of this book, that is, aligning lesbian with a critical pliancy in the visual field. Even if not "about" lesbians in an obvious way, *Exile Shanghai* nevertheless records a lesbian impression of exile and of history, a lesbian's impression of the world around her. Moreover, I see the lesbian impression as inextricable from the affective politics of the archive associated with the extermination of the Jews and others in the Holocaust in Europe. By those politics I mean to suggest that the film condenses a number of crucial questions regarding the place of Europe versus the diaspora (the time and attention given to Europe more generally, as opposed to that given to Asia or elsewhere); the legacy of colonial power in the formation of twentieth-century international formations (including the international division of labor maintained by post-Fordist *multinational* capitalism); the political economy of hatred (in the comparative calculus of competition among forms of suffering); the insufficiency of *Holocaust* or *Shoah* as general terms to condense the history of Nazi and fascist practices;[6] and, to borrow Marcia Landy's phrase, the cinematic uses of the past, specifically the Second World War, for present politics or for the future.[7]

Ottinger has managed to find a subject, in other words, that seeks to evade the repetition-compulsion indicative of acting-out or the melodramatic pleasure in the familiar, a pleasure not to be dismissed but analyzed, that characterizes other popular modes of reckoning with the past or, in the German context, mastering the past (*Vergangenheitsbewälti-gung*). My goal in this chapter is to bring to this subject, the Jews of Shanghai, a critical analysis of the specificity of marginality and the possibilities of ethicopolitical alignment, reading their history and *Exile Shanghai* in the context of the archive. What *matters* is precisely the difference lesbian might make, however oblique the *presence* of lesbian might be in its making. I see the archive in terms of Ottinger's contribution to an expanded history of Jews, of exile, of diaspora, and of the effects of the Second World War, but also in terms of investigating under what system and according to what principles one consigns the Shanghai exiles specifically to a record of persecution or survival. With what interests does

Ottinger approach such a task *in terms of a documentary practice,* and how does one gain access to them? I do not here seek to account for Ottinger's oeuvre in its entirety, for others have written magnificently about her work from the point of view of authorial study, as I have noted; my aim is a more modest look at this single film in context. To provide that context for the critical analysis of the Shanghai exiles, then, I want first to return to the mundane, even "practical" matters of distribution and exhibition made visible in my epigraph, and then to turn to the time in exile that is the basis for Ottinger's documentary.

Archives and Exhibition

Many of Ottinger's films are distributed in the United States by the New York-based Women Make Movies, a nonprofit media arts organization that, unlike most of its counterparts founded in the 1970s, has gloriously survived the assaults on radical culture of the past quarter century. Women Make Movies distributes major feminist and lesbian films and videos. Despite their survival, the public sphere is still, however, under attack, especially in its media vectors. Massive arts de-funding in the past decade reduces the production of counterimages to commercial culture: the New York State Council on the Arts (the oldest such arts organization in the country as well as the model for the National Endowment for the Arts) alone has cut funding by over 50 percent since 1989.[8] Controlled by transnational media conglomerates (Time/Warner/AOL), circuits on the so-called information highway are also relays for corporate interests, while the few exits or detours of alternative media—such as Pacifica radio—are threatened by takeovers in the name of "management" and "the bottom line."

But, as Patricia Zimmermann documents in her book, *States of Emergency: Documentaries, Wars, Democracies,* counterattacks, guerilla assaults, media pirates, and critical interventions are also on American screens, and they bear little resemblance to the counterculture for which the left wing frequently harbors nostalgia. As a result, she asks her reader to ricochet *productively* between binarized poles: "we need to explain an intricately layered set of contradictions: the changing transnationalized economic sphere of commercial media on the one hand and the emergence of new technologies, new subjectivities, new discourses, new wars, and new ambushes on the other. These contradictions oscillate between utter despair and ecstatic hope."[9] In this oscillation, ossified

distinctions collapse—between "demonized corporate media and sanctified pure independent media" (160), especially now between analog
and digital, indeed, between rigidly separate disciplines and modes of
thinking-working (making media and making criticism, for example).
Our indices of value need to be recalibrated to these risks and possibilities if we are to recognize the transformations of which we are a
part, and that recalibration may change our sense of what questions
matter.[10]

The programmers and activists of the San Francisco Jewish Film Festival, like those at their gay and lesbian counterpart festivals, risk ex-
tinction.[11] They must base their decisions upon their knowledge of audiences' tolerances, preferences, and histories, and they must rely on ticket
sales (despite increasing corporate sponsorships) to stay alive. Distributors similarly respond to their constituents' demands in making acquisi-
tion decisions, decisions that in turn determine and frequently constrict
programmers' choices. Women Make Movies survived because it generates (still) the bulk of its profits directly from video sales and rentals
rather than from grants and project development.[12] In short, audiences
matter. If it is the case, then, that within the independent sector of
production and distribution, there is decidedly more mingling between
genres, lengths, and budgets than within the commercial mainstream,[13]
it is also the case that the film *exhibition* sector continues to rely on the
two-hour slot, standardized by the conversion to multiplex theatres in
the commercial sector throughout the late 1960s and adopted by the art
house and festival sectors.[14] Reared and naturalized within the practices
of the multiplex *and* the art house, audiences rarely commit to screenings
in excess of two hours. The 275-minute *Exile Shanghai* is not distributed
by Women Make Movies, for reasons to which I will turn shortly.[15] Instead, it has been acquired by the distribution wing, Atara Releasing, of
the San Francisco Jewish Film Festival; Atara will permit the exhibition
of the film in two chunks of 140 and 135 minutes, respectively. Among
its programmers is the author of my epigraph, "D," and their courtesy allowed me access to the film for close analysis; when there are few copies
in circulation, academic scrutiny is purchased at the cost of a much more
lucrative rental. Writing academic articles with commercially released
videocassettes and DVDs can but ought not obscure our role as intellectuals; my own time with *Exile Shanghai*, on the other hand, cannot escape
the circuits of its travel as a commodity in embattled exchange, and it
becomes the time of luxury.

The substitution of Atara Releasing for Women Make Movies as distributor might seem to provide material ground for arguing that *Exile Shanghai* be critically realigned neatly with its "parent" organization's new identity category: to see it in the context of "Jewish" film rather than "feminist" or "lesbian" film, and, indeed, a new audience came to Ottinger's work through that shift in distribution, an audience for whom Ottinger is (perhaps nothing other than) a "Jewish" filmmaker. To make such a claim, of course, would be necessarily to ground the film and the oeuvre to which it belongs in a lineage that is not self-evident but is continually produced and reproduced within antagonisms over what it means to "be" or "represent" Jewish(ness), within the limits of representation itself, and within institutions with their own histories. Over and again, that is, we produce and remake "Jewish" film, just as communities, makers, and intellectuals redefine "feminist" or "lesbian" film. On the other hand, to isolate the film for textual analysis without inquiring at all into the circumstances of its movement and, to borrow Marx's phrase, its "form of appearance," is, I think, to mystify both its critical function in the world and our critical task.

The reason for which Women Make Movies declined to distribute the film is, however, just as tied to residual identity categories: the organization distributes *only* films that are by *and* about women. At the same time, to make the counterclaim that Ottinger's work *must* be understood as feminist or lesbian would simply be to impose a false coherence through these similarly contested terms, and for obvious reasons; that is, *Exile Shanghai*, like Ottinger's previous work, is clearly informed by a host of political and aesthetic determinations and commitments that ought not to be bent to the will of a single signifier.[16] To acknowledge the importance of feminist and lesbian contexts alongside those of Jewish history and Jewish audiences to the present work is quite a different matter than deciding among them, and yet such a proposal raises further questions, affectively laden particularly in relation to a German filmmaker whose "mother is Jewish."[17] In what follows I seek to resist the tug of these identity categories in favor of a different framing of "the Jewish issue" in *Exile Shanghai*; instead of confirming Ottinger's own romantic conception of "the wandering Jew," I seek in what follows to demystify that figure through the specificity of the Shanghai exile.[18]

A critical practice informed by the contradictions Zimmermann diagrams in *States of Emergency* cannot, however, remain blind to the work of activists and organizers of a festival such as San Francisco's with its annual attendance of 32,000 filmgoers.[19] Our writing and teaching depend upon them. Another reason to have dwelled for a moment on the particular fate for the distribution and exhibition of *Exile Shanghai* in the United States is, finally, even more compelling: its travel from the Europe of its director, to the Shanghai of its content, to the San Francisco of its parent organization, mimics precisely the direction of movement of the Jews of Shanghai, to whose story we now turn.

The Jews of Shanghai

Ottinger's film takes as its occasion what hardboiled screenwriters might call a helluva good story, one with which she had become familiar by following the Trans-Siberian railroad for *Johanna d'arc of Mongolia.* A landscape that yielded for the earlier film a playful lesbian/feminist romp now yields, in other words, a very different story, still tied to its origins in lesbian cultural production of place. The challenge of this story, for the documentary form in particular, is that its visible evidence has vanished; in some cases it has been obliterated. It is, like many stories of survival during World War II, a story of recollection and reconstruction, with its attendant ambiguity and vagueness. Here is that story in its barest, dubiously scientific/historical bones, but documentary "pre-understanding" often begins here, in excavation.[20]

By the time of World War II, Shanghai was home to a large and varied Jewish community. In the mid-nineteenth century's first movement of Jews to the eastern shore of China, Sephardic Jews from the former British colonies, predominantly from India, rushed to capitalize on the opium trade, newly sanctioned by the British free trade agreement, the Treaty of Nanking, in 1842. These families (the Sassoons, Hardoons, and the Kadoories most renowned among them) amassed great fortunes, enormous by present-day standards, but also established the social and cultural hierarchy and infrastructure that would sustain the last ripples of quasi-imperial power through the next century. The second movement of Ashkenazi Jews (Eastern Europeans and White Russians, fleeing pogroms and the Revolution) eased into the slots for professionals and merchants in the thriving and prosperous international colonial outpost in the first decades of the twentieth century, and they became a forceful support for the first wave's social structure, contributing especially to the city's metropolitan and decadent prewar feel. If we are not steeped in that version of Shanghai through more recent films such as Zhang

Yimou's *Shanghai Triad* (1985), it has been memorialized in von Stern-berg's films, *Shanghai Express* (1932) and *The Shanghai Gesture* (1941). It also appears in Orson Welles's *Lady from Shanghai* (1948); the tagline for the latter film was "I told you . . . you know nothing about wickedness." *Shanghai'ed*, also a title of a Charlie Chaplin short, was widely used as a synonym for kidnapping, a sense bolstered by the city's aura of dan-ger. "In any event" (in the way Geoffrey Heller, one of the interviewees in *Exile Shanghai*, often nervously makes a transition), these two Jewish populations occupied monumental positions and places within the map of decadent "Old Shanghai." They built hotels and civic and mercantile institutions along the Bund, Shanghai's "Gold Coast" and symbol of its role as financial center of the first part of this century. They designed couture clothes and fitted furs, directing their fortunes toward luxury and philanthropy, though not in equal measure, in horse races, country clubs, aid societies, and schools alike.

The Jews, like other colonial settlers, were, in other words, rich, pam-pered, and feeling adventurous. "Old Shanghai," in its colonial partitions and administration (the International Settlement—comprised of British and American expatriates, the French Concession, and the Chinese por-tions of the city), accommodated the Sephardic and Russian Jews into its oxymoronic hierarchy of profit and debauchery easily, and there the Jews mastered the tongues of international power and the etiquette of a gen-eralized European gentility. There, too, the Jews danced and drank and screwed their way into all but a few of Shanghai's most venerable social organizations (the British Country Club being the most exclusive among them, as it alone restricted its membership to British subjects).[21]

The third movement of Jews into Shanghai began in 1937 and ended in 1941, when 17,000 or more European Jews entered the last open port of the world after the closing of Palestine, in flight from Nazi persecu-tion. They were largely German and Austrian, and they came "stateless," meaning both "without papers" and with papers overstamped with the red "J." They were often literally penniless. Social relief organizations, founded by Sephardic families and fed by White Russian support, at-tempted to integrate their numbers into the fabric of Shanghai Jewish life, mercantile and cultural, yet the "floods" overwhelmed the struc-tures of benevolence built by a century's investment, and the relief orga-nizations were woefully mismanaged. When the Japanese occupied the city, in late 1942 into 1943, they interned Allied civilians (British and American) and confined the new Jewish exiles to a "segregation area,"

Figure 13. Still from *Exile Shanghai.* Courtesy of the Offices of
Ulrike Ottinger.

Figure 14. Still from *Exile Shanghai*. Courtesy of the Offices of Ulrike Ottinger.

the former turf of the Americans before they joined the British in the International Settlement and an area heavily bombed by the Japanese in the Sino-Japanese war of the previous decade. Hongkew, or what was only retrospectively called the Jewish ghetto, housed the European Jews, living in squalor and with severely restricted movement, while the Sephardic and Russian Jews maintained their relative freedom, though many had to relinquish their living quarters to the Japanese during its occupation of the city, in wartime Shanghai. Most of the European Jews suffered tremendously; many died.

The coda to the story in this form is that those surviving Shanghai Jews of whatever origin fled after the war, many relocating to Israel or to the United States, where a dwindling number of former Shanghai residents exists in the San Francisco/Bay Area (following patterns of Asian migration in the Pacific Rim). There they have rekindled a community of exiles *from* Shanghai, meeting for reunions (including one, incongruously, in Las Vegas) and recording their recollections and testimonies of their exile in films such as Ottinger's and Grossman and Rosdy's film, *Port of Last Resort*. Ethnographers from the University of Nevada brought tape recorders to that Nevada reunion to gather oral histories. Several survivors of the exile have written memoirs (including, in English, Ernest G. Heppner's *Shanghai Refuge: A Memoir of the WWII Jewish Ghetto* and Ottinger interviewee Rena Krasno's *Strangers Always*), and historians have documented the complex issues of foreign aid and the administration of the "segregation area" by the Chinese and Japanese during the seven years of the encounter between European Jews and the city of Shanghai.[22]

The commodification of the Jewish exiles' community continues unabated in Shanghai itself, where tourists may hire, for $50 U.S. ("toward local charity"), a personal tour guide for "The Hongkou Ghetto."

> Flora Amiel, a member of our present-day Jewish Community of Shanghai, leads tours throughout the sights of "Old Jewish Shanghai" in English, Hebrew, Spanish and Portuguese, complete with explanation and vivid description of life . . . Pointing out the differences in lifestyle between the Jewish refugees and the successful Jewish businessmen, you will get a clear picture of the day to day experiences of life in "Old Shanghai."[23]

Or, in the tourism of the daily news, one can follow former First Lady Hillary Clinton and former Secretary of State Madeleine Albright to Shanghai, where they visited a restored synagogue early in July 1999, hailing it "as an example of a new respect in China for religious differences."[24] Note, though, that the Othel Rachel Synagogue visited by Clinton and Albright was in a shambles three months prior to their visit, and that the Chinese had not yet granted official permission to practice the Jewish faith in Shanghai, much less to worship at this particular synagogue.

These strands of the Jews' history in Shanghai remain, therefore, alive in the present day, with their attendant contradictions. Each thread is complexly mediated by the vagaries of memory, by the interests of historians, by the discourses of Holocaust studies, as well as by the larger discourses of nation and religion in which these histories are enjoined. The lesbian filmmaker encounters this fabric as her archive and records her impression of its texture. The history this lesbian filmmaker confronts is, moreover, inextricable from the *politics* of memory, the ethical necessity for witness. One way, then, of consolidating the problematic for subsequent analysis of the lesbian impression in *Exile Shanghai* is through theorizations of the archive itself, to which I now turn.

Archive Fever

> Like the question of the proper name, the question of [Jewish] exemplarity . . . situates here the place of all violences. Because if it is just to remember the future and the injunction to remember, namely the archontic injunction to guard and to gather the archive, it is no less just to remember the others, the other others and the others in oneself, and that the other peoples could say the same thing—in another way. And that *tout autre est tout autre*, as we can say in French: every other is every other other, is altogether other. (50)

To leap from the Jews of Shanghai to Jacques Derrida's essay, "Archive Fever: A Freudian Impression," requires some explanation, to be sure, but Derrida's essay helps to guide my reading strategy and lends me my chapter's title. Originally titled "Mal d'archive: Une impression freudienne," Derrida presented this occasional lecture at a symposium held on 5 June 1994 at Freud's house in London, entitled "Memory: The Question of Archives." His primary consideration in the essay is, for this occasion, at least a two-fold understanding of the archive: first, as an inscription of all that will have come under the name and authority of Freudian psychoanalysis and, second, following upon the first, modes of understanding the function and processes of the psychic apparatus and of memory *as* archivization(s). The first emphasis encompasses an inquiry into the proper name of Freud, his legacy, his relation in particular to his own father, his Jewishness, "his" science. As Lacan famously quipped, "one has only to remember that Freud's discovery puts truth into question, and there is no one who is not personally concerned with truth."[25] There is *no one* for whom the archive is *not* relevant.

The second emphasis, in related but different terms, guides us toward an understanding of memories both sanctioned and illegitimate, modes of claiming authority not only in behalf of the past but in relation to the future, technologies of inscription that change over time, from Freud's mystic writing pad to e-mail, and the ethical/political issues associated with the archive more generally. Enmeshed in this second emphasis are questions having to do with the technologies of memory and of fantasy, the very mechanisms by which the unconscious and conscious life archive or store their materials. One obvious arena that interests me in this emphasis is the work of documentary cinema in archiving or logging an evanescent experience of exile that leaves traces: distorted, condensed, displaced. Along, then, with Derrida's interest in memory devices, we note the changing technologies of archivization from latent image-recording (including that done on film) to digital storage; these enter into the calculus of a literal and figurative *investment* that interested Freud, captures Derrida's rhetorical attention in his essay, and prompts consideration of a filmmaker's investment in her subject.

Lodged within these larger questions guiding the lecture having to do with memory, Jewishness, psychoanalysis, and Freud (and alongside a host of references to previous of his works and preoccupations), Derrida reads Yosef Hayim Yerushalmi's book on Freud, *Freud's Moses: Judaism Terminable and Interminable,* a book that, according to Yerushalmi, "is not an attempt to prove that psychoanalysis is 'Jewish,' though eventually it is concerned to inquire whether Freud thought it to be so, which is a very different matter."[26] By devoting the bulk of his lecture to Yerushalmi, indeed by dedicating it to him, Derrida foregrounds the particularly pressing link between Jewishness and memory, and he also foregrounds the gesture of dedication that is Yerushalmi's subject: a dedication made on a flyleaf of a Bible from Jacob Freud to his son, Sigmund. Derrida also confronts directly, as I have cited above, the violent effects of claiming "exemplarity." He does not treat the Holocaust directly, but, as is his practice let us say since *Glas* (1974), allows his listeners and subsequent readers to work with the "impressions" of his text. It is therefore crucial to note that he *invokes* the Holocaust: the last word of "Archive Fever" is "ash."[27]

Derrida's essay takes as one of its organizing ideas, then, the *impression* left by the Freudian signature. He does not mean, thereby, to restrict himself to the proper name of Freud, as though one could know precisely what is gathered there, how that signature would mark its limits, how one could restrain what is gathered there to a particular place or location. Rather, he allows that signature to extend to the invention of psychoanalysis (as): "project of knowledge, of practice and of institution, community, family, domiciliation, consignation, 'house' or 'museum'" (11).

Three meanings are condensed in the word *impression* and in the phrase *Freudian impression,* beyond the idea of a signature. First, an impression has a typographic meaning, an inscription on a surface: the foundation, the substrate of the archive, the place of an inscription or a recording. This "typographic" meaning also invokes or evokes Freud's distinction between "repression" and "suppression" (*Verdrängung* and *Unterdrückung*), a distinction that directly concerns the psychic apparatus in terms of the way in which we imagine the relationship between conscious processes, the substrate of the unconscious, and its relation to displacements of affect in the mechanisms of "suppression." The second meaning of "impression" opposes it to the robust and formal status of the specifically philosophical concept (*Begriff,* nowhere in Derrida's essay in German, however); an impression suggests the "vagueness or the open imprecision, the relative indetermination of . . . a *notion*" (24). By insisting on the unstable, fleeting, or indefinite figure of an impression, Derrida does not thereby mean to diminish its significance, impact, complexity, or urgency. To the contrary, it is central to a deconstructive understanding of the concept in general to remark the founding violence, the irreducible disjunction and division at its core.

Finally, the third meaning Derrida summons in *impression* has to do with the impression left by Freud, the impression that Sigmund Freud will have made on "anyone, after him, who speaks *of him* or speaks *to him,* and who must then, accepting it or not, be thus marked" (24). To speak of Freud is, in other words, to join the Freudian archive, even if or especially if one speaks to deny or denounce.

To speak, as I am doing, of a lesbian impression is, first, to speak of an inscription, a recording made "by" a lesbian if not in her name; it is to disseminate the very name *of* lesbian across a textual body that bears a trace but need not limit itself to the meanings tied previously to the signature, for example of "Ulrike Ottinger." Because this is an Ottinger film, her viewers will keep the lesbian in mind, even when she is not in sight in *Exile Shanghai*. To speak of a lesbian impression is also to notice the force exerted in particular by psychoanalysis, since that science has been vital to delimiting and domesticating lesbian. Psychoanalysis, in turn, also bears upon the project of knowledge of Holocaust studies by seeing memory as one of the key elements of both, by seeing trauma as fundamental to both, by seeing Freud's own preoccupation with the question of a "Jewish science" as crucially connected to the history of the Jews in Europe, and, for that matter, to Freud's own history as a writer in exile. To speak of a lesbian impression is additionally to see sexual difference and sexuality as crucial to the processes of subjectification and desubjectification which structure memory and history more generally; it is to introduce sexual and gendered being into the meditations on Being meant to drive straight to the core of witness, testimony, and survival. The lesson, after all, of psychoanalysis is that one cannot *not* make such an inflection. In this lesbian impression, then, I realign what appears to be an autonomous inquiry into the Jews of Shanghai with feminist and lesbian interests, with philosophy and with psychoanalysis, asking simply what it means that a feminist/lesbian mark might be part of the project that is *Exile Shanghai*. In this lesbian impression, one can also hear the voices of the Shanghai Jews, as they are deposited in the public documents of official history and in the perhaps private voices of recollection, interspersed with the authoritative commentary of exegesis and theory.

Derrida's own metaphorics lend themselves to meditations on the role of gender in archiving, in memory, and in its sciences, since his essay is structured principally around "eco-nomics," literally *oikos + nomos,* the name/law associated with the house (Freud's name and Freud's house), the law of the house, and therefore around the distinction between the public and the private, and the gendered division which frequently accompanies it. Derrida is interested throughout the essay in the patriarchal (the law or Law in psychoanalysis and in Judaism), in the signature of the patriarch, and in the legacies of the father of psychoanalysis. For Derrida's reading in this essay, that distinction between the private and the public, however, risks collapsing upon another: the difference between the secret and the nonsecret.

There is a way to see the unhinging of the feminization of the private sphere in the noncoincidence of the distinction between secret/

nonsecret and that between the private/public. Indeed, a name for the hinge is "patri-archic," the archive that cannot be detached from the name of the father. Derrida cites Sonia Combe: "I hope to be pardoned for granting some credit to the following observation, but it does not seem to me to be due to pure chance that the corporation of well-known historians of contemporary France is essentially, apart from a few exceptions, masculine . . . But I hope to be understood also" (11). It would seem, however, that the public/private distinction is also a techno-effect, one, for example, in the process of being if not undone than absolutely transformed by digital technologies such as e-mail. With attendant juridical and political implications, the radical transformations of media through digital technologies similarly present us with upheavals that are not "merely" technological, but they transform in their turn the status of privacy, publicity, the workplace, and home. The "home" reverberates all the more powerfully in the German, of course, a translation whose effects are diminished in the essay.[28]

These oppositions that seem to pile up in Derrida's text lend themselves to a number of levels of reading in turn, from the abstractions of the "philosophical" categories a chapter such as this one cannot touch, to the notes of a few survivors of exile or a moment of a film about them. Those distinctions, between the secret and the nonsecret, between the public and the private, between the law and the home, can appear in the particular cruelty of a guard or in his kindness, in the banality of a comparison or in its violence, in the far reaches of theology or in the grassroots efforts of a relief committee. To take but one example of "exemplarity," where what is at stake is *explicitly* the measurement of the value of Jewish life against others: in the Shanghai Jewish community, there were a group of students from the Mir Yeshiva, who continued with their studies while in Shanghai and who received top priority from the Joint Distribution Committee (JDC) due to pressure from rabbi and other Jewish officials in the west. In Ross' account:

> JDC's position was that all refugees should be treated equally; there should be no special treatment for groups with powerful representation in the United States. But Va'ad Hahatzalah and other groups had argued that rescuing the rabbis and students, the scholars who would preserve the future of Judaism, was far more important than rescuing others. Their lives had more value, they claimed, than other refugees.[29]

The question of the archive is the question of the outside: how does one mark boundaries, cause, effect? One way to think that question is this: How is it possible to delineate the interior of the body and the outside, its environment? This is simply the question of memory, of "internal archivization" (15), its structure and its model. Freud's own model, a way, as Derrida reminds us, of representing on the outside what memory is doing internally, is the Magic Mystic Pad, *der Wunderblock.* It should not come as a surprise to learn that mechanisms of inscription were at the core of the encounter between the Jews in Shanghai and their Chinese citymates. Please forgive a very long citation, but it returns us to the scene and allows us to see that these developments are not autonomous and discrete but rather shared and inserted into systems of meaning-making elsewhere. A Shanghai exile remembers:

> I met two Korean businessmen who were buying supplies and who complained about the shortage and rising prices of paper products. I inquired whether they would be interested in financing a writing pad I knew about, on which one could write without using paper. After several weeks of negotiations we struck a deal giving me a cash advance and obligating me to come up with a sample of this mysterious writing tablet. I was supposed to be paid for my assistance during the manufacturing phase.
>
> Liu, the bookkeeper, warned me to be extremely careful. Although Korean and Chinese dialects are quite different, Liu had overheard the men say that they had no intention of paying me; they intended to cheat me out of the balance of the money. I hunted around until I found a waxy substance, blackened it and covered it with cellophane. I had duplicated the magic slate I had used as a boy. You could write on the cellophane cover with any instrument, even your fingernail; when you lifted the cover, the writing would be gone, and the pad could be used again and again. Mindful of Liu's warning, I negotiated an additional installment, and only after I received the cash did I happily turn the gadget over to the two men, never to see them again. (Heppner, 65–66)

Heppner's recollections reveal a number of layers of connection to Derrida's exploration of the inside and the outside of the archive: the retrospective shaping of one's personal story as it is inserted into history of more monumental proportions, the reliance on technologies of archivization for that retrospective insertion, and the role of memory in

generalizing from the individual to the group (here Korean). Derrida's invocation of the mystic writing pad opens to two related questions: is the
psychic apparatus affected by changes in techno-science, i.e., do transformations in the speed of processing of information or changes in the
"prostheses of memory" which are meanwhile becoming more "refined,
complicated, powerful" change the modes by which our internal archivization proceeds? Second, how is psychoanalysis (itself) archived, and
has its archivization been similarly determined by states of technology
and communication? Derrida is aware that the modes of archivization,
the technologies of recording, transmitting, printing, inscribing, cipher-
ing, en- and decoding, editing, perceiving, receiving, and the like do not
simply transform a process; they determine content, as we saw in the
previous chapter with regard to what photography, as an apparatus, develops. And, therefore, had Freud recourse to other models (e-mail, AT&T
phone cards), the content of the history of psychoanalysis would have
been different; this is the limited version of the claim. The larger implication is that our modes of conceiving of memory must respond to
changes in techno-science, to the ways in which we experience, think,
model, and survive the very relation between the outside and the inside.

The limit case of that distinction has been marked in the word *Auschwitz*, the place, as Hannah Arendt put it, where anything is possible. It
remains for us to understand how the Shanghai Jews' exile can be archived alongside that limit case, for the history Ottinger confronts in her
lesbian impression is inseparable from the Holocaust, bound to its history and its unspeakability, even while she deposits a trace of its effects.

Memory and Official History: The Figure of the *Muselmann*

There are links between both the official history of the exile in Shanghai
and its popular forms (memoir, tourism, film) and the memorialization
of Nazi genocide more generally. These links program the shape of documentary practices, and they set another piece of the background against
which Ottinger's impression of the Shanghai Jews appears. The history
of the Shanghai exile, like the history of European Jews and other persecuted groups, lies suspended between Primo Levi's insistence on the
importance of memory ("even in this place one can survive, and therefore one must want to survive, to tell the story, to bear witness") and Saul
Friedländer's observation that the proliferation of stories about the Nazi
genocide and its traumas obliterates specificity and tends to freeze the

past into murky tableaux.[30] Levi, Friedländer, and other survivors and historians writing on the Shoah thus struggle against the domestication of the past and the blunting of its impact, for example through a strategy Friedländer calls juxtaposing "entirely different levels of reality—for example high-level anti-Jewish policy debates and decisions next to routine scenes of persecution—with the aim of creating a sense of estrangement counteracting our tendency to 'domesticate' that particular past."[31] Yet, they recognize that speech itself threatens to negate the very force of the history it seeks to represent. In *Remnants of Auschwitz*, Giorgio Agamben condenses this impossibility of speech, as he puts it, the lacuna in which "the survivors bore testimony to something it is impossible to bear witness to," into a series of reflections on the concentration camp.[32] He focuses, more particularly, on the figure of *der Muselmann*, the "Muslim," the mummy-man, the living dead. Agamben's thought transforms the terms under which it is possible to think about Nazi genocide, the work of memory, and the archive of history, and to it I turn now to situate Derrida's formulation of the archive in relation to Agamben's perhaps "anarchival" understanding of testimony.

With a word of caution: it may appear unnecessary to align a film about Jewish survival far afield from the atrocities of the concentration camps in Europe with theoretical reflection on the limit case the latter illustrates. It is precisely that appearance, however, that *Exile Shanghai* confronts; it is precisely that appearance that determines the choices the film makes about its own inside knowledge and outside stakes, its own authority, its own movement backward as recollection (an archiving prosthesis), and its own look toward the future. To mark the Shanghai exiles as less significant because peripheral is, not to put too fine a point on it, to reduplicate the claims to exemplarity that endanger our collective future; to overvalue their experiences is, similarly, to evade the atrocious. To understand their "case," as Agamben will suggest, requires instead the investigation of the limit case, the Muselmann. Through that case, we can begin to understand survival itself, and to return to the instance of it Ottinger has recorded.

Muselmann was concentration- and extermination-camp jargon for the inmate on the edge of death, the walking dead or the inhuman human, who had given up on survival and provided the grimmest possible reminder (remainder, example) of the loss of the will to survive and the certain death to come. As such, Agamben suggests that the Muselmann might figure as the impossible witness for whom others must testify; the Muselmann reminds us, at the same time, that the survivors are not the true witnesses. This is the paradox of testimony set forth by Primo Levi. In Agamben's thinking, it is a complicated one: the "*Muselmann* is the complete witness," which implies "1) the *Muselmann* is the non-human, the one who could never bear witness, and 2) the one who cannot bear witness is the true witness, the absolute witness" (150). Embedded in this lacuna are a number of meanings: "At times a medical figure or an ethical category, at times a political limit or an anthropological concept, the *Muselmann* is an indefinite being in whom not only humanity and non-humanity, but also vegetative existence and relation, physiology and ethics, medicine and politics, and life and death, continuously pass through each other" (48). Agamben's analysis here calls attention to a number of transformations which make the Muselmann a crucial figure for ethicopolitical engagement. In sum, however, the Muselmann marks the full transition from, as Foucault describes it, the exercise of sovereign power to "biopower" or "biopolitics" but with an extension of Foucault's thesis, wherein what is at stake, as Agamben reads Foucault, is no longer the power "to make die and let live" (155), or even "to make live and let die." In the camps, in the Muselmann, Agamben argues, we confront the distillation of survival itself; it is "now" the insignia and task of biopower to "make survive."

Survival, in Agamben's extraordinary series of meditations, must not be understood therefore as extrinsic to life but as interior to it. The witness can survive the inhuman, the Muselmann, just as the Muselmann can survive the human: "what can be infinitely destroyed is what can infinitely survive" (151). "In our time" (155): Agamben over and again locates his readings and his analysis of the camps and the limit-figure of the Muselmann in a particular time, a "now" that is both after Auschwitz and, to use his language, a remnant of it, as are its witnesses.[33] In that "now" we confront the impossibility of speech, the horrors not of the unsaid but of the unsayable, that which, in his view, cannot be *archived*. For the archive, following Agamben's rereading of linguistic theory, resides in the relationship between *langue* and *parole*. It is the unsaid "inscribed in everything said by virtue of being enunciated; it is the fragment of memory that is always forgotten in the act of saying 'I'" (144). In that gap, in the system of relations between discourse and its taking place, there is the archive. Agamben, however, locates testimony *outside* the archive, in the relationship instead between *langue* and its taking place, "between a pure possibility of speaking and its existence as such" (144).

Within *that* disjunction, not within the archive, is produced the witness; what prevents the cleavage of survival from life is testimony. Otherwise, in the figure of the Muselmann one might have seen the essence of "a survival separated from every possibility of testimony, a kind of absolute biopolitical substance that, in its isolation, allows for the attribution of demographic, ethnic, national, and political identity" (156).

Agamben thus resists the cleavage of what he elsewhere calls "naked life" from "forms of life," which are then abstractly coded as "social-juridical identities (the voter, the worker, the journalist, the student, but also the HIV-positive, the transvestite, the porno star, the elderly, the woman)" (*Means,* 6–7). He seeks, then, in *Remnants of Auschwitz,* to strengthen the tie that binds life to form-of-life against modes of power, including fascism, that isolate naked life as "biopolitical substance." Against the attribution of nationality and citizen markers, Agamben is therefore interested in the possibility of non-statist politics and in the figure of the refugee who, like the Muselmann, becomes emblematic. Following Arendt, he sees in the refugee the paradigm of a new historical consciousness, yet one need not follow with a reading that merely celebrates the figure of the refugee where he is found; it is possible, instead, to locate that figure more broadly both conceptually and historically, as Ottinger's film also seeks to do.

The concentration camps were, after all, built initially as spaces for controlling refugees; the camps became possible directly due to the failure of national and international aid organizations.

> What is essential is that each and every time refugees no longer represent individual cases but rather a mass phenomenon (as was the case between the two world wars and is now once again), these [international] organizations as well as the single states—all the solemn invocations of the unalienable rights of human beings notwithstanding—have proved to be absolutely incapable not solely of solving the problem but also of facing it in an adequate manner. The whole question, therefore, was handed over to the humanitarian organizations and to the police. (18–9)

The camps allowed a process, to put it somewhat awkwardly but more precisely, of "refugee-ization," or of "de-citizen-ization"; indeed, the Nuremberg laws were one set of many such denationalizing tools.

Agamben's interest in the refugee can be seen thus to align him with, rather than separate him from, Derrida's considerations in "Archive Fever." Both confront the crucial question of the substance or the substrate on which inscription (of nationality, of citizenship) takes place, whether that ground is "testimony" that resists the "biopolitical" exercise of power that fragments forms-of-life into refugees, or whether that ground is the affirmative itself, the "yes" that opens to the future, and that is for Derrida the horror presented by claims for Jewish exemplarity. In Yerushalmi's sentence, "Only in Israel and nowhere else is the injunction to remember felt as a religious imperative to an entire people."[34]

Agamben characterizes well Derrida's conception of the archive as that which is structured between langue and parole; in "Archive Fever," Derrida stresses over and again the performative and enunciative dimensions of the archive he seeks to consider. What Agamben does not confront directly is the question Derrida poses in the face of the transformations (technological but not "merely" so) both he and Agamben explicitly mark.

> How can [one] claim to *prove* an absence of archive? How does one prove in general an absence of archive, if not in relying on classical norms (presence/absence of literal and explicit reference to this or to that, to a this or to a that which one supposes to be identical to themselves, and simply absent, *actually* absent, if they are not simply present, *actually* present; how can one not, and why not take into account *unconscious* and more generally *virtual* archives)? ("Archive Fever" 43)

I take Derrida to here be reminding us of the dimensions of archivization beyond the protocols of rational deliberation, classical scholarship, and scientific (or historiographic) conventions; he is wondering, at this point in the text, how it is possible for Yerushalmi to have the chutzpah (Derrida calls it the merit, or temerity [43]) to mount the argument that if the Biblical Israelites had wanted to kill Moses, what counts is that they did not "actually" do so. Derrida's larger concern remains, then, the distinction between a conscious, willful, patent act of memory and its other, call it repression or suppression (displacement). This is at any rate the very distinction that founds psychoanalysis and must be accommodated within a challenge to its systematicity. Whether finally marked by the language of the unconscious or the language of virtuality, the larger point would appear to be that memory does not stand in transparent relation to the archive, to testimony, to witness. To the contrary, all of these enjoin ethical, political, philosophical, and historical reflection; to archive is to enter into a structured and over-determined field within which one must nonetheless maneuver. To archive the Jewish diaspora during World War II is, moreover, to risk memory in the face of at least one injunction that might have precisely the opposite effect: never to forget.

Documenting Relationships

Facing the story of the Shanghai Jews entails entering this field of history, witness, testimony, affect, identification, memory (conscious and "virtual"), and lineage. It is to align oneself with the question Derrida posed in *Right of Inspection*, "who possesses this right, who possesses the other, holding it as the object of its gaze or within its sights?"[35] Ottinger, whose "mother is a Jew," has inscribed her point of entry as I have already described by elevating the figure of the wandering Jew to the status of a conceptual ideal, thereby, we might add, elevating herself. It would be possible, I think, to read *Exile Shanghai* as a film that does, indeed, romanticize exile or the figure of the refugee and thereby reinforce the exemplary status of Jewish displacement, were it not also for the fact that Ottinger's camera resolutely lingers on the Chinese. Her attention to Shanghai makes that reading less plausible. The film is structured as a series of experiences of Shanghai set in motion by the recollections of surviving Jews, but Ottinger's camera alone ultimately becomes responsible for the film's documentary voice.[36] *Exile Shanghai* allows us, as Ottinger has put it, "a certain amount of time to understand the whole system."[37] Without denying the extent to which she is inserted into that system, Ottinger nonetheless displaces a relation of directly sanctioned authority, while braiding the strands of testimony and historiographic evidence regarding the Shanghai exiles into a chain made available for our understanding. As is Derrida's, Ottinger's "method" is impressionistic. She confronts the following fragments, and she uses them to craft a commentary on the experience of the Jews in exile.

Ottinger faces a world in which the Jews of Shanghai stand in for the Jews of Europe, but as their shamed or guilty counterparts. Impossibly bound to a metonymic relation, the Jews of Shanghai cannot, however, become synecdoches for the Jews of Europe, for that grammar would obliterate the trace of the latter's specificity that archivization seeks to preserve. To analogize suffering and persecution requires a suspension of the conclusive voice:

> But he never escaped the fears and nightmares from the Bridge House —they would haunt him for the rest of his life. He woke up Hella on many nights with his screaming and would sometimes run in terror if he saw a Japanese soldier on the streets. He was not a hero, but a surviving victim. Perhaps, some in the community later suggested, Herman Natowic also was a victim of fate, chosen to suffer for the Jews of Hongkew as millions of Jews who remained in Europe suffered far greater horrors. (Ross 193)

As in the camps, furthermore, the administrators of the Hongkew segregation area relied upon the Jews to police one another, through a brigade known as the *pao chia*, a border patrol, which "brought out the worst German militarism" of some of the refugees (Ross 208). The pao chia thus present an obstacle to idealization. Ottinger puzzles over how to film reluctant analogy and guilty complicity.

Shanghai was a world, like the pre-unification Germany of *Countdown*, where value fluctuated wildly, where the substitution of one thing for another could not be guaranteed by the universal equivalent or by a coherent system of exchange, and where currencies migrated across national borders. Ottinger puzzles over how to film this abstract but real fluctuation and migration. A representative account:

> By the spring of 1944, eggs cost more than $1 (U.S.) apiece, pork nearly $20 a pound, a loaf of bread $2.50, and milk nearly $10 a quart. Refugees adapted to the inflation by hoarding commodities, such as flints and kerosene, since cash had become almost worthless. The commodities themselves sometimes proved to have little value. One refugee bought several tins of kerosene from a Chinese friend as a hedge against inflation, but decided to splurge during a cold winter week and use one tin as fuel. He opened it to find it filled with water. The refugee returned the tin to his friend and demanded an explanation. "I thought you wanted this as a commodity, not to use," his friend said. "If you wanted kerosene for heating, you should have told me."[38]

To get a feel for the "system," it is necessary to think about value as an abstraction, as Ottinger had done in *Countdown*, concentrating on the

Figure 15. Still from *Countdown.* Courtesy of Women Make Movies.

language of hand signs. One could conclude for the present film, as Alter does for *Countdown,* that what distinguishes Ottinger's meditation on value is "the loving, critical care it takes in its extensive shots of the 'the people'–as well as inanimate structures and objects—which . . . stand in for various kinds of animate 'otherness.'"[39]

Ottinger confronts, too, the already concrete history of this encounter between the Chinese and the Jews. The Chinese, in Kranzler's account, are understood to be fully embracing: "The long history of China's tolerance toward all religions and the generally excellent economic relations which the refugees maintained with their neighbors kept trouble at a minimum" (154), while the Jews confronted the unsympathetic attitudes of Shanghai's wealthy quasi-colonialist "international" community: "'Loss of face' was suffered in general by the white community with the arrival of the refugees: in a society where the white man was respected only for his power and wealth, manual labor on his part was unthinkable. The impoverished refugees, therefore, lowered the already weakened status of the Occidentals in China" (155). A number of Japanese, similarly, placed the responsibility and blame for increasing westernization on Jews; in the literature of ultra-nationalist expansionists, it was the "Jewish vices of the three S's (Screen, Sex, Sports) that eroded traditional morals and corrupted the traditional family and community. These were propagated by those students with Western or liberal leanings referred to as the 'Karl Marx boys'!" (Kranzler 198).

Finally, Ottinger confronts Freud's relation to Shanghai:

> *Die Gelbe Post,* a monthly under the very able journalist A. J. Storfer, who was also a psychologist and a student of Freud, was considered one of the best-edited papers in Asia. Most of its contents were devoted to articles of a cultural nature, as well as political and local news. (Kranzler 365)

After mutating from a monthly to a weekly to a daily paper, Storfer's paper began to suffer; he was not geared, apparently, to the pace of a daily, and he suffered a heart attack in September, 1940 (ibid.). Ottinger's shot of the front page captures a headline announcing Freud's interest in the Jewish question.

The closing words of Kranzler's account open onto Ottinger's task: "Like the *Kikayon* plant in the Book of Jonah that grew and blossomed for only one day, the twentieth-century settlement of Jews among the one billion Chinese will have been only an ephemeral phenomenon in the Diaspora history of the Jewish People" (582). In the tense of the archive (the future perfect) Kranzler enjoins the archive in the most predictable fashion possible, urging us to remember, to cherish the document he has bestowed in the place of the Kikayon. Ottinger will remember otherwise.

Impression, Displacement, Translation

Ottinger's orchestration of Jewish exiles' recollections with extended glimpses into the life of Shanghai as it is now provides a critical apparatus with which to displace or dislodge the authority of the archive as dead repository and to effect a mode of direct translation from the past to the present, from Europe to Asia, from memory to a kind of documentary presence. It is a film of "live" memory in a rhythm of the future, produced through a lesbian impression. It bears repeating that *Exile Shanghai* is not a film "about" lesbians, but my argument seeks to draw attention to what and how lesbians see and record, or archive, their impressions. An impression: "the feeling inspired by this excessive and ultimately gratuitous investment in a perhaps useless archive" (Derrida, "Archive Fever," 12). *Exile Shanghai* renders the "extraterritorial" status of Shanghai that was bought with a quasi-colonial authority reciprocal, bringing into being a visual counterpart to what Agamben calls "aterritoriality" (*Means*, 24).

The first shot of the film is likely one of the "pointless" ones, though it provides both a point of entry and a point regarding the graphic force and ideological direction of much of the contemporary footage: an endless stream of bicyclists and pedestrians, wearing brightly colored ponchos, parades in front of Ottinger's camera. While the viewer is to learn of Shanghai's endless rains from other sources, this shot serves no function other than to introduce us to the city/mise-en-scène in what will be its emblematic state: wet, crowded, dense, though brimming with beauty (pattern, color, contrast, direction, movement) and with life. To invoke a city-symphonic resonance, it is Joris Ivens' *Rain* (1929) in brilliant color. The musical score echoes the immediate temporal dislocation of a film "about" memories of Shanghai introduced with a direct lingering recording of the city: a faintly "Asian" impression lent by strings gives way to a cartoonish, almost circus-like whistle laid over a waltz, a kind of aural pastiche. And as the score shifts locales and becomes driven by the voice-over of the first interviewee, Rena Krasno, the graphic dimensions of the ponchos yield to Chinese calligraphy, a photograph of the young Rena in Shanghai, and a tale of origins and a postal coincidence. In effect, Rena tells us that she was born and raised in China, a member of a Russian Jewish family. With the camera still lingering on a surface of Chinese characters, Rena must begin the history of Jews in Shanghai in order to explain the surprise of such a revelation: a "Shanghai Jew"? One imagines Ottinger's prompt here ("tell us"); it will be foregrounded in other testimony to reveal the guidance of an authorial hand.

The story of the Shanghai Jews gains momentum as the camera turns to Rena in close-up, whereupon she explains the history of one of Shanghai's most prominent Jewish families, the Sassoons. David Sassoon, an Iraqi who had made a fortune trading with England on the cotton market in India, in his quirky self-reliance seems to have fetched his own mail from the post office in Bombay. There he noticed that his competitors were getting letters from China, and he found out that Shanghai was an open port; he immediately sent his son to exploit trade there, and thus was founded the Sephardic Jewish community in Shanghai in the mid-nineteenth century. A secret made nonsecret, but not public. Rena's eyes in smiling close-up register the delight in the story: of deviousness or cleverness, of the coincidence of a misrouted post, of an improbable origin at the macro-level that ties her micro-history to that of a monumental figure in Shanghai and, more significantly, a striated Jewish community. Dissolve to photographs of those early tycoons.

Through this brief introductory sequence, Ottinger seems to me to provide a tutorial in reading the rest of her film. It is not so much that the initial shots of streams of ponchos provide a graphic transition from the new to the old, from the now to the then, as much as that they remain a layered reminder of the contradictory dimensions of recollection itself. Rena Krasno's testimonial, that is, will have been founded on supporting visual evidence, as in the conventional cutaways to old photographs, newspapers, or other documents, *as well as* visual challenges to the legitimacy or coherence of her recollections. Shots of the contemporary city thus introduce a rebus of authority that functions politically: Rena's *relative* privilege along with that of many of the other interviewees in relation to the fate of other Jews during the war, her Orientalism (for Jewish Orientalism has its own dense history), her class allegiances, and her cultural snobbery are neither exposed as ideological in the pejorative sense nor are they dialectically set against poverty and despair as, say, with Vigo's *A Propos de Nice*. Instead they are set *trembling* by testimony, reverberating critically in the face of the ethical imperatives to decide, through the dense stream that becomes Shanghai. Tracing further obstacles of recollection and access inherent in the western encounter with Asia, the film is begun with a juxtaposition of the emblematic or the iconographic, insofar as the brightly colored ponchos as elements of an abstract canvas become emblems of the city's dominant "feel," with the corresponding "unintelligible" calligraphy. Those who cannot read or understand Chinese, those who know little or nothing of Shanghai or who know it through the movies, are consigned to swerve between the semiotic registers through which epistemic violence is wrought, "mistaking" the detail as representative, investing in the dream of a universal signification.

To criticize Ottinger's gaze as *exotisme pur* in this instance would be to miss the alignment of gazes in the sequence: the viewer sees not as a distant observer, not through the lens of an authoritative interpretation or an imperializing aestheticism. Ottinger's viewers see as the exiles have seen. We reauthorize their misrecognitions in our own. They perhaps could not have read Chinese, as we perhaps cannot now, and their gazes upon Shanghai may have been awash in color but muted in understanding as ours are certainly in the opening minutes of Ottinger's film. This temporal layering of gazes, the extent to which they refuse the separation of then and now, is sustained throughout *Exile Shanghai,* and in it I mark the outline of a lesbian impression. Ottinger, in other words, refuses the authority of the past as convention (old photographs, maps) but similarly refuses the continuity of the present as identity (we, Jews, then and now). A different ethical alignment is at work, a different coding of affective value, in the disjunction that is a testimony to that which cannot be grasped and instead is approached through a swerve. Ottinger's camera records the possibility of a mistake rather than endorsing the orthodoxy of a position. The critical work of Hansen, Hake, Mayne, and others would seem to reinforce this strategy of reading against identity-driven certainty, to see Ottinger in a feminist and queer lineage yet as resisting the aesthetic prescriptions of social movements.[40]

Three further examples illustrate Ottinger's anti-identitarian "take" on cross-cultural exchange and affective alignment. Here is Rena Krasno again, on the encounter between the high cultural sphere of the White Russian émigrés with the Shanghai Chinese:

> It was really fantastic because the Chinese are very very gifted. As soon as we saw a nice dress we liked in a movie, we went to our tailor and asked him to copy it. They never needed a pattern, you could explain it to him, and there was this man to whom we spoke pidgin English and he answered in pidgin English, and he knew exactly what we wanted and it would fit. By the way, it was also marvelous with Chinese cooks: that they hated the food that they cooked for us, but they cooked delicious food according to our tastes.

This narration precedes a single shot of roughly three minutes in which Ottinger's camera settles on a cook in a blue-lit backroom in Shanghai now. He begins to manipulate a round of dough, slowly dividing it by pulling it horizontally, then folding the strands vertically to repeat the process. As the strands multiply, the cook allows them to lengthen as well, whipping them like licorice against the floured kneading surface, until he ultimately holds in his hands a skein of perfectly even strings. They are, of course, tossed into a pot of simmering liquid, only to become . . . chicken noodle soup? Or its Chinese "equivalent"? It becomes difficult *not* to see the overdetermination at work in the fantasy of an identification between his labor and that old staple of Jewish cuisine. The fantasy is, moreover, neither dismissed by the film nor sanctioned as a "real" equation: it allows us the disjunctive rhythm of recollection and diaspora, at once.

Examples could be multiplied through the interview with Rena alone: her story about her experiences as a medical student buying bodies for dissection that had been found on the streets is followed in a manner similar to the noodle store sequence by roughly a five-minute sequence in the interior of a Chinese pharmacy. Where Rena's tone in her interviews is matter-of-fact with a twinge of shock, Geoffrey Heller's later interview is more poignant: "The things I never got used to were the fact that, on a winter morning, you would leave your little place and you would find people frozen to death in the streets." These bodies, at once an index of the misery, starvation, and disease that obtained for the Chinese in Shanghai during the war and increasingly for the Jews consigned to the Hongkew "ghetto," have immanent potential to signify primitivism, lack of civilizing institutions, the cannibalizing force of contagion, and the like. The sequence that in effect answers these under- or overtones in Rena Krasno's description, however, contains them in a curious distance: here, says the camera, is Chinese medicine. The voice-over has halted to focus attention. The shot remains in a pharmacy. Here, in bins and drawers and jars and weights and measures and packets, is a system of medicine; here is a mixture of herbs, here is chopping; here is a bundle tied with twine. What do you know of it, then or now? And where lies judgment?

"As Only a Sixteen-Year-Old Can Sleep"

Another part of Exile Shanghai's critical force lies in the ways it foregrounds the distance between the exiles' adolescent experiences and their recollections of them as adults, mirroring the distance I have been discussing between images or recollections of Shanghai during the war and Shanghai now. Adolescence is seen as a fertile moment for the imagination, as well as a time when the rearrangement of thought and desire is most possible. One of the film's second set of interviewees, Gertrude Alexander (who appears with her rabbi husband, Theodor), tells a marvelous story of her journey to Shanghai on a boat from London, as many of the exiles traveled through an itinerary of stops that become a litany in the film: Port Said, the Suez Canal, Capetown, New London, Durbin, Bombay, Colombo, Singapore, Hong Kong, Shanghai. After the story, Gertrude tells us, "Today I can say that I've been to all these places, but I've never seen them. I've never gone ashore." Counterpoint/implication: and neither has the viewer gone ashore to Shanghai; haven't his/her glimpses, too, been stops on an itinerary of a diaspora that remains at the far side of a docking ramp or the end of Ottinger's lens? At Liverpool, the first port on that voyage, Gertrude, who had been in London with other children sent from Vienna until the raids began, awoke suddenly to the sound of an air-raid siren. Panicked, she turned to her shipmates to confirm that they were under fire; her compatriots, she tells us, laughed and laughed, until they finally could regain the composure to tell her that what she was hearing was the sound of the "all-clear." She had slept through the entire harbor raid, "as only a sixteen-year-old can sleep."

A Shanghai Bildungsroman: most of the film's interviewees stress the sense of adventure, the opportunity for exploration and learning, and the pleasure in the new (and the debauched) afforded by the journey to and encounter with Shanghai. Geoffrey Heller and his brother were befriended by a German Jesuit priest who taught them Japanese; his recollection of the journey through the same ports is that "it was magical for a boy of sixteen: all the joys of adolescence, the miracle of eating in the dining room [where you could] pick *everything* on the menu, eat yourself under the table . . . We became adults, [we] started smoking at that time." A few of the interviewees are able to locate their adolescent impressions in another context; Heller continues,

> I'm sure there are other people who had a terrible time in this Shanghai experience. I must say that for me at seventeen it was an absolute eye-opener, it was high adventure, it was an unbelievable juxtaposition of exotic and fantastic things . . . It looked to me almost like a mini-United World, with the coexistence of so many nationalities . . . On the other hand, it was not melding . . . the International Settlement was kind of the last ripple of the quasi-colonial period.

Inna Mink, like Rena Krasno of a more privileged Russian Jewish background, is more critical in her retrospection:

> It's strange for me now looking back and seeing things as an adult, not as a kid, how horrible it was for the Chinese people who were very suppressed. Here we were, living in their country in the lap of luxury where they had either everything (only a small percentage of the Chinese people) or nothing at all; who basically waited on us hand and foot, who took care of us, and this is what colonialization was all about . . . I can't really fathom what the heck was going on with my

brains why I never saw any of it that way then that I see today. It's just absolutely amazing.

As with Rena Krasno's story of the Chinese gift for the copy, these are moments of self-incrimination, of the adult indicting the excesses and privileges not only of colonial power but of adolescent naiveté or blindness. Rena earlier had told us explicitly, "I think people's impressions are different according to their age," but the question the film poses, then, is this: how are we to counter the impressions of age/race/ethnicity/religion/gender/class/sexuality as they are recoded as Jewishness itself in the archive of victimhood? Testimony refuses the certainty of such codings.

One strategy the film adopts toward this end, as I have suggested, is to juxtapose the images consigned to official history in the dead past with living "translations" into the present. These are abundant, indeed, especially in shots of what was the Hongkew "ghetto," seen through photographs that serve as recollection-images edited in parallel fashion with its teeming life in the film's present. In a park with a marker commemorating the Jewish internment, kids play in a "ball room" filled with plastic, brightly colored balls, men and women in gray garb practice martial arts, a band picks up and leaves off. Another exemplary sequence answers the wedding stories of the Jewish exiles with a contemporary Shanghai wedding-photo shop. In a sequence of almost ten minutes, "pointless" for certain, Ottinger lingers on tawdry vinyl tablecloths, rhinestone pins, outlandish "western" garb (overdone wedding dresses and the ubiquitous polyester tuxes of the middle classes), hairpieces, tired and hapless brides standing before a *Heavenly Creatures* movie poster (the murderous lesbian in the odd detail!). Ottinger discovers here all the detritus of western culture's obsession with fabricating the fantasy of the perfect commodity-wedding as it creeps into the crevices of Communist China.

The more powerful method the film invokes of reading the exiles' adolescent glee and concomitant blindness, however, is the use of the close-up: after five hours of *Exile Shanghai*, one *knows* Rena and Gertrude and Theodor and Inna and Georges and Geoffrey. Lanzmann's *Shoah* relies on a similar intimacy, a similar mode of knowing affect, not only in the more melodramatic moments when tears are shed, but in the tics of the face, the strained tale completed. Quirks of speech become familiar, such as Geoffrey Heller's nervous transition through "in any event." Faces reveal themselves in their age and, precisely, in their distance from

Figure 16. Still from *Exile Shanghai*. Courtesy of the Offices of Ulrike Ottinger.

the events narrated. The affect generated by the knowledge that these are old people is not, in fact, to be dismissed; it is one of several modes of legitimizing the stories "in their own right," the length of their telling and the need for us to lend an ear, even or especially for five hours. *Exile Shanghai,* however, poses one substantial challenge to the sentimental-izing imperative of the dying Jew: in the interview with Georges Spunt, it recalibrates Shanghai's sinful pleasures and victimhood through the lens of a gay man, who died in San Francisco in 1996. I turn to his recol-lections to conclude, honing in on the remaining elements in Ottinger's repertoire for archivization and translation in *Exile Shanghai.* In so doing, my emphasis is on the possibilities of alignment.

And What Is a Lady without Her Boudoir?

The testimony provided by Georges conforms to the tales of the other more privileged Jews of Sephardic and Russian descent in the film. Unlike those of his temporary compatriots, however, his recollections are nothing if not camp: his Shanghai was divided not by the Garden

Bridge that segregated Hongkew but by movie theaters tied to Hollywood studios, his icon not the notoriously lesbian Anna Mae Wong but Bette Davis. The language and style of cinematic life shape the city he recalls even more forcefully: the Paramount nightclub was the hub of gay life before the war, and the Deco architecture of Shanghai is lovingly traced by his narrative. Even while much of gay culture was hidden, "*en cachette*" he tells us, Georges' own affect and descriptions are outrageously queer, tied as they are to a young gay man's fascination with couture, with his aunt Lisa's flamboyant femininity: "she was very much a clothes horse." (My subsection's title is one of the segues to a photo of the same aunt's boudoir.) As much as Georges may provide the obviously queer kernel—melodramatic, fantastic—of *Exile Shanghai,* however, it is the images of Shanghai that accompany his particular testimony that produce the force of the film's impression. To make the point clear, I am not arguing that the "lesbian impression" comes in Ottinger's obvious delight in filming the gay man; her delight, to the absolute contrary, extends to all of the interviewees and is palpable in each of the interviews. It is not, to underline, in the processes of *identification,* but in alignment, and particularly in alignment with the Chinese rather than with Georges in this segment, that Ottinger's intervention is best glimpsed. More than any other, this interview segment discloses Ottinger's strategies of juxtaposition and alignment that contribute to the film's lesbian impression. In this closing section on *Exile Shanghai,* I trace a counterpoint in the curiosity that unsettles identificatory pleasure and the more conventional cutaways that confirm Georges' recollections.

There are thus two elements of this section of the film: a gay "character," in both senses, and a city, edited in a sequence as complex as the sequence in the Potsdamer Platz in Ottinger's earlier film, *Countdown.* It is important to a reading of *Exile Shanghai* to note that many of the other exiles' interviews are set into motion, as is Rena Krasno's, by courtship and marriage. These are without doubt the rituals, if melodramatized, linking Jewish marginalized and/or suffering peoples to their brethren in the heterocentric rest of the West. The narratives of both Georges and the final interviewee, Geoffrey Heller, thus rely less upon recognizable appeals to an ostensibly common bond of love under strenuous conditions than to the strains of experience produced through jobs, leisure, and the intricate nature of survival during wartime. In these strains, for Georges in particular, are production and literal exchange, a scheme of value, and a problematic of remembrance. There is a lot to unpack in this claim. To begin, Georges is the only interviewee who addresses directly the status of the Jew in terms of national belonging; Georges' father managed, by way of his financial contributions to the Allied Red Cross, to wrangle for himself and for his child French citizenship. "He wanted to belong to a country, not to a race or religion." Georges was therefore raised as French (hence the name with an "s"), following a French curriculum, living in the French Concession, enlarging his larger sense of European belonging with the study of Italian, and the like. That French, unlike British, citizenship could be bought, however, introduces a trembling leitmotif of exchange that will be heard throughout Georges' testimony: "[Shanghai was] sort of a city that was not raped like Nanking because the Japanese had a purpose for Shanghai: they wanted to keep a city where they could make transactions and have sort of a freedom for themselves." What Georges remembers about the increasing restrictions imposed by the Japanese occupation is similarly tied to transactions, to currency: due to the astonishing rates of inflation, money was carried in bundles rather than in single bills, "a taxi ride cost 5 million CRB" (Chinese Reserve Bank currency).

There are already contradictions, condensations at play in the testimony. Citizenships are traded like commodities, racial/ethnic identities are set in motion in exchange, producing unsettling equivalences. Freedom for the Japanese meant preserving the structures of imperial settlement founded upon expropriation; by implication, the "devil may care" freedom of the gay community rested upon the same scaffolds. The general equivalent, money (currency, wads of bills), veils both the materiality of the signifier *and* the social relations through which such an abstraction is produced. The case of Georges demands that we ask after the political economy of gay life, national identity, and Jewish remembrance, but his testimony, it must be stressed, is not offered by way of critique. To the contrary, Georges' fascination with Shanghai as mise-en-scène for a camp reading embeds, as camp does more generally, the pain of nostalgia, of translating despair into an excessive and excessively funny lavishness of description and recollection. The critical task falls to Ottinger, in the images she selects by way of instrumentation. In these images, the cinematic production of gayness becomes more clearly for her a question of archivization.

One long sequence stands out. While Georges describes his apprenticeship to fashion designers (he was the first to put Dietrich in slacks, he claims against more received gossip), what we see are Chinese couples dancing, western-style, on the Bund. They are costumed in Maoist sim-plicity; most are middle-aged and most appear slightly disinterested in the orchestrated proceedings. The chord Ottinger strikes in this se-quence at first appears to be an analogical one: the Shanghai of Georges' remembrance (Deco, neon, "devil-may-care" gay nightlife) is to contem-porary Shanghai's regimented and controlled forms of leisure what Ori-entalism is to Communist "reality." The film would thus seem to align gayness with Orientalism, just as Ottinger had previously revealed a strain of particularly Jewish Orientalism, yielding a "take-home" indict-ment of Chinese repression as against the excessive opportunities of fad-ing imperial Shanghai, as with a certain kind of nostalgia for Weimar Germany as freedom-before-fascism. Such would be one version of a critical understanding of gay identity in wartime Shanghai, one which notices the complicity of gayness with so-called larger structures of his-torical belonging. Yet a quick analogical maneuver would fail to acknowl-edge the reciprocal nature of exchange. In the sequences of contem-porary Shanghai accompanying Georges' recollections, what Ottinger instead offers is the extent to which historicizing as archivization yields stasis: domiciliation, the domestication of historical antagonisms, can-not be contained in what Ottinger describes as the "live" translation, of bodies, if disaffected ones, moving to music in a now that spills onto the archival testimony of the then. This is not to posit, incidentally, an "outside" to archivization or the "meta-archive" denied by Derrida; to the contrary, the impression left by the Mao-jackets waltzing is precisely the *questioning* of gay bodies dancing in Deco palaces built by Chinese hands. If there is anything to this rhythm, it is a challenge to rote mantras of inclusion, *naturalized* habits of historicization, conventions of read-ing "gay" as liberatory. There is no meta-archive, but there remains an impression.

There are also, to be sure, more conventional relationships that obtain between recollection and image in the testimony of Georges, as there are in the other segments of the film. His memories of his aunt are accompa-nied by photographs of her villa (the Villa Mona Lisa) and by glamorous photographs of her as a singer in the early 1920s; his mapping of Shang-hai through movie theaters and Deco architecture is answered by images of the city lit by neon, the moon reflecting upon the harbor waters sliced by a boat. One could obviously invoke the image in *Un Chien Andalou* as inspiration. But we are never certain that these rhythms will not yield to others, challenges to the confirming and conforming laxity of orthodox documentary form. One final example, from the following interviewee, Geoffrey Heller—whether it is because Heller is the last interviewee, the final impression, or because his self-presentation is the most awkward, his voice remains with me.

Heller, rummaging through his memorabilia in preparation for the interview with Ottinger, had come upon a book of his father's entitled *Shanghai Country Walks*, written by a "charming, humorous, thoughtful Englishman." Heller had often walked with his father, following the "quite ingenious" maps with their little landmarks of bridges and stones through the countryside surrounding Shanghai, until their mobility was restricted by the Chinese to Hongkew and to Heller's daily commute across the Garden Bridge to work. Both the book and the walks Heller took with his father are relegated to the past, to the world of fading imperialism and the sense of mastery and leisure it produced; insofar as they are beyond retrieval, they mark, as does the film more generally, the contradiction at the heart of the archival project. On the one hand, Heller muses thoughtfully, "the landmarks really worked. We found our way." The sensuous delight Heller takes in the memory of these walks is palpable and for the viewer to share: what a pleasure, for this young man, to breathe country air with his father, blissfully unaware of the brutality around the corner. And yet, of course, these maps could show him nothing, they reveal to the viewer nothing, of the lives of the Chinese in imperial Shanghai or now, much less of the structural relations that obtain between the hand that draws on another continent or the persecution awaiting Heller's family in Europe. Ottinger therefore answers twice: first in another long sequence, this time of rural China, following the verbal cues of Heller's recollection of landmarks that in images become dissociated from the path Heller followed and instead come to function as the tracing of a map we will never have seen. As with the sequence of the Chinese pharmacy, it says, "here is grain sifted in the sun, here are fishing boats, here the fish comes to market." What does one know of these exchanges, what does one exchange for this knowledge? The second answer comes from Heller, in his final thoughts:

> But when I think about the dreadful fate of millions in Europe, it seems so utterly trivial, it seems like a picnic in a way, and I never thought, during these times at least, of myself as a victim other than to be embroiled in the uncertainties and hardships of this dreadful war. Then when the war was over came the discoveries of terrible tales

that we had not perhaps been privy to while we were cut off from all news of the world. I discovered that my grandmother had been killed at Auschwitz, my other relatives likewise, my great-aunt, my great-uncle, all sorts of other people. It's very searing, in fact I don't recall quite just how the knowledge of all this ultimately became a reality. It took a *Life* magazine here, and a story there, but those were very terrible times.

How does the knowledge become a reality? Is this not, indeed, the kernel of the question of the prosthesis of the mystic writing pad, the question of the archive coming to be? Heller's narration cannot sustain coherence in the face of these "terrible tales," but not only or simply or even primarily because he confronts atrocity. Instead, what he confronts is the rhythm of a life lived otherwise, wherein all the memories, photographs, newsreels, articles, monographs, official histories, and documentary films cannot stop the trembling of something beyond, from the past and toward the future, "if it will have been." Ottinger's imperative seems to be to keep this trembling alive, through necessarily incomplete translation.

Chapter 4

Absolut Queer: Cuba and its Spectators

The future will have to have been one of struggle.—Raúl Castro in "The Sexual Politics of Reinaldo Arenas," Jon Hillson

Art can transgress death.—Julian Schnabel, *New York Times Magazine,* 25 March 2001

The migration of the Shanghai exiles of the preceding chapter follows a pattern carved by their Pacific Rim counterparts, from China's eastern shore to America's west. The early frost of the Cold War, however, deadened many of those exiles' ideas about a future in the ostensibly free world; postwar immigration quotas thwarted a large number from reuniting with families in the United States, and many of the Shanghai Jews reluctantly settled for berths on ships to Australia and Israel where they now remain. The promised routes thus revealed older, other, traces of political determinations and alliances that set parameters on the futures of exiles, as well as on our readings.

Though their numbers are tiny, the Shanghai exiles nonetheless remind us of the roundabout, unpredictable, and layered nature of diaspora even as it is forged through macro-political events, discourses, and interests. Place generates a problematic. Each story of exile embeds these layers and forms of historicizing: some banal, some melodramatic, some monumental, some horrifying, some menacing, some heartening. Each attempt to document these layers faces similar questions: through what grid are these experiences intelligible? How and according to what rules are they recorded, archived, deposited, documented? Through what strategies does one declare one's own location and interests? And toward what ends, with what violences wrought by the apparatus of representation and the traps of visibility I have discussed in the preceding chapters?

Though Shanghai and Havana may conjure similar images of decadent vice, the ideological distance from Ottinger's Shanghai to the Cuba of several documentaries that I investigate in this chapter is significant, greater perhaps than the physical distance that separates Cuba from the shores of its largest diaspora in southern Florida.[1] Where Ottinger sought to reveal the mechanisms of our affective and political cartographies, involved as she is in a practice of exchange (that is, two-way travel and recording between continents and cultures, with the attendant certainty of misunderstanding), dominant cinematic treatments of Cuba largely mystify the gap separating the island from the United States, and they do so precisely in the name of understanding. Indeed, those ninety miles of sea between us, traced as they are by almost a half century of the particular turbulence associated with the Cuban Revolution and attempts on the part of the United States to sabotage its gains, are also carved with a pattern of recent migration, one that obscures the layered exchanges of which that distance is a product. Almost uniformly, that is, in cinema as in western media more generally, that migration appears as one-way, exodus, flight or, more precisely, drift: from totalitarianism to democracy, from repression to freedom, from scarcity to plenty, from the dreary past to the glorious present. Routinely the cinema indicts Cuba and its figurehead or synecdoche, Fidel Castro, as do those right-wing communities in greater Miami who constitute a horrifying caricature or cartoon of the Cuban people's struggle; routinely, the drift is naturalized, rendered commonsensical. Cuba, like Shanghai, becomes the static mise-en-scène of oppression, backwardness, totalitarianism: outside of time, outside of the enlightened history of which our gaze is both product and confirmation.

Or so it would appear. The ideological project of naturalizing drift, of condemning Cuba and the Revolution in the names of capitalism and democracy requires ammunition, and it has come in a surprising, indeed astonishing, alternate name: one that I shall call *gays-and-lesbians*. The hyphens are necessary, since this weapon, I shall argue, is precisely a melding together of rights-based discourses of Euro-American emancipatory struggles on behalf of lesbians and gay men, deployed now in the service of anti-Revolutionary rhetoric, in the service of anti-Revolutionary politics. The most recent instance of such a maneuver comes in Julian Schnabel's 2000 narrative film, *Before Night Falls*, but a history of documentary film provides the ground for, as well as incipient challenge to, Schnabel's sympathetic, at times beautiful portrait of the gay Cuban writer Reinaldo Arenas.[2] In what follows, I track that history to examine the production of a peculiar equivalence: between Cuban Revolutionary society and the repression of gays-and-lesbians, forged through a documentary practice. In our names, that is, in the name of *lesbian,* the most pernicious conservatism restricts the production of counterdiscourses to that equivalence and reinforces the condemnations of socialist possibility. What is worse, the counterdiscourses when they do appear seem merely to repeat the move in different terms, whereby under the cover of an *endorsement* of gay-and-lesbian comes either homophobia and stultifying moralism, or identity-based obliterations of difference.

The documentary scaffold upon which *Before Night Falls* climbs to new heights of anti-Revolutionary fervor is well-known to several scholars of Cuban cinema and culture, John Hess, José Estéban Muñoz, Jon Hillson, and B. Ruby Rich among them. The work of this chapter is indebted to their differently provocative analyses and is driven by the imperative of situating that work within the limits of rights- and identity-based discourses dependent upon the paradigm of visibility. Beginning, then, with the viciously anti-Castro film that inaugurated the equivalence between the Cuban Revolution and the repression of "gays-and-lesbians" and that persists as a reference point, *Mauvaise conduite/Improper Conduct* (Nestor Almendros and Orlando Jimenez Leal 1984), the chapter moves to two American documentaries more evidently allied with gay and lesbian interests, *No porque lo diga Fidel Castro/Not Because Fidel Castro Says So* (Graciela Sánchez 1988) and *Gay Cuba* (Sonja deVries 1995). I turn finally to the very first Cuban documentary on queer issues, *Mariposas en el Andamio/Butterflies on the Scaffold* (Margaret Gilpin and Luis Felipe Bernaza 1996), learning from its elaboration of a transformative sexual difference how to reinvigorate a sense of lesbian as the possibility of something else.

I visit these films (and describe my stakes in them further) in this chapter to urge queer intellectual work on cinema, again particularly on documentary, to broaden its purview in two more specific directions. First, by attending as I did in the previous chapter to the exigencies of exhibition and to the particular circuits of gay and lesbian film festival exhibition, I relocate the critical task from the more restricted moves of textual analysis to a contextual practice of reading visibility, attending to the difference of enunciation. In Cuba, after all, the most vigorous conversation about homosexuality in recent years followed the release of a *film,* Tomas Gutierrez Alea's *Fresa y chocolate/Strawberry and Chocolate* (1993); more than a million Cubans saw the film, perhaps the most widely seen on the island. By placing these films within these arenas of exhibition both at home and abroad, however, I am not thereby endorsing a reductive notion of subcultural community reception, or pleasure, or *necessarily* camp re-evaluation of derisive portraits of queer lives. No one is in a better position to caution us against the dangers of romanticizing art house spectators, or the communities of queers-on-the-town at gay and lesbian film festivals than B. Ruby Rich, and I join her in the task of stoking a sense of wonder, attending films "in search of new experiences" within these contexts, against the limits of orthodoxy and continued audience demands for the already known and for "positive images." [3]

Because film festivals are the central organ for elaborating gay and lesbian film culture, and because I encountered the documentaries of this chapter through that organ, a further word is perhaps in order regarding my investments. For about five years in the mid-1990s, I worked as programmer and board president for the Pittsburgh International Lesbian and Gay Film Festival, one of the oldest in the country. That work prompted a number of concerns that echo Rich's above, primarily regarding the idealization or overestimation of independent cinema for the gay and lesbian community, a community forged largely as a "commodity audience." I borrow Eileen Meehan's term coined to address the television audience to designate an audience forged by the commodification of their collective attention; that is, their collective attention can be sold, as a commodity, to corporate sponsors, who in turn provide enough money to supply whatever "programming" might fill in between commercial appeals. [4] I repeat Rich's observation, then, that bringing the pessimism of the culture industry to the euphoria designated in the idea of a "festival" may itself be a perverse gesture, but it is a necessary one. Due to decreasing public funding for the arts in the United States, it has become imperative for arts organizations to seek corporate support in order to make possible their survival. Yet at the moment of this economic transformation, which prompts further questions about the equivalence of state subsidy and private benevolence, other transformations are resulting in the production, distribution, and exhibition of gay and lesbian or queer cinema, metamorphoses that might receive better attention through contextual work than the invocation of a necessary "visibility."

In addition to enlivening textual analysis with that contextual work, then, I follow this set of documentaries that provide the ground for *Before Night Falls* for another, perhaps more pressing, reason having to do with the production of a "theory of sexuality." The case of Cuba, that is, provides an extremely exciting if shopworn knot of questions to which we need not be drawn on identitarian grounds: what form does a revolutionary conception of sexuality take? To what extent has Cuba embraced an emancipatory sexual politics? What are the contours of the sexual in a revolutionary context? What, in short, does Cuba teach us, and how do we embrace its lesson? There is, moreover, a subsidiary set of questions that undergirds these more abstract formulations, having to do with what it means to belong in one way or another to a community of lesbian and gay (queer, trans, bi: the question is not dependent right now upon the naming) spectators in the United States, a community daily complicit with the trade embargo against Cuba, a community only annually and likely through film festivals encountering Cuba in substantive ways. As I try to invoke in the chapter title, what does it mean to encounter "Cuba" under the sign of corporate America or its art venues, particularly as it invests in the very same category of "gays-and-lesbians" as niche market that the films on Cuba figure as victim?

As I have, members of the left in my community have followed the revolution as closely as any life-and-death experiment—Castro indeed frequently uses the language of the laboratory to describe the ongoing struggle. Their views have more recently been tinged with nostalgia or, perhaps better, the sense that one is losing contact with a once-dear friend. This chapter seeks to re-establish contact, with one eye open to the daily struggles of the Cuban people and the other eye fixed directly on the historical reality of their Revolution, not to romanticize but to investigate and imagine.

The Beginnings of "Arteurism": *Mauvaise Conduite*

A Cuban exile, Nestor Almendros was a cinematographer who worked on acclaimed films such as *Days of Heaven* (Terence Malick 1978), *The Last Metro* (François Truffaut 1981), and *The Marquise of O* (Eric Rohmer 1976). Orlando Jimenez-Leal is the director of *El Super* (1979), the first Spanish-language film made in New York City and a film that thematizes the experience of Cuban exile; he later directed *8-A Ochoa* (1992), a film about the 1989 trial and execution of Cuban former General Arnaldo Ochoa. Together in 1984, Almendros and Leal made *Improper Conduct*, coproduced with and screened on French television's Antenne 2, on 24 May 1984. Just thereafter, the film opened in the United States at the "New Directors/New Films" New York festival. Distributed by Cinevista,

a Miami-based distribution firm, *Improper Conduct* traveled the film festival, art house, and museum circuit for several years after its initial release. Though it is now screened less frequently than upon its release,
Improper Conduct retains a certain notoriety, earned through the vicious-
ness with which it attacks its putative subject, the repression of gays and
lesbians in Cuba, and the accompanying venom which Almendros and
Jimenez-Leal directed toward critics of the film.

In one such exchange of the latter, in the magazine *American Film,* the
directors of *Improper Conduct* respond to B. Ruby Rich's critical article,
"Bay of Pix." They allege that Rich has proffered "redundant political
rhetoric" as opposed to "actual film criticism," of which Rich is reputed
to have offered only "four lines."[5] The tone of Almendros and Jimenez-
Leal's response to Rich's piece is representative of the inflated and in-
flammatory discourse of the film itself; to identify only two of its strategies, it attacks individuals, and it makes charged historical comparisons.
To wit: "Ms. Rich should see our film again. Does she have wax in her
ears, impaired vision, or are all her senses blocked?"[6] And: "Our conso-
lation is that George Orwell and Arthur Koestler were also accused in
their time of being right-wingers for having criticized Stalinist methods
'too early.'"[7] It is, unfortunately, as easy to dismiss such hyperbole as it
is to greet it with more of the same, yet to do either is to miss a chance at
understanding how such rhetoric, in fact, succeeds: how it gains hold, retains force, determines subsequent discussions, haunts every step. One
cannot overestimate the extent to which *Improper Conduct* remains the
touchstone text for many discussions of gay and lesbian life in Cuba. It
becomes, therefore, necessary to engage in some "actual film criticism,"
not to endorse Almendros and Jimenez-Leal's attack, or even to defend
Rich, but to see how the film works.[8]

My contention is that *Improper Conduct* manufactures a site for its
enunciation that I shall call *arteurism*.[9] By this term I mean to invoke
a combination of a generalized discourse of art and the particular assumptions of intent, coherence, and individual will that coalesce under
the film-theoretical term *auteurism,* derived from the *politique des auteurs.*
The characteristic emphases of arteurism are, I think, as follows:

1. Timelessness. Art (film, literature, poetry, drawing, and painting)
   is timeless, meaning both that art is not located within time, and
   that it can, as Schnabel says, transgress time, or death. Art survives
   as testimony, and the survival of artists is necessary—is, indeed,

the future. From art's point of view, as with any good narcissist, time is above all ordered by art's progression or art's production and not by other events such as social change or revolution.

2. Individual value. Individuals produce art, and the survival of the idea of the individual is therefore necessary to art. Individuals harbor genius, and individual genius can be ranked, as in "greatest living writer." Because individuals are understood to be coherent and fully intentional, moreover, individuals can speak truthfully and finally about the art they produce; there is no disjunction between what an individual means and what he says. There is, furthermore, no disjunction between what an individual says and truth.

3. Intellectual value. Intellectuals are individuals, not functions, and they are located within a generalized western metropole. They are surrounded by books and/or nature, they speak several (European) languages, and they are sometimes but not always artists. The role of the intellectual is to expose lies by standing above propaganda, popular belief, and opinion; indeed, intellectuals oppose the popular by making visible art and higher forms of thought. In this category, belonging to the French by language or by funding is an important link between the intellectual work of the critic as elaborated by auteurism and the work of the intellectual-as-filmmaker as represented by Almendros.

4. History. History is a resource for intellectual derring-do: the greater one's citational familiarity with history, the greater one's persuasive power and authority. In contradictory fashion, history is both a factual reservoir, as opposed to an interpretive domain or rigorous discipline, and a writerly practice, as opposed to a factual domain or sequenced causality, one that can be used to provoke higher thought and understanding.

Improper Conduct is an arteurist product. With what consequences? To read the film through the lens of arteurism is to make visible the extent to which it produces a generalized and seemingly left-wing indictment of "human rights violations" in Cuba precisely through a bourgeois aesthetic vision and an elitist (antipopular) cinematic practice. This perhaps comes as no surprise, given the explicit indictment of Castro and the Revolution the film makes, and it is hardly shocking that in the wake of

such an indictment would come the reification of history, the mobiliza-
tion of common sense, the melodramatization of repression, and a large
measure of disdain for popular struggle and modes of understanding.
But to understand the film is also to grasp how the politics of authorship
embedded in arteurism are also, to paraphrase Judith Mayne's reminder,
sexual politics.[10] Before examining how it is that gay-and-lesbian enters
as support for the film's restricted vision and practice, I therefore need
to demonstrate the mechanisms of the ruse by which *Improper Conduct*
eschews the very "politics" in form it thinks or acts as though it espouses.

From the first moments of the film, time loses all coherence. Here
are the first eight minutes of *Improper Conduct:* we are in the Havana
streets in 1980 (the Mariel boatlifts), then in Paris in 1966 (the Cuban
ballet dancers' defections), then in an interview with Julio Medina (one
of the dancers) in the present of the film, then in 1959 (guerilla war-
fare, Fidel), back to the film's present (an interviewee in New York), 1965
(a story of purges at the University of Havana), 1961 (the Revolutionary
agenda shifts), a map of Cuba, and back to the film's present. During this
period of eight minutes we have learned (1) that art in Cuba is "politically committed" ("you can't express things freely") and therefore non-
arteurist; (2) the history of Cuba's occupation and the complexity of the
Revolutionary overthrow of Fulgencio Batista's United States–supported
repressive regime; (3) that Cuba is not a dream, "a golden island in the
sun with palm trees"; (4) the history of Marxist-Leninism in Cuba as well
as the history of emigration; and (5) that the revolutionary government
in its "Marxist-Leninist" form established forced labor camps, the UMAP
(Units to Aid Military Production) in 1965 in the province of Camagüey.
These will become significant points for elaboration, both in the film
and in my discussion, yet in these initial moments they are but fleeting
glimpses one might glean from the rapid-fire cutting through disparate
times and locales.

Throughout *Improper Conduct* we are asked to follow these wild leaps
in chronology, none of which appears as explicitly deceptive or rhetorically motivated as is, for example, the cross-cutting in which Castro is
shown to deny the very testimony we have heard and will hear. The effect
of these willy-nilly leaps in time, however, is to create a swirling map of
time or chronotope in which specificity begins to appear simply pedan-
tic: as if one's preoccupation with causality, sequence, lines of influence,
and possibilities for change were irritating demands in the face of what
is simply true. The simple cuts contribute to the seamlessness of time:

rather than calling attention to temporal ellipses through dissolves or fades, the film throughout moves swiftly and without reflexive gestures accomplished through editing. When necessary, time is even mistranslated to intensify a sense of mistreatment or of repressive practice. In a French television report on a Cuban political prisoner freed through the "personal" intervention of François Mitterand, the duration of the prisoner's separation from his wife, *"trois ans,"* is subtitled as "thirteen." What becomes clear, however, is that, despite the switchbacks and repetitions, we have absolutely no trouble following along. Our orientation owes thanks to two further strategies through which the film secures spectatorial consent: first, the use of dialogue, in particular to confirm an impression of stasis, and second, the film's strong authorial voice, both in the presence of a voice-over narration and an interviewer shown several times with the talking-head interviewees.

The film is replete with present-tense statements of stagnancy. "All Cubans are scared." "Nothing in Cuba changes." "I doubt if it's better now. Nothing improves there. All you get are variations on the same theme." "The Cuban social system is racist." "[Cuban] cops have a fascist mentality." "Little value is placed on Cuban women." "It's obvious. You have to be blind not to see it." "Imagine your whole life controlled." "In a way, the [Cuban] state has become the new pimp." Combined with the film's spiraling sense of time, these truisms tend to produce an image of Cuba identified with an immobile past and a future tied to it as repetition. The task *Improper Conduct* sets for itself is to save Cuba for its own vision of the future: capitalist, "free," democratic. Just like ours, and saved through art.

The voice-over is used as conventionally as the film uses talking-head interviews with its participants. Despite the directors' claims that their film practice shares more with Jean Rouch or Marcel Ophuls than with the montage school, the fact is that the film is woefully uninteresting in terms of style or innovation in film language.[11] Unlike the work of either Rouch or Ophuls the film's overall emphasis is on telling rather than showing; because it relies entirely on second-hand accounts of Cuban life, it lacks the immersive and direct appeal of ethnographic witness, relying instead upon an interviewer as viewer-surrogate in order to ground its point of view. That interviewer (I am assuming Almendros, though he is nowhere named) both defines and enforces the film's arteurism; in two particular instances, to turn now to the film's explicit linkages, we begin to see how arteurism props itself on gay-and-lesbian interests.

To take his first appearance, the interviewer speaks with José Mario, a Cuban exile in Madrid who was "the first" to write about the UMAP camps. The voice-over ominously intones that "as with Stalin's concentration camps, few people believed what he described" in those accounts. Following this hyperbolic historical comparison, the interviewer joins Mario for shot/reverse shot conversation in a bucolic park, replete with a bubbling fountain:

> *Interviewer:* Were you interrogated when you were arrested?
> *Mario:* Yes, by a soldier who told me with a sneer that I was in the Writers and Artists Union and that artists, intellectuals, writers are all faggots [*maricones*].
> *Interviewer:* You're a faggot because you're a writer? [peals of laughter]
> *Mario:* All faggots. I didn't say a word. [laughter]
> [cut to interviewer shaking his head in disbelief]

The conversation continues as Mario tells the interviewer that the soldier then asked him to walk around the interrogation room, that in his walk the soldier could see something "dangerous" in him, that the soldier then told him, "we're going to make a man out of you." To which the interviewer, again incredulous, responds: "From your walk he could see . . . ?"

The arteurist function of the interviewer is here twofold: on the one hand, through him the film secures its own testimony as the *only* authoritative visible evidence we will be able to trust in an argument about Cuba's repression of gays and lesbians. Neither the soldier in the narrative above nor any other source of information will prove to make good sense out of what one sees; the film locates knowledge and authority in the perception of its director alone. Thus the film asserts the preposterous nature of the idea that one could perceive gayness in a walk; thus that idea is attributed to an unnamed man assumed to be a functionary in a repressive regime identified with Castro; thus the film confirms its own superior knowledge and visual truth, at the expense of an unthinking coarse mouthpiece of machismo who is stupid enough to think one can *see* homosexuality.

Improper Conduct seeks to indict Castro specifically for his policy of interring homosexuals and other marginalized people (prostitutes, Jehovah's Witnesses, tramps, delinquents, people who demonstrate "extravagant behavior") in camps which the film consistently compares with Stalin's concentration camps, by which the film further solicits an implicit comparison with Nazi death camps. The UMAP camps, located initially in the province of Camagüey, gathered their inmates through a ruse of military induction, and they required forced agricultural labor under apparently horrendous conditions.[12] During the same period of the late sixties, many intellectuals, artists, and writers, homosexuals and pros- titutes were imprisoned in similar or worse conditions in Havana. That these internments and imprisonments are made to resemble the atroci- ties of World War II is essential to the French appeal of the film, since *Improper Conduct* borrows the affect resulting from collaboration (guilt, the necessity of popular memory, and direct testimony regarding repres- sion) for its punch. Aligning Castro with mid-century dictators, the film also aligns the Cuban policies of internment—which lasted for fewer than three years, 1965–68, during a push to increase agricultural pro- ductivity—necessarily with Nazi, fascist, and Communist bloc positions toward homosexuality, in an undifferentiated sweep of condemnation.

The question in the film quickly becomes, "what is the relation, and is it nonexclusive, between (male) homosexuals and artist/intellectuals?" Many of the interviewees in *Improper Conduct* are gay, and as many or more are not. The interviewees do not produce legitimated knowledge equally: the drag queen Caracol, for example, can tell a story about his tight pants but not about high-level political scandal, while Susan Son- tag can speak in measured French about the disregard on the left for questions about femininity. Accepting clear-cut divisions between its two categories, gay people and intellectuals, the film oscillates uncom- fortably between, on the one hand, laughing at Castro's crude universal- izing of effeminate or extravagant traits and behavior as homosexual, as in the interview example above, and, on the other hand, expressing out- rage at the internments and imprisonments as human rights violations. The twisted logic becomes, "I'm not gay (although some of my friends are), but I'm a writer, and isn't that a ridiculous reason to have been per- secuted?" or "I'm gay, but those people think they know I'm gay because I wear tight pants; they must therefore be backward tyrants."

These causal ruses foreclose on the very questions of the process of social upheaval the film raises obliquely through its interviews: how is a gay man or lesbian identified and for what purposes (flirting, consen- sual sex, labor, repression)? What effects does "ostentatious" or "extrava- gant" behavior or "improper conduct" have on social participation, and might it enable or block specific forms of labor? How does sexual differ- ence interrupt or displace subject-predication based on labor? Is a homo- sexual "sensibility" tied to artistic production or intellectual expression in any intrinsic way, and if so how? Are common sense gender or sexual mores, such as machismo, or the location of normative sexual expression in reproductive practices, in fact dominant? How are they produced historically, and are they subject to change? How are these common sense assumptions processed through a Revolutionary imaginary, or through ostensibly simpatico left intellectuals in the northern metropole?

Improper Conduct does not provide any answers to these questions, and it instead turns its lens on unexamined testimony from exiles who oppose by blurring beyond recognition the (past) repressive apparatus of Cuban Revolutionary society to the (present) implicit freedoms of the United States and Europe. There is an occasional nod of pathos: toward an accomplished artist, for instance, who is "reduced" to selling ice-cream cones on Broadway, or to the writer Reinaldo Arenas, to whom Schnabel will devote his entire film, based on similarly blurred testimony provided in Arenas's memoirs after which Schnabel also titles his film. But these moments serve only to amplify the discord between victimized intellectuals who proffer privileged analyses and the duped or repressed population at large, struggling to escape the island, as in the lengthy sequence leading up to the Mariel exodus. There is no analysis whatsoever of the dynamics of exile or displacement, despite a short sequence in the film traversing "Little Havana" in Miami, which, despite the directors' protestations to the contrary, is seen as a mirror and not as a retrospective recoding of a pre-Revolutionary fantasy. There is no doubt some kernel of insight in Arenas's statement that "when Fidel Castro speaks even to proclaim laws that condemn homosexuals or other human beings, these people must go . . . and applaud these laws." The manufacture of consent, the production of a self-disciplining populace (through the Committees to Defend the Revolution, for example) are not unfamiliar critical problems in the maintenance of hegemony. But the statement is isomorphic to the logic the film itself invokes: when a hyperbolic film is made to condemn the practices of a Revolutionary society, the intellectual stratum of the international left wing—the implied audience—must go to the film and applaud these indictments. The translation to gay-and-lesbian audience only intensifies the problem, since the exposé form reiterates traditional understandings of "our" self-hatred and, to borrow a phrase beloved by Oprah Winfrey, "low self-esteem."

Hyperbole gives way in *Improper Conduct* to mockery, and it is finally this generalized attitude of contempt which permeates the film and prevents it from listening even to what its own subjects provide by way of inroads into substantial historical and theoretical questions. The moment of the extreme expression of this scorn comes late in the film in the second appearance of the interviewer in a discussion with writer Heberto Padilla. This discussion, worth reading in some detail, is set predictably amidst books, framing both the interviewer and Padilla himself as claustrophobic authority. Padilla, a renowned novelist, has been in exile since 1979, but his interview focuses initially on the inspiration for the UMAP camps in the early 1960s, pointing to a visit that Raúl Castro (Fidel's brother) took to Bulgaria, where he learned of their "solution" to the problem of homosexuality in internment camps. Padilla suggests, much to Almendros's glee, that many of the new leaders of Cuba were themselves homosexuals, but "macho" men who were socially tolerated and unmarked as gay. After describing the "Pavlovian" tests given to men to cure them of homosexual desire, Padilla directly addresses Almendros's laughter at his description of the new leadership: "This Cuban trait of laughing at serious matters, that we in Cuba call *jojedor,* and which in English could be translated as a gift for mockery, this trait enabled Cubans to endure some of the misery. But the misery was real." This national but not strictly homosexual gift, something like a scheme of translation of sensuous apprehension, is then opposed to the fetish in Padilla's following comment: "Lesbians [unlike gay men] excited [the new leaders]. Nothing so appeals to the primitive Cuban mind as two women in bed. And they seem so innocent as they have no weapons. [Almendros laughing hysterically.]"

Again analogizing, Almendros asks, "The 'scientific' aspect reminds one of Hitler's Germany, no?" Padilla continues, "Sartre once said to us, 'In Cuba, there are no Jews, but there are homosexuals.' Homosexuals, and this is my own unscientific opinion, always question the world they live in. They are by nature active, they're never sad. On the other hand, heterosexuals tend to be melancholic. They get over-attached to things, say, a landscape, an old shoe. [Almendros laughs.]" Almendros wonders whether Padilla ever takes offense at the presumption that he is gay. No, says Padilla, it doesn't bother him at all. Enlightened heterosexual benevolence, bought at the cost of an historical analogy, eclipses any assessment, whether psychoanalytic or unscientific (read, whimsical), of affect, attachment, critique.

One might, alternatively, allow the gift of jojedor to provide a gloss on these didactic assessments, for it has some continuity with the over-attachment of the fetishist, who is not, strictly speaking, a melancholic heterosexual. For this gift, like the fetish itself, seems to interrupt the circuit of analysis and "unscientific opinion," as well as to put a halt to the tornado of time within which *Improper Conduct* swirls. Jojedor, like camp, like the fetish, appears to represent something the "primitive" Cuban mind has devised in order to endure real misery as a process of comprehension. While it may not, in Padilla's mind or in Almendros's or Leal's, have any connection to gay men, it does seem to designate a resource, an intellectual and affective function, a scheme of value-coding which might be historically tied not only to imaginative gay activity but also to the entirely ignored world of lesbians, whose "weapons" may indeed be hidden to the straight male mind. If jojedor is aligned with melodrama, with the spirit if not the letter of a language of affect that speaks in its silence and in its gestures, it is this realm of expression that is forsaken, indeed degraded, in *Improper Conduct*'s valorization of *gauchiste* pseudo-intellectualism. In the name of gay-and-lesbian, gay is disciplined into normativity and lesbian disappears. In the name of gay-and-lesbian, modes of survival and feeling linked to gay and lesbian life are dismissed in favor of knowing condemnation. Though the form of appearance of heteronormative absolutism in this case is temporal displacement (that is, the way that the film enunciates its heteronormative logic is through its manipulation of time), its tentacles stretch elsewhere into the forms of thought upon which the film relies. Even Susan Sontag's invocation of Rosa Luxembourg reduplicates a gesture of dismissal with a long history in so-called Marxist analysis: relegating affect to the sphere of women's work, social reproduction, or the trivial, and preserving a strict division between proper politics and "gender" or "sexuality."

Improper Conduct, in sum, builds the artist from scraps of didacticism and mockery and saves him in the name of gays-and-lesbians. One need not invoke the "real" Cuba or the "real" lives of its gay and lesbian peoples to notice that questions are absent from the film, most notably any inquiry into the relationship between socialism and sexuality, although *Improper Conduct* nonetheless reveals the mechanisms by which such questions might be generated. The film's ethical absolutism, in other words, might be undone by jojedor, but its unraveling would have only begun in the candid declaration of stakes and the willingness also to abandon judgment. I turn now to a video that is both resolutely clear in its stakes and open to its subject; it also happens to confirm Padilla's unscientific hunch about homosexuals' inquisitive nature!

"Going Strong": *No Porque lo Diga Fidel Castro*

Graciela Sanchez borrows the title of her short, no-budget video from the testimony of one of her unnamed interview subjects, whose remarks also provide the subtitle of this section. The interviewee is taped in mid-shot but outdoors in clear lighting, rendering her one of the more "out" subjects of the video, since many of the interviewees are shot in shadow. A black woman, she stands next to another woman who remains silent.

> We are gay. But we must try as much as possible for people not to real-ize it. If not, we are repressed. Not because Fidel Castro says so [wags finger], but for example . . . If you ask for a job and you're seen "going strong," because that's the way we say it, "going strong," they say, "No, she's a homosexual, strike her out." Understand? Not because Fidel Castro says so [wags finger] but because society, that is, the people, have no sexual education and we are discriminated [against].

These comments lay bare the tentacles with which *No porque* works as well. First, against the assertions regarding blanket repression in *Improper Conduct* and against that film's melodramatizing of the Cuban closet, *No porque* presents, without question and without discomfort, out gay men and lesbians in Cuba *now*. Sanchez shot the film in Cuba with the support of the Cuban television school and therefore (more like Rouch and Ophuls than Almendros and Leal) offers her document as immersed testimony rather than objective recollection. Furthermore, unlike the majority of texts on the repression of "gays-and-lesbians" in Cuba, lesbians are central to the videotape's direct address. Also, against Almendros and Leal's emphasis on personal experience and psychologi-cal explanation, Sanchez highlights, as do the Cuban people, the terri-tory of *labor* as the primary scene of social definition and participation. Finally, against the exclusive focus in *Improper Conduct* on Fidel Castro as an individual who directs national law and is seen to determine, from the top down, national structures of feeling,[13] Sanchez illuminates the stratified relationship between the knowledge of the people (education, common sense, ranges of understanding) and national policy.

Sanchez reveals these stakes as her own in the opening moments of the tape. The first image is a graphic, a quotation from Zora Neale Hurston: "Man, like all animals, fears and rejects all that he doesn't understand, and anything unusual may be considered as evil." Following Hurston's words with flashing screens of bright colors overlaid with jazz, Sanchez establishes a problematic involving knowledge, self-representation, and simple claims to visibility, even while she speaks portions of identity. In voice-over, Sanchez identifies herself as a Latin-born lesbian raised in San Antonio, Texas. She is "a person like everyone else" when people don't know that she's a lesbian, but she is subjected to scorn, derision, and homophobia ("a worldwide illness") when it is known that she is. "Having been affected," she says, "as a Latin lesbian I must dispute all that I have heard and read about the repression of homosexuals in Cuba. I can't conceive it as something the socialist government has implemented as part of its policy." Illuminating Hurston's declaration of a natural, animalistic fear of the unknown, Sanchez sets a version of socially situated critique, born of experience, and Sanchez joins Hurston as American women of color with something to say about the epistemology of violence. As she inserts these investments, which are initially defined not as finding Cuban lesbian counterparts to herself but instead as a critique of received and dominant positions, she also inserts images of homophobic posters, clips of text on the alleged repression of gays and lesbians in Cuba, and an image of Rich's aforementioned notorious review of *Improper Conduct*, "Bay of Pix." The latter reads, "*Mauvaise Conduite*, a new documentary, is an explosive mixture of seductive images, gay politics, and anti-Castro propaganda." As much as *Improper Conduct* thus appears as the precursor target of this videotape's address, through this citation Sanchez also enchains Rich in critique, linking herself to feminist and lesbian intellectual work on cinema. Finally, to drive home its understanding of its context, the video turns to a Cuban immigrant come to the United States and asks the question Almendros and Leal forbid but consistently beg: "Do you think it's any better here?"

The question frames the testimonials that follow. The position from which Sanchez inquires into Cuban gay life becomes something like the implicit "no" in answer to it, but Sanchez is not reductive or judgmental in the comparison between Cuba and the United States. What is remarkable about *No porque* is, in fact, the brevity with which Sanchez jettisons the predictable. The point is to get to the point: not to be lodged within the ground established by Almendros, Leal, and homophobic propaganda but to probe the questions of labor, education, and social value embedded in the current moment, to provide what is forbidden to the American audience by the weight of inveighing against violations of civil liberties. Sanchez offers, that is, glimpses of how the phenomenon of homosexuality can be *revolutionary* and not simply "included" or "incorporated" into Cuban society. She relies upon a traditional talking head of the documentary genre to do so: Monika Krause, the director of the Grupo Nacional Educacion Sexual. (What Sanchez obscures in her presentation of Krause, upon whom Lumsden and Young also rely, is the extent to which Cuban sexual policy and education derives, as Krause's name would suggest, from the East German advisors and experts the Cuban government consulted and hired in formulating its current sexual pedagogy.)

A tracking shot of a Spanish Catholic church cuts to a close-up of Krause:

> It's a harmful addiction. The Spaniards imposed their standards, their ethical and moral standards, based on the catholic [not capitalized in the subtitles] religion. And even if the catholic church never worked with the great majority of the Cuban population . . . those standards took root very deeply, these ethical and moral standards on human sexuality in the sense that it is right if it serves for reproductive purposes. We also have to consider the homophobia element, how it appeared and developed in the country. It didn't appear after the victory of the Revolution, as many of our enemies are trying to make believe, but in Cuba it's an ancestral, an ancient phenomenon.

If there is a problem, in other words, it is in understanding the layered and stratified nature of this common sense, filtered as it is through religious belief, colonial practices, and the uncertainties of revolutionary society and ideology. Contrast such a historical form of understanding with, for example, the August 1999 statement on the status of Cuban homosexuals from the United States Immigration and Naturalization Service (INS), which opens: "During the first three decades of the Cuban Revolution, homosexuality was outlawed and gay people were persecuted—severely during the 1960s—ridiculed, and marginalized."[14] In the discourse of human rights, one begins with what is assumed to be the repressive formation, unless a preexisting attitude such as machismo may be thought to be "reinforced by decades of government persecution."[15]

Against these incessant attempts contradictorily to locate the present in the past and to invoke the past to authorize regressive views of the present, Sanchez sets her videotape resolutely in the present views of her interviewees, who introduce themselves at the beginning of the tape curiously in the style of Alcoholics Anonymous: "My name is René (Maricela, Robert, George, etc.), I'm gay." Despite the formal similarities, Sanchez mobilizes nothing of the confessional mode that marks recovery movements. Many interviewees see no pathos in their lives; many have never experienced any difficulty with the state. Some detail practical problems having to do with social sanctions or with the housing shortage in Havana, such as finding a place to express affection or have sex: "In Cuba, the one who hasn't a house for love really has nothing." Even such criticisms of Cuban life are tame given the scarcity of resources in the "crisis" period of the late 1980s and 1990s. Most of their comments refuse self-loathing and instead emphasize the lack of preparation of the people for certain forms of what we might call queer expression (such as transvestism). In contrast to *Improper Conduct, No porque* is playful and not moralistic about the pressures of machismo: the images of straight men draped around one another's arms as they condemn homosexuality are seen by Sanchez as visually identical to the affections of gay men on the beach, revealing the kernel of the homosocial even or especially in *machista* culture. Even the staple element of individual suffering is sent up, in an interview with a melodramatic queen on the street, who displaces the burden of ill health onto society as its responsibility: "Even if I've been given the opportunity to feel well, I can't, because as everyone knows we are internally rejected. We receive no help. We should be helped, because I feel that if we were helped, if work was done with us, we could be very useful to society."

The moral and ethical education of the populace becomes the focus of the remaining remarks in the video, though Sanchez is oblique about the terrain on which common sense transmutes into good sense. Some interviewees who are not gay use the language of normalcy ("It's not normal") or fear of contagion ("They spread venereal disease"), but most express their views about gay men and lesbians in the language of cultural transformation wrought through pedagogy. Over and again, man-on-the-street interviews disclose the necessity for constant analysis and intellectual work in the language of revolutionary change: "I think that one is always prejudiced toward homosexuals. But I feel that we are now liberating ourselves from prejudice and starting to see them socially as normal people, useful and not harmful to society, as acceptable people." Even those gay men and lesbians who experience familial and social rejection see homophobia in political terms, see gayness as an axis of work and an element of life that must be inserted into a larger scheme of political prioritizing. The closing remarks of the video, in voice-over against a street party of gay men and lesbians dancing at dusk, respect and listen to the terms of revolutionary priorities.

Really the situation of homosexuals in Cuba is not as chaotic as considered by some people always pretending to be interested in our situation. If you take your job seriously, if you care about not having ideological or political problems, nothing happens. Thus, attacks on the Revolution on the issue of homophobia are frequently undeserved. But, in truth, life for homosexuals is not as easy as for heterosexuals. I think that this is cause for concern, and we should start educating the people on what is a homosexual. And why he shouldn't be rejected. This is something that should be done, not only in Cuba but worldwide. There are important things to be concerned about, really negative things much more important to be concerned about than the private life of a person and judging him negatively.

Even while the party in Havana is "going strong," the video departs from the ethnographic pretense of interest in the local scene, moving instead to worldwide (hence also local) priorities to be taken up at home, in context. These remarks remind us, first, that the repression of gay men and lesbians is not, a priori, an equivalent issue everywhere, and, second, that the everyday language even of revolutionary culture will list as powerfully toward "the private" as toward "the visible" when confronted with the difference homosexuality might make. The lyrics of the song fading out into the credits, "My love for you is difficult, different!" are reductive and melodramatic but indicate the pull of popular forms and modes of understanding.

As a summation of the video, however, the song may be understood in two divergent ways, aside from providing a nice segue from the party sequence to the video's credits. On the one hand, the conclusion of the film literally acknowledges both realities of gay life in Cuba: that it is difficult, due to homophobia, and that it is different, meaning potentially transformative of our conceptions of sexuality and its relationship to sociality. In this reading, the video might be thought usefully to insist upon the bind between affect and labor which many of the film's interviewees foreground and which some refuse in their more rational Revolutionary language. The video closes, then, on a note of radical hope for the Revolutionary project and the affirmation of sexual difference in a socialist society, while also affirming popular understanding through song. On the other hand, the conclusion makes the most obvious reach for United States audiences, with songs in our hearts and dancing in the streets and a candid declaration of banality in the song's lyrics. In this reading, the video hitches itself to its United States gay and lesbian spectators, to an emphasis upon what Eve Sedgwick calls a minoritizing conception of sexuality, as either private or an issue of "rights" for gay people, rather than understanding sexual difference also as a universalizing, socially transformative practice that might be mobilized for critique, as the film's opening moments would suggest. The next two documentaries more fully define these two poles, oscillating productively between this constitutive tension: *Gay Cuba* provides a model of the Yanqui bid for understanding, to which I turn now before concluding with a discussion of *Mariposas*.

Gay Cuba

Like *No porque*, *Gay Cuba* responds to *Improper Conduct*. Unlike *No porque*, *Gay Cuba* has received relatively wide distribution and, in its titular claims and its sweeping scope, has aspirations toward a more definitive take on the subject. The low-budget video is distributed by Frameline, which runs the San Francisco International Lesbian and Gay Film Festival. Due to that festival's size and longevity (twenty-five years in 2001, at which festival *Gay Cuba* enjoyed a screening as part of a "Homo Retro" celebration of the Bay Area Video Coalition), Frameline exerts tremendous influence upon the selection of films available for other festivals and academic venues. Also unlike *No porque*, *Gay Cuba* unwittingly repeats many of the tactics of *Improper Conduct* even as it declares its opposition to Almendros and Leal. It combines forms of traditional history—including a continuist voice-over contributed by Jennifer Maytorena Taylor, then-director of the distribution and festival organization, CineAcción—individuating interviews, and revisionist history. The amalgam jeopardizes the indictment of the regressive narrative the video seeks to make.

The most vexing tension in *Gay Cuba* derives from its juxtaposition of crucial information regarding United States intervention in and policy on Cuba with a series of psychologized and interiorized portraits of gay and lesbian interviewees, to which I also return at the end of this section. The former functions radically to implicate United States audiences in repression, exploitation, and economic degradation via the trade embargo against Cuba, in stark contrast to that which French or "international" audiences are spared in *Improper Conduct*. In deVries's video, the blockade is understood to cause suffering for gay and lesbian Cubans, and for Cubans more generally, just as do homophobia, legislation, misguided education, and direct repression. As one gay male interviewee says, picking up on the interviewer's language of cultural exchange, "The gay community in the U.S. could help the gay community in Cuba by breaking the blockade to allow more exchange between the communities."

This interviewee's plea contrasts sharply with the rights-based discourse of liberation that would see in Cuban gay men and lesbians the counterparts to a gay "community" in the United States, since it indicts us for economic policy derived from Cold War illogic and expansionist capitalism. Rather than provide spectators with political education, however, deVries tempers the radical potential of this critical inroad with humanist portraits of gay and lesbian Cubans; with them, she offers individual, familial, New Age, and pop psychology explications of the lingering homophobia of Revolutionary Cuban society. The video thereby duplicates an ethnographic sense that politics, while derived from Cuba as a kind of subject matter, obtain not there but instead in the larger, layered machinations of the northern economic order and state policy. The gay and lesbian people of Cuba, on the other hand, are marked in humanist terms as struggling for dignity, acceptance, and worth, not in the transformative grammar of revolutionary society but in the sloganeering of United States identity politics.

Gay Cuba builds its historical case against the United States by invoking, in gendered voice-over, our tyrannies against Cuba through the kind of liberal language of progress used in reference to Vietnam where, as Lily Tomlin joked, the people "just wanted to live happily in their rice paddies." According to *Gay Cuba*, the Cuban Revolution above all ends a history of poverty and exploitation, and it represents a struggle for self-determination. The video therefore, and, I think, rightly, celebrates Cuba's redistribution of health care, the movement for national literacy, the attempts to redress gender and racial inequality, and the Revolution's other "visionary transformations." Overt United States aggression, such as the invasion known as the Bay of Pigs, and the defensive Cuban militarism it spawned thwart these progressive revolutionary changes, yet the video places internal blame on the early years of the Revolution for sustaining those "oppressive attitudes toward homosexuality" that went unchallenged. The video then builds quickly through the use of archival footage toward the events of the late sixties and early seventies chronicled in *Improper Conduct:* the purges of homosexuals in the university and the relegation of marginalized peoples to the UMAP camps. Cinema itself ruptures the narrative of past oppression as we leap forward two decades: Alea's film *Fresa y chocolate/Strawberry and Chocolate* forces debate, opens a gate for a public discussion, in the narrator's words surpasses "a cinematic phenomenon to become a social phenomenon."

The effects, however, of military and police severity of thirty or forty years ago, initially credited to the United States, become free-floating aspects of Cuban social repression of homosexuality. Interviewees, much as in *Improper Conduct,* testify to raids on Havana night clubs and gay beaches and to subsequent unjust imprisonment. Though nowhere is the vision of prison as hellish as in *Before Night Falls,* the punctuating rhetoric of repetition drives home a sense of indignation. One of deVries's lesbian interviewees remembers:

> It was a long time ago, when this was more repressed. There was a club in Havana called El Intermezzo. It was raided. Without distinction, they picked up everyone they thought was gay, and they took us to jail. We had a trial, an indictment really, because we didn't have the right to speak or call a lawyer or our family or to communicate with anyone. Of the people there, there were those that got three months, others six months. I got six months. I was incarcerated for six months simply for being homosexual.

One notices a discursive shift in this story, from the recollection of repression that resembles something like a pre-Stonewall raid to the violation of human rights: to a trial, a lawyer, a phone call, a defense. The video solicits our rancor both in response to rights-violations but also to the criminalization of homosexual *identity:* "I was incarcerated for six months simply for being homosexual." Stitching the two together, the video breezes over the legal grounds for arrest and detainment (such as those detailed in Cuba's Public Ostentation Law of 1938) as well as the mechanisms through which the expression and regulation of homosexuality "a long time ago" likely complicate this memory of blanket repression. Almendros and Leal escalate precisely this condensation of rights and identity in order to allege that Castro had "disappeared" one of the *Improper Conduct* interviewees, borrowing affect resulting from the particular violation of human *presence* (legal, familial) that routinely takes place in other Latin American (United States–supported) countries.

It comes as no surprise, then, when Taylor's voice-over informs us that the Public Ostentation Law was repealed in 1988, freeing the way for homosexual expression. From twilight to limelight, this freedom comes in a Havana performance—inserted fully into *Gay Cuba* as a music video—by Cuban superstar Pablo Milanes of his song dedicated to gay people, "Original Sin." Milanes's performance underscores the role of culture and music in particular in Cuban struggles. Its incorporation into *Gay Cuba* also provides the American audience with the spectacle of a professional endorsement of *Gay Cuba* by Pablo Milanes, and by extension an endorsement of *Gay Cuba*'s versions of history by a Cuban musician-cum-celebrity spokesman. *Gay Cuba* borrows the credibility of Alea's film *Fresa y chocolate/Strawberry and Chocolate* in similar ways, using clips to buttress the video's claims, and thereby aligning itself with Alea's importance and popularity.

Before the video turns to the embargo, it takes on briefly the education of the people, and more particularly of Cuban youth. Because the video has established the need for further progress in Cuba in combating prejudice and embracing gay men and lesbians, it seeks pedagogical authority through an interview with Lourdes Flores, of the National Center for Sex Education. Like Monika Krause, Flores organizes workshops on sexuality, including sexual orientation; unlike Krause, she emphasizes homosexuals' capacity to "give and receive love" rather than the effects of homophobia. But when deVries turns her camera on the youth—law students at the University of Havana—for whom sexual education is geared, they appear not to need it at all, displaying within a range of attitudes the consistently shared understanding that one must work to combat homophobia. An interviewee comments, "I don't think that in Cuba the situation is as critical as it is in other countries," a sentiment then confirmed by an expert, Jorge Cortinas, of the International Gay and Lesbian Human Rights Commission. He reminds us, from his United States office, that Cuba is *not* a human rights emergency. Contradicting its earlier interviewee, the video then resolves that the problem is not the violation of human rights, but the embargo.

Over images of deteriorating or empty shops, Taylor's voice-over details the history of the trade embargo, from the beginning of the United States military occupation of Cuba in 1898 through the United States' Torricelli Bill in 1992, which imposes sanctions on any country that trades with Cuba. The video illuminates Cuba's vulnerability to the embargo and its literal costs: according to the video's statistics, forty billion dollars since 1960. Without reflecting on the video makers' own access to Cuba or perspective on it, the video relates the Cuban attempts to reinvigorate its tourist industry in the face of United States punishments of ten years' jail time or $250,000 in fines for unauthorized travel to Cuba. What is significant in this discussion is that the invocation of tourism in the name of bridge-building or exchange appears to invite but in fact glosses over an analysis of uneven economic *and* epistemological positions: the lived consequences of the embargo, access to information, modes of dissemination of the history and present circumstances of Cuban life, and the violences made possible by the touristic gaze. As waves wash over Havana's Malecón and beaches, the barriers to tourism are seen only to mark a loss for Cuba, yet the video then launches a discussion about what one can only read as the underside to tourism: HIV and AIDS. Largely in sympathy with Cuba's early policy of segregating seropositive and AIDS-symptomatic people, the video reminds us via screen graphics of the extremely low incidence of HIV infection on the island (roughly 1,200 infected out of a population of eleven million).[16] In the words of an HIV-positive doctor, the video indicts the restrictions on mobility associated with the segregation, although "quarantine" is obviously the more ideologically loaded term the video prefers. The video's final endorsement of Cuban health policy, however, comes in its plea for "choice" as the operative chunk of ideology, or ideologeme, borrowed again from United States discourses of healthcare as a free marketplace.

Throughout *Gay Cuba*, deVries provides identificatory spectator surrogates such as the HIV-positive doctor, imbued fully with warmth, humor, pathos, desire, and, not least, artistry. Racially diverse and split between gay men and lesbians, the video's interviewees seem to represent an inclusive and exhaustive vision of gay Cuba: a New Age radio show host (of a program called *Casa de Crystal,* no less), an interpreter, a singer/songwriter, a visual artist. The tack the video takes is thus to split the difference sexuality might make into two separate and distinct flows: on the one hand, the monumental history of revolutionary nation-formation and its attendant official discourses, and on the other hand, gay and lesbian people whose sexualities are exterior to the revolutionary project until incorporated as either private or tolerated. No doubt *Gay Cuba* challenges the relegation of Cuba to a primitive and unenlightened past, and no doubt *Gay Cuba* dispels for an audience in the United States myths of ongoing horrendous oppression and tyranny, but it does both at a cost. Retaining the very coherence of the bourgeois subject it thinks it dissolves, *Gay Cuba* forsakes an opportunity—one not granted to all—to explore the potentially transformative uses of homosexuality for another future.

Mariposas en el andamio/Butterflies on the Scaffold

Another version of *Gay Cuba*'s valorization of the humanist subject comes in what is an otherwise astute assessment of sexual politics in Cuba in light of Schnabel's film, and a snippet of that assessment provides a useful bridge to the final, and to my mind most exciting, documentary on gay Cuba I shall examine in this chapter. Jon Hillson, a Los Angeles union and political activist, launches a thorough, full-scale defense of the Cuban struggle in his article, posted on SeeingRed.com, "The Sexual Politics of Reinaldo Arenas: Fact, Fiction and the Real Record of the Cuban Revolution." As the title indicates, Hillson meets Schnabel's anti-Castro fervor with facts, exposing its errors of omission and commission and dispelling its outrageous lies with carefully reasoned evidence to the contrary. An exemplary writer with a vast knowledge of Cuban history, Hillson implicitly poses this question: how did Arenas's vision (anti-Castro, in the name of gay-and-lesbian) win? That is, how did the version of the Cuban Revolution we receive in *Before Night Falls*, what Hillson cleverly dubs the "slick, bionic offspring" of *Improper Conduct*, become once again accepted?[17]

The failures of counterdiscourses to the attacks on Cuba in the name of gay-and-lesbian are not limited to the warm, fuzzy school of *Gay Cuba*, which reaffirms monumental history and bourgeois autonomy, thereby excluding any sustained analysis of sexuality as a social formation. Hillson's essay, to my mind, makes a rather similar move in a different key, defending a humanist conception of self-worth, now against sexual expression. Regarding Arenas, Hillson writes (and I quote necessarily at length):

> For Arenas, the struggle for women's liberation did not exist. Numberless sexual encounters (in his case, between men)—with the sole criterion of quantity—is a version shared by many self-proclaimed advocates of "the sexual revolution." This definition has served only to gut the concept of its historic substance and curdle its revolutionary social content into an unrelenting search for individual sexual satiation as the center of life. There is nothing at all progressive about this

—it is the pornographic response to sexual repression that dehuman-
izes both genders, irrespective of sexual orientation . . . Human sexual
liberation, freed from the fetters of repressive norms, requires such
a dignified starting point as negation of the alienating and abusive
fetishism that defines sex and sexuality.

Hillson follows this moralizing attribution of sexual promiscuity to capitalist decadence with (what else?) a citation from Engels, imagining the
evanescence and eventual obsolescence of prostitution and notions of
sexual ownership when the revolution is a generation old. Unlike Engels,
Hillson, however, is not primarily concerned in the above citation with
women's oppression, the economics or politics of prostitution and other
sex work, or the necessity of theorizing sexuality in relation to issues of
labor and domestic organization. Instead, his task is prudish dismissal,
rendering Arenas (who, there is no question, was an unpleasant fellow in
many respects) an excessive sex-obsessed exterior to acceptable homosexual life in Cuba.[18] As with the parallels in form we have seen between
Improper Conduct and *Gay Cuba*, one can also, reluctantly, acknowledge
continuity between the knowing dismissal of what we might call queer
knowledges or modes of knowing drawn from lesbian and gay lives that
characterizes the former film and Hillson's sex-conservative soi-disant
radicalism. To put it differently, it is hard to see how the left can win
the battle over representations of gay Cuba with normatively anti-queer
arguments such as Hillson's. Thankfully, a different rhetoric is on the
horizon, in Margaret Gilpin and Luis Felipe Bernaza's video, *Mariposas
en el andamio/Butterflies on the Scaffold*.

By contrast to *Improper Conduct, No porque,* and *Gay Cuba, Mariposas*
(a slang term for gay men) is a "Cuban" independent production, in
the restricted sense that one of its directors, Luis Felipe Bernaza, is a
Cuba and Moscow-trained director with vast experience at ICAIC (the
Cuban Film Institute). He is also a renowned Cuban novelist (*Busca-
guerra, Buscavidas,* and *The Detroit Tigers Love Tosca*). The crew of the
video was entirely Cuban, and the other of the directors, Margaret Gilpin,
though only a third-time filmmaker, has strong ties to Cuban culture and
politics as a healthcare expert and advisor. In the case of Gilpin, the distinction of national belonging is important not necessarily as extratex-
tual background trivia, accessible only to those with the directors' biog-
raphies at hand, but as determining the stakes of this video. The video
declares to the audience at the outset that it speaks on *both* sides of the

gulf separating Cuba from its comrades in the capitalist west. Since it has been exhibited at European and United States festivals, its audience is international; at the same time, it is dedicated to "the workers of the community of La Güinera, Havana, Cuba," who made the film (possible). It is also dedicated "to Fifi, with love." Fifi, as will become clear, is in large measure the video's protagonist, and she is absolutely its affective center.

Unlike the Cook's tour approach of *Gay Cuba* and the more personalized interests and resultant eclecticism of *No porque, Mariposas* is built around a story: of the birth and growth of the transvestite movement in the marginalized community of La Güinera, Havana, and of the transformation of the community when it welcomes drag as a form of revolutionary labor. Performing in the workers' cafeteria, in other words, La Güinera's drag queens lodge themselves in the very infrastructure of revolutionary society, and the community embraces them. The terms are clear: the embrace, it must be emphasized, not the tolerance, of homosexuality. Enrique Pineda, a filmmaker and the video's first interviewee, as with the other films and videos in traditional, talking-head form, remarks, "We don't seek tolerance. Tolerance is a misguided notion. Tolerance is smug and arrogant." Interwoven throughout the film as if providing visual evidence of its commitment to something other than tolerance are images of drag queens preparing for performances. The queens provide the video's rhythm and its raison d'être, which it never forgets. At the start, then, the video tracks the community of La Güinera following the Revolution, a community, that is, of shacks and shanties in the shadow of a slaughterhouse. In the words of its local doctor, interviewed in the community before a backdrop of fronds:

> Compared to other places, La Güinera is relatively homogeneous, but it has its peculiarities. For ten to fifteen years after the Revolution, La Güinera was still a marginal area. This place was hidden behind a slaughterhouse, with lots of land, bushes and insects [the visual cuts to historical black-and-white footage]. Squatters came here from the provinces and formed an association. They said, "We'll build your house today and mine tomorrow . . ." As a marginal area, La Güinera had a high incidence of delinquency which luckily we eradicated. Cultural levels were very low and the birth rate was very high. Has it dropped? [in response to Gilpin's question in background] Yes, and we are very proud of our infant mortality rate. It's two, in our clinic.

Reminiscent of an Italian neo-realist imperative or its extension in the films of the Tavianis, especially *Padre Padrone* (1977), *Mariposas* takes care to establish the community of La Güinera as a specific place, as land with a history and with contours, angles, people, workers of all types, light and darkness, signs and images. While *Gay Cuba* and even *No porque* tend to collapse "Cuba" into one big undifferentiated block of urban space or stretch of beach, *Mariposas* delineates both temporal and spatial differences. The transformation from the black-and-white footage shot in 1980 to the present footage thus becomes all the more striking in the color shots of the new apartments in La Güinera, built as part of the revolutionary housing initiative by crews predominantly of women (70 percent), headed by Josefina ("Fifí") Bocourt. This is the mise-en-scène for the story that will unfold concerning Fifí, the construction workers, and the drag queens the viewer is about to meet.

That introduction takes place with the credits interspersed, and throughout the scenes of the queens' preparation for their performances, the film brandishes images and stories of scarcity, the traces of the embargo, and signs of the crisis of the late 1980s and 1990s. In the face of such shortages, the queens, to borrow Ru Paul's anthem, *work*. Armando/ Mandy displays his new dress on the stage of a pagoda, lovingly explaining its construction from dyed goose feathers; underneath, he reveals a crinoline made from the plastic used for garbage bags. "Airy and functional!" Others, applying their makeup, explain that "real eyelash glue has vanished from our world"; so, too, have they found a substitute for fingernail glue in *"el baje,"* the glue used for shoes. Molded and cut carbon paper substitutes for commercial false eyelashes. These are the tools necessary for the labor — psychological, physical — of becoming; incorporated in the most intimate fashion, these elements of innovation contribute to the labor of the women these drag queens become.[19] While deVries visited the drag queens of La Güinera (because she saw Gilpin and Bernaza's film crews there),[20] her camera never found a home in the queens' preparations in the manner of *Mariposas*. Even when the performers paint the last nail and take the stage, they remain in contact and in conversation with the camera, shooting it a proud or defiant look, camping up a particularly hyperbolic moment for the spectator's pleasure.

Music, of course, punctuates these performances, and the filmmakers also include a folksong about gay life toward the end of the film. In *Mariposas*, the music does not derive its impact from the lyrics alone, although the lyrics frequently provide counterpoint, through masterful editing, to the images of drag performances. Nor does music serve as a unity bridge to Euro-American spectators. In addition to the running commentary provided by the lyrics, the music instead offers a glimpse of traveling cultural forms, where the popular American songs "Power of Love" (recorded by Celine Dion) and "Total Eclipse of the Heart" (recorded by Bonnie Tyler) are rewritten with lyrics in Spanish and a Latin beat. They underscore not only how superior the remakes are to the originals (so superior that the soundtrack to *Mariposas* was pirated in Miami!),[21] but also how music functions as a backdrop, both banal and achingly pertinent, for social expression. As in the folksong, it can often become a direct means for social commentary. Finally, *Mariposas*'s music provides the *melos* of melodrama, providing an occasion for the movement of bodies through dance, the posturing of the queens in the scenarios they enact with one another as well as in relation to the audience, and the beat to which the costumes jiggle, fly, and twirl about the stage. As these performances weave through the more conventional talking-head interviews, the interviews acquire a surprising sense of movement themselves, a trajectory of change which is also the focus of the videotape's story, to which I now turn in more detail.

Following on the introduction of the drag queens and their performances, Fifi stitches together the site of transformation—La Güinera and its new apartment buildings—the documentary explores: "This [the two new buildings] met the needs of the neighborhood. We set out to build new homes and to build the 'new man' in our 'new society.' [cut to shot of children on a carousel] Something I don't want to leave out . . . the drag queen performances in the workers' cafeteria." The video then cuts to a performance in that cafeteria, which provides both food and entertainment for the workers, again, a majority of them women. A visit to the cafeteria also functions as a reward for the most accomplished workers of a given period: they are *invited* to the cafeteria for these performances. In a marvelous coincidence, the camera captures a shot of a drag performer who is also the object of the gaze of the requisite poster of Fidel Castro hanging on the cafeteria's wall.[22] The queen's face and arched eyebrows provide commentary enough! While the shot records the fabricated desire implicit in Castro's gaze, the video does not burden that desire with straightforward assertions, as in *Gay Cuba* or *Improper Conduct*, that the Revolution's leaders were/are gay but instead allows that gaze, like the melodrama of the performance, to do its own work of suggestion, implication, amplification, play, accusation, solicitation all at once. *Mariposas* in this regard is more akin to *No porque* in its playfulness, recalling that video's presentation of the affections of the homophobic male teenagers on the beach. Several short interviews with young gay men follow this sequence, including one with a novice drag queen on the day of his debut, amplifying the melodrama of the performance into the everyday: "I'm so nervous, I've got a stomachache. I'm dying!" The lyrics of the accompanying song contaminate the real: "lies, falsehoods, dishonest caresses, not one more!" We return to Fifi, not as the real opposed to these falsehoods, but as another locus of transformation.

The video charts Fifi's gradual recognition of the drag queens' labor in a number of interviews, and because she becomes exemplary of what it means to be open to change, her comments and presence carry a great deal of weight in the structure of *Mariposas*. A black woman of middle age, interviewed on the construction site wearing a bandana around her head, she begins with her resistance:

> At first I rebelled. I'm an older woman. I wasn't accustomed to running around with "this class of people" . . . It seemed to me I wasn't doing my duty to society. I said, "No! Keep them away. I don't want to hear about people with a 'double façade.'" The workers brought me "one" to show me. I said, "No, please. I can't be around you guys. I wouldn't be doing my duty to society. I'm too old for this stuff. I've never been involved in these things."

The story unfolds that another member of the construction staff, Marisela, had learned of the private, home performances of a group of drag queens in La Güinera, to which a group of women workers in the dining room were invited. Because the Cuban government had seized control of the acts in cabarets (which alone were licensed by the state, including the permission to sell alcohol), the drag performances were forced into clandestine, private venues with meager resources. Audiences brought their own chairs, sometimes couches, and paid a modest fee to the performers. It was this type of performance Marisela saw and pleaded to Fifi should be the showcase of the workers' cafeteria.

Fifi's decision to invite the drag queens to perform in the cafeteria earns their undying respect for her. One enthuses in an interview:

> Fifi is the zone chief for housing construction at La Güinera. She opened a cabaret in the workers' cafeteria and brought us into it. She

made us face the herds of public we were afraid to face. She reassured us. She said, "Do it, face them, you'll see, nothing will happen." [lyrics of song: "Decide! Go on, man, tell me!"] . . . and that's how it was. Fifi should be honored by us. She'll always be close to our hearts for the wonderful way she treated us.

Not only does Fifi emerge as accepting the drag performances as socially useful, but she is also enlisted in the melodrama that accompanies performance anxiety! The honor due to her derives in large measure from the position she occupies now in society after a representatively embattled past: "I started to work when I was nine years old. I was one of the 70,000 maids Cuba had before 1959. I couldn't enjoy much of my childhood. Now I've had the opportunity to work on the development of La Güinera, and I feel like a new woman."

What emerges in *Mariposas* after the moment of Fifi's transformation is a dense and urgent look at who these drag queens are, who the workers are, and how their various strands of understanding, prejudice, and history function in a bounded space, drawn by the careful hands of the filmmakers. As with *Exile Shanghai*, it is tempting to recreate the entire text, so lovingly does it savor every surprise, every word, every performance its subjects offer. As with *Exile Shanghai*, too, one cannot not enter it intimately if one enters it with open eyes. But where *Mariposas* mobilizes its central affective response is in the figure of Fifi who by virtue (for she makes of it a virtue) of her position with respect to age, social position before the Revolution, common sense appeal, strength as exemplified in her bearing and in her forthright assessments, makes of the chance happenings at La Güinera an opening for new social possibilities. In enabling the institutionalization of drag performances in the workers' cafeteria, Fifi literally makes the predication of the "new man" an expansive and not yet decided form of labor, since the work of drag is indissoluble from the "affectively necessary labor" (Spivak's term discussed in the first chapter) of transforming social responses to homosexuality, nurturing gay children to open paths for their own social contributions, and redrawing the outlines of the family in the process.

The video's intimacy with the drag queens is then established along these lines through interviews with them and their families, investigating drag as work, both in its preparation through rehearsal and make-up and the performances themselves, along with the work of the day jobs most of these queens also hold. The smatterings of common sense (apho-

Figure 17. *Mariposas en el andamio/Butterflies on the Scaffold*. Courtesy of Water Bearer Films.

risms, truisms, clichés) to which we are treated in these sequences do not, as in *Improper Conduct*, verify the timelessness of repression or indicate the nature of an unthinking populace. Instead, they demonstrate the persistence of formulations of difference that are not *yet* subject to translation through new categories, and the persistence, as well, of generational difference: "At the bottom of the grave, we're all buried in the same clothes"; "Despite this, he's my son and I would give my life for him"; "Everyone is as God wills, and he has chosen a good career, hasn't he?"

Finally, it is in the understanding of drag as work that the workers and families of the community come together to embrace homosexuality as a vital axis of social participation. The father of one of the queens remarks: "Here you can do anything but you have to do it well. If you're going to make cigars, make good ones. If you're going to steal, really steal. They can shoot you if they catch you! Just to have a good time or be the laughingstock, no." Fifi echoes this disdain for irresponsibility in her own two sets of closing comments, stitching the realm of socially useful labor to affectively necessary labors assigned to the domain of social reproduction. I have combined them:

I think this type of work should go on all over the country, because of the respect, pride and responsibility with which [the drag queens] work. They never say, for example, "We're transvestites, let's misbehave!" If the nation accepts these cultural workers, these workers for society, as we did here in La Güinera, we'll be successful as a nation . . . I think that our kids will grow up according to what we teach them. We have to explain the variety of lifestyles in the world. They have to choose among them. If our kids get used to seeing men in drag, they'll see it as normal. We'll explain what a transvestite is, and that child will choose a path to which their education leads, and we'll create the new man. Besides, the new man will be brought up completely without any taboos!

The force of the transformation Fifi suggests, of the new man who was the subject of exclusionary revolutionary practice in her earlier comments to this new man as *maricón* or drag queen, comes by her own example. The former maid now construction chief is the gendered and raced instantiation of revolutionary change, and the video implicitly grafts the affect Fifi herself solicits onto the struggles of the queens, struggles which then are seen to permeate the community and society at large. That Fifi and the La Güinera construction brigades were recognized with an award from the United Nations Environment Program in 1995, as the closing title tells us, retrospectively confers distinction on the entire work of the community, including the drag performances. (In the several public screenings of the video I have attended, the closing title inaugurates lively applause.) In the video's closing song and number, "Vivir, vivir" (Live, live), dedicated to "everyone living with HIV/AIDS," the "life" of La Güinera as a community is celebrated in a fashion that gathers to the meaning of community a number of its prismatic facets without, however, reducing it to one. We applaud the lives of gay people, the lives of HIV-positive people, people living with AIDS, and those of communities indeed forged through the cinema.

It would be misguided, in the end, to call *Mariposas* propaganda, in that the word's very origin is implicated in colonizing missions of the Catholic church against which the Cuban Revolution battled and battles still.[23] It certainly addresses the distortions of films such as that of Almendros and Leal, and in its focus on the story of the drag movement begun in La Güinera serves as reproach to the cursory survey that cannot adequately solicit support of *Gay Cuba*. What is most power-

ful, however, about *Mariposas* is that it is willing to listen to and learn
the lesson of this community's transformation—a local but not micro-
cosmic example of revolutionary change—without a single judgmental
shot, without the urge to preach empty slogans of globalism, without elevating Cuban society to a utopian solution in totalizing fashion, without
the certainty that gay-and-lesbian is the ground on which connections
across ninety miles or 3,000 miles may be forged. It is, as its title tells
us in linguistically playing upon the construction efforts, a scaffold for
thought: regarding Marxism, regarding sexuality, regarding materialist
filmmaking, in that the video responds to the urgency of the movement
begun in La Güinera by writing its own essay and distributing its contributions to the historical unfolding of the Revolution.

To return to the question of naming with which this section on lesbian
place began, *Mariposas* is not a film on the gay and lesbian film circuit
that would be dubbed "lesbian." It does not, as *Gay Cuba* does, presume
that gay-and-lesbian is a traveling unity, an organizing principle for social change, or a hyphenated whole with any coherence. Instead, *Mariposas* provokes—through the figure of Fifi—a different sort of alignment
between women and men, between the new woman and the new man,
where affectively necessary labor becomes distributed across a range of
subject positions, modes of value-coding difference, and ways of intervening in social processes. The hyperbolic or excessive registers of drag,
as they become anchoring nodes for transformation, provide an index to
the *mobility* of social markings (gender, race, sexuality, labor, kinship, affective positionings), all of which require elucidation in the name of an
ethicopolitics of pliancy.

Unlike the other films and videos I have discussed in this chapter,
Mariposas is not "about" lesbians in any explicit way, nor does it include lesbians as a gesture of parity to its focus on gay men. Instead, the
video probes dimensions of gendering as a transformative social process,
whereby a debased *identity* becomes a celebrated *function*. That transformative grammar is crucial to what I understand as a queer politics: queer
is not a string of nouns (gay, lesbian, bisexual, transgendered, etc.), but
a syntax yet to be elaborated within specific moments, practices, locales.
Mariposas does not make lesbian visible; instead it promotes the mobility
of the "new man" and "new woman" as revolutionary projects-in-process,
opening new horizons of imagination, understanding, and desire that
are not founded upon static identity categories. American viewers, of

whatever nominative sexuality or gender, may find in *Mariposas* a document of that sociosexual mobility necessary to queer struggles on our
own shores. Had the project of this section been to look for lesbians in
films, I would have missed—as *many* "lesbian" audiences at festivals have
missed—*Mariposas en el andamio* and its love for change.

Chapter 5

Forbidden Love: Pulp as Lesbian History

The New *Pocket* Books that may revolutionize New York's reading habits.

Today is the most important literary coming-out party in the memory of New York's oldest book lover. Today your 25-cent piece leaps to a par with dollar bills.

Now for less than the few cents you spend each week for your morning newspaper you can own one of the great books for which thousands of people have paid from $2 to $4.

These new Pocket Books are designed to fit both the tempo of our times and the needs of New Yorkers. They're as handy as a pencil, as modern and convenient as a portable radio—and as good looking. They were designed especially for busy people—people who are continually on the go, yet who want to make the most of every minute.

Never again need you say, "I wish I had time to read" because Pocket Books gives you the time. Never again need you dawdle idly in reception rooms, fret on train or bus rides, sit vacantly staring at a restaurant table. The books you have always meant to read "when you had time" will fill the waits with enjoyment.

—*New York Times* advertisement, 19 June 1939

New York, time, leisure, urban anxiety, leaps of value, book-loving, and coming out, condensed neatly in the debut of a new commodity: these will be the subjects of this chapter, which moves from the mass-market paperback of the 1940s to 1960s to a relatively contemporary documentary that returns us to them, and to the fantasies of lesbian history they invoke—the 1992 film financed by the National Film Board of Canada, *Forbidden Love* (Aerlynn Weissman and Lynn Fernie). If we had time to read *Forbidden Love* as something like a pulp *film*, we would be ushered toward a set of questions about pulp's specificity, its transformations across media, its way of rendering the clandestine spectacular. If we had time to read more closely, we might focus on a single sequence at the outset of *Forbidden Love,* which begins with a titillating track across the covers of a group of forties and fifties mass-market paperbacks: *Women of Evil, The Girls in 3-B, Satan's Daughter, Women's Barracks, How Dark My Love, Duet in Darkness, Private School, Queer Patterns.* The tracking shot then cuts to individual shots, ending in tight focus, of exemplary paperback covers: *Queer Patterns* and *Women's Barracks* (again), *Girls' Dormitory, Man Hater,* and *Lesbians in Black Lace.* If we had time to examine these covers (for the sequence is very brief) or read these books, we might wonder how they become ephemeral proxies for defining what is generally at stake for lesbian and gay historiography in its incessant return to the mid-century, and how these lurid covers and titles, in particular, therefore function not only as a form of history and historicizing but also as a visual form of static classification, of synchronicity, in *Forbidden Love.*[1] And if we had time to displace the paradigms of history which mark the synecdoche "Stonewall" as a rupture between the period of "twilight lovers," shame, and shadows these novels evoke and that of self-proclaimed enlightened urban lesbian identity the film boasts, we might continue to probe the nature of history as commodity, affectively invested and circulated as value, within the vast matrix of postwar American culture.

But what gives us time, according at least to the logic of the advertisement, is the new commodity itself, which envelops and distributes, fills and makes time. The commodity, the mass-market paperback, is time's design; design gives time, and design sets value "leaping." Crises of value inhere in time's design: no wonder that the most frequent word used to describe the covers of mass-market paperbacks of the forties and fifties is *salacious,* which derives from *salire,* meaning "to leap." The advertisement heralds the mutation of value along contradictory axes, both tied to the problematic of speed, time's new rate of motion, in the city: on the one hand, the book as commodity remains tied to literary value (only obliquely summoned, however, through reference to "great books") yet promises class mobility. The book will now serve, on the other hand, an ancillary if not competing function, produced by acceleration and deceleration within modernity itself, of "filling time," "killing time," "occupying time" when urban isolation (stasis) threatens to engulf.[2] An encapsulated morsel of the modern moment, the commodity thus conjures a new reader—not a book reader, but a reader of mass publications (newspapers, magazines, and the new paperback books), an isolated, modern, urban creature beset with anxieties (fretting, busy, loathe to be dawdling idly or staring vacantly) that will be soothed by this new product. And time's design as paperback produces the masses themselves: this Pocket Book reader will become a comrade-consumer in the "paperback revolution."

What, though, is the "queer pattern" (if there is one) in the web of design, books, modernity, cinema, history, and value? Where are we to discover the lesbian lurking, and at what cost does she become visible? The paperbacks on display in the film *Forbidden Love* share a lesbian "theme," or so it would appear from their covers and titles, and there are gay-themed counterparts, though fewer of them, that partake of the same tropes of torment, shame, sin, lust, and shadows in their titles and cover illustrations. But why should we assume something as coherent as a group of "lesbian pulps" or "gay pulps," and authored by lesbians or gay men, no less? As a literary or filmic critical gesture, isolating these books or films with identifiable lesbian or gay themes against a presumed-stable heterosexual majority results, I shall argue, in at least three layers of misguided analysis. First, thematic analysis in its hermeticism ignores the social determinations and circuits of textual production. Second, the isolation of lesbian- or gay-themed novels severs their connections to other forms of social abjection (alcoholism, drug addiction, other forms of vice) that are central to the novels' history and regulation. And third, there is a convergence between the critical gesture of isolation with the postwar social production of isolation, a mimetic relation whereby the lesbian text is isolated as the lesbian herself was, a convergence that further sequesters critical commentary from the domain of the popular that is its subject.

To underscore against such thematic treatments: the novels themselves (as materials products — things — as well as literary or popular cultural texts) are artifacts of postwar and Cold War culture, evoking but not simply "reflecting" dominant concerns with anxiety and paranoia, while they, at the same time, are products of industrial innovation and the reorganization of mass consumers and mass taste. Central to their emergence, heyday, and decline are codings of sexuality, of emergent urban conflicts and sexualized enclaves, and therefore of suburban mythologies, as well, and of work and leisure. Sexuality is seen as a component of both work and leisure, as a matter of fact, and therefore of time's own design through Fordist industrial organization but also belonging to a nostalgia for sedimented myths of nineteenth-century pastoral idylls. Yet the "form of appearance," again to borrow Marx's conception, of sexuality is caught within a set of undisclosed determinations, within lingering forms of mass literature from the previous century, prewar conceptions of the city (including contradictory responses to the "great migration" of the twenties), and massive reorganizations of leisure. What would it mean to read within this matrix?

The novels both appeal to and shape what Antonio Gramsci calls common sense: a conception of the world that "contains Stone Age elements and principles from a more advanced science, prejudices from all past phases of history at the local level and intuitions of a future philosophy."[3] The challenge in understanding the novels "in a Gramscian way"[4] is to make visible the tentacles of common sense, its modes of transformation, and its complex determinations within the conjuncture. The challenge involves remaining mobile. Indeed, what may be occluded by a certain fidelity to Gramsci—the tendency, in other words, to historicize his writings—is his insistence on the mutability of institutions, the speed of transformation of the social landscape, and the consequent need to develop flexible critical methodologies to track the lines of metamorphosis of popular and mass culture.[5] Gramsci's comments on the intellectual function, on Americanism and Fordism, his attention to cinema as a powerful popular cultural force, and his awareness of the molar as well as "molecular" dimensions of sexuality demonstrate his capacity to turn a critical eye on emergent forms.[6] Reading "in a Gramscian way" provides a beginning point for an analysis of these mass-market paperbacks and their contemporary circulations and translations, including their cinematic movement into the documentary. While some scholars have been critical of the polarizing nature of (mis)readings of Gramsci, it is possible, I think, to retain his insights into the stratified and heterogeneous nature of popular cultural forms, while articulating his work with Marxist projects of recent decades.[7] In particular, it seems crucial to assess the ways in which "the fantasy world [of the popular novel] acquires a particular fabulous concreteness in popular intellectual life."[8] I consequently consider the particular modes of sensation, adventure, affect, and emotion these novels embed not only in their ostensible content but also as commodities which circulate now.[9]

Pulp Fiction

Gramsci's oxymoron, "fabulous concreteness," beckons us toward the dynamism that seems structurally constitutive of pulp. As narrative,

Quentin Tarantino's 1994 *Pulp Fiction* returns to that world of tempta-
tion, violence, and redemption of 1940s mass-market paperbacks, strad-
dling as it does realism and escapism—a binary I will trouble a bit later in
this chapter—in its fixation on drugs, mobsters, and crooked boxers. As
phenomenon, the film rekindled John Travolta's flagging career, stimu-
lated older modes of naming alienation and prurience, and strengthened
the petit bourgeois populist imaginary associated with the group of films
and filmmakers known as the new independents, whereby the unoffi-
cial knowledge of the video store clerk (Tarantino's former occupation)
is validated as superceding that of the outmoded corporate marketeer,
the Hollywood mogul. Easily commodified, pulp has entered the mainstream at alarming speed as a new "postmodern" buzzword, despite the
longtime interest in pulp novels by collectors and *bricoleurs* hot on the
trail of mid-century cultural artifacts and debris. Aligned with but not
equivalent to camp and kitsch, pulp seems to secure at minimum a procedure of circulating and transforming abjection, bad taste, outrageous-
ness, criminality, and despair. It does so, historically at least, at the level
of the cover (as artifact and metaphor), to which I must turn now by way
of defining pulp fiction.

Robert deGraff launched Pocket Books with the *New York Times* advertisement that appears as the epigraph to this chapter. While, according to Janice Radway, deGraff has wrongly been heralded as the initiator
of the paperback's "second revolution" (Radway contends that Mercury
Books, and their line of Mercury Mysteries begun in 1937, deserve the
honor), the influence of deGraff upon the field is uncontestable.[10] His
initial list for Pocket Books included ten books, a hodgepodge of titles
ranging from classics to bestsellers, mysteries to self-help: *Lost Horizon* by James Hilton, *Wake Up and Live!* by Dorothea Brande, *Five Great
Tragedies* by William Shakespeare, *Topper* by Thorne Smith, *The Murder of Roger Ackroyd* by Agatha Christie, *Enough Rope* by Dorothy Parker,
Wuthering Heights by Emily Brontë, *The Way of All Flesh* by Samuel Butler, *The Bridge of San Luis Rey* by Thornton Wilder, and *Bambi* by Felix
Salten.[11] What unified this eclectic group was simply and only the books'
design: a uniform size,[12] a recognizable imprint colophon (Gertrude the
Kangaroo), high quality print and binding, and eye-catching cover illustrations under a Perma Gloss coating which, in many cases, endures
more than sixty years later. Despite the differences among deGraff's and
Pocket Books's imitators, the paperbacks published from the year 1939
to the late 1950s are significant for the purposes of this chapter precisely

because of the cover: as analytical touchstone, as signifier (though un-reliable, or "slippery" as the critical tradition would have it) of their "thematic" interests, as historiographic text, as source of titillation or fasci-nation, and, importantly, as focal point of industrial organization.

What does a cover do? Its foremost function is to lure the potential reader at the "point of sale," the moment of transaction between retailer and consumer. But the cover has traveled through a number of ancil-lary functions before that crucial encounter, moving as it does from pub-lisher to distributor to retailer. At the design stage (the focus of much of *Hardboiled America*), the publisher's art director and stable of artists create an image thought to be "appropriate" for the book in question. In that design stage are involved labors of artistic creation, layout, self-censorship, and promotional decisions. These labors congeal in the cover image and tend to remain anonymous. In the development of marketing schemes for mass-market paperbacks in the early 1940s, deGraff made a decision that erased the gap between a potential and an actual mass audience: he devised a distribution system that went outside the parame-ters of hardcover distribution to retail bookstores, and he instead em-ployed independent distributors (IDs), who sold newspapers and maga-zines to drugstores, corner stores, and the like. This system promised Pocket Books a truly mass audience, not concentrated in the larger cities and not limited to higher-income hardcover buyers (the lack of a limit does not, however, render the phenomenon "working class"). The paper-back book cover underwent a second transformation at the stage of sale from publisher to ID: it had to represent the *promise* of a new title, without accompanying page proofs, except in the case of anticipated bestsellers. IDs selected the titles they would promote to their customers, then, fre-quently on the basis of the cover alone; they would favor some illustra-tions over others, since they could not include every title of every imprint in their offerings. While O'Brien sees the importance of the cover art in determining a book's future as an occasion to elevate the artists them-selves to the status of active producers of cultural taste (a worthy project indeed), what I want to mark about the cover's function at this stage is the weight of the economic function, the place the cover marks within the circulation of value, ensconced as it is within the cover itself, to the *exclusion* of the paperback's "content," whether Shakespeare's five trage-dies or, to heighten the contrast, *Seven Footprints to Satan*. Of course, the IDs' knowledge of the novels' quality is not limited to the cover alone, but its *functional* role in distribution at this moment in its circulation, consonant with the uniformity of design, troubles the distinction between "quality" and "trash" on the basis of presumed "content."

After the cover performs its marketing function to distributors, it moves to retailers, who display the book: in racks designed to fit the uniform size of the paperbacks and, more important, in groupings suggested by the imprints' signifiers of genre. It would not be an overstatement to suggest that design determines genre, and genre likewise subsumes the coherent category of the author. As with the color-codings of Albatross's line, the mass-market paperbacks of the "second revolution" were distinguished by genre on the cover itself: a Red Arrow Thriller, or Dell Mystery, or, more familiar to us due to its longevity and Radway's study, a Harlequin Romance. The cover art sought to confirm the genre designation (keyhole conventions for mysteries, gothic palaces looming in the background for romances), and the imprint's name and colophon became indices of generic division along with the image. Many publishers issued series, and most of the imprints numbered their volumes for reference, with the effect of enhancing the pattern of repetitive consumption of a single imprint. Retailers, too, chose their stock from distributors' selections on the basis of covers, although they were, and are, more often sold blocks of titles dependent on distributors' earlier choices, a practice which was soon contested.

To continue to follow the chain of circulation, then, in the hands of retailers, the cover later came to serve yet another function, as a substitution for the book upon its return. After a number of days, in other words, if a mass-market paperback fails to sell, a retailer may return only the cover for reimbursement by the publisher of the book's price to the retailer (itself dependent on volume), a practice instituted to save money on the shipping costs of returns. In the case of the commodity's failure to complete its circuit, at this stage, then, the final step in the loop that returns us to publisher, the cover is a metonymy, a substitution for the book's congealed value: the physical book remains (to be read, to be traded, to be resold illegally), but it has shed its value within the sphere of legal circulation.

The cover thus organizes the movement of the commodity from publisher to distributor to consumer. As Marx stresses in the chapter in volume 2 of *Capital* titled "Circulation Time," however, the form of appearance of value (of productive capital, of money capital, and of commodity capital) mutates at every step of the cycle from circulation to production and back to circulation.[13] Rather than a linear model, such as one might deduce from the direct movement of the book from publisher to consumer, Marx emphasizes a multilayered model, wherein at every synchronic freezing of the movement, the form of appearance of value is distributed over productive, money, *and* commodity capital. Mediating the cycle, of course, is time: when a number of books, for example, are unable to be sold as commodities, they are stalled as value in the commodity form, which cannot be returned to the publisher as money capital to reinvest in the next production cycle, and yet money capital must be available to reinvest in production, and productive capital must also be available to continue production until it, too, can be replaced. The cover, as we have seen, stands in for the death of the commodity (its death only *within* the circuit of capital) at its final destination, and it returns to the publisher as a signifier of his loss.

Marx stresses two imbricated or mutually dependent elements in *Capital* that are crucial to further understanding the cover at every stage (a term that is *not* a misnomer only when one makes an artificial synchronic cut) of the cycle production-circulation-consumption: first, the social character of the commodity, reified through fetishistic relations, and, second, the role of time in determining value's form of appearance. Recall Marx's restatement of fetishism in the second volume: it "transforms the social, economic character that things are stamped with in the process of social production into a natural character arising from the material nature of these things," replacing social relations with relations among things.[14] The *predication* of the fetish is substitution; the *effect* of fetishism is stasis, the freezing, reifying (thing-ifying) of a process wherein elements only truly acquire significance or meaning in relation to their functions over time. Marx is at pains to emphasize function over the categorical imperative, time and social processes over the stagnancy of fetishistic bourgeois economy. What is important, I think, to mark in his treatment of function is that, from within the capitalist mode of production of value itself, each element of capital value mutates at any given time. In the world of the mass-market paperback, this mutation happens "under the cover."

Under the Cover: Salaciousness Regulated

The most frequent adjectives used to describe the covers of mass market paperbacks of the 1940s and 1950s are *lurid* (a pale version of the color yellow, metaphorically associated with ghostliness, the unknown, or the mysterious) and *salacious,* a word (literally, again, "to leap") that stitches the *New York Times* advertisement's "leap of value" (where a quarter becomes a dollar) to the leap into the forbidden, the voyeuristic, the prurient, or the streets, where one does not "properly" belong. For whom and by whom is this leap made possible? There is little record of publishers' internal comments regarding the covers' design, but, in *Hardboiled America,* O'Brien develops an archaeology of the mass-market paperback cover through interviews with publishers and the few artists whom he was able to find. What O'Brien uncovers, as it were, is the relative devaluation of the cover at the level of the individual artist. While a few of the imprints included the name of the artist along with the cover art or on a blurb, most of the artists went unacknowledged, and, indeed, most of the cover art was destroyed by the publishing houses some years after the penchant for original illustration waned. O'Brien argues that "of all the things that may be considered when looking at this art, personal style is probably the least significant."[15]

We do know, from an author's testimony, that authors were absolutely excluded from the production of their paperbacks. According to Ann Bannon:

> In my own experience, it was the editors who had sole discretion over the cover art: whether painting or photography would be used, which artist to hire, which scene to illustrate, how much to exaggerate or distort, etc. And they clearly had learned to calibrate the level of desired sleaze as precisely as a Swiss horologist. We authors were permitted no input whatsoever to this process. Louche as my original covers (and even some of the reprints) are, I escaped the worst of the editors' excesses. But some of my colleagues were not so fortunate, and few of us, upon pulling off the brown wrapping paper, were gratified by our first glimpse of a new title.[16]

What is more available than production histories for analysis is at the more general iconographic level: conventions that developed over the course of the mass-market paperback's life from 1939 into the 1950s. From the highly stylized conventions of the mystery novel, whereby the cover simply reduced to the barest possible degree the pertinent narrative features (a formalist rendering of a cat, or the central position of the falcon in the first cover of *The Maltese Falcon*), to the more airbrushed

"Deco-style" covers and back-cover extensive maps of mysteries developed by Dell, the cover artists tended to adopt recognizable patterns and styles repeated by a number of imprints.

The hallmarks of the covers taken collectively are, of course, memorable and noted as scenes of sex and violence: scantily clad women in diaphanous flowing skirts holding cigarettes or guns (most often pointed toward men, but occasionally threatening each other), scenes of the streets, men in trench coats, pools of blood and murdered corpses, tenements, piles of cash, public parks, blond sirens, hotel rooms, docks, and so forth. The colors are bold, and indeed often lurid in its literal sense, yellow or chartreuse (both integral to mid-century design).[17] This iconography intensified in the early years of the 1950s in order to combat declining sales: "Art Deco abstractions and cityscapes . . . gave way very quickly to photographic realism and expanses of bare flesh."[18] No matter whether the cover illustrated a classic by James Baldwin, a hardboiled mystery by Raymond Chandler, or an exposé of life in a women's prison by then-unknown Tereska Torres: the covers partook of the same style and imagery no matter what the ostensible "content." The correspondence, moreover, between the covers' illustrations and the books' narratives or themes was slight, so much so that the conventions of cover illustration took on lives of their own and became amplified in the 1950s. To the extent that the covers were an index of industrial innovation or product differentiation, they obeyed the market dictum that "sex sells," a trend that had the paradoxical effect of flattening distinctions between covers, genres, and imprints.

It was during the early 1950s that the "excesses" of the covers (more flesh, more blood, more "realist" depictions of the sordid worlds the novels investigate) became indicators of the novels' lessened value as measured against literary standards popularly understood. The more, that is, the covers became what they were, or the more they obeyed the conventions that distinguished them from hardcover literature, the more they fell into disrepute. If the monetary "leap of value" promised by the Pocket Books advertisement elevated the mass-market paperback to the status of a hardcover, where a quarter becomes a dollar, the covers came to signify a fall in moral value, which fall resulted in a call for the law. In 1952, a congressional committee (the Select Committee on Current Pornographic Materials, known after its chair as the Gathings Committee) was convened to investigate the conjunction of sex and violence the covers appeared to signify.

The Gathings Committee was neither exemplary nor an isolated in-stance of disciplinary fervor. Other such regulatory efforts and inves-tigations popped up throughout the country at the state level, and the Kefauver hearings (the televised senate investigation of government corruption by the mob) captured public attention with their own lurid scandals. In 1955 a California state senate subcommittee, called the Kraft Commission, investigated a group of scandal magazines. Later in the de-cade, then–Attorney General of California Edmund "Pat" Brown brought the enormously successful scandal sheet *Confidential* to trial on charges of "conspiracy to publish criminally libelous, obscene and otherwise ob-jectionable material."[19] Although the *Confidential* trial occurred five years after the Gathings Committee inaugurated its investigation, the circula-tion numbers in several of the intervening years disclose the extent to which tabloid, sensational, or pulp writing grabbed American readers as a widespread phenomenon. According to Jeannette Walls, "From 1952 to 1955, *Confidential*'s circulation went from 150,000 to 3.7 million an issue. In the same period, the *Saturday Evening Post* dropped from 1,742,311 to 1,547,341 an issue, and *Look* magazine fell from 1,153,525 to 1,001,068." *Confidential* sold only on newsstands, had very little advertising and low overhead costs (since it bought the basis for its stories from stringers) and used cheap paper, "super newsprint," rather than the slick stock used by its competitors.[20] *Confidential*, in other words, belonged precisely to the world of pulp, a world increasingly popular and under increasing attack during the decade of the 1950s.

To return, then, to the Gathings Committee: it was charged with in-vestigating a more limited purview of mass-market paperbacks, maga-zines, and comic books that were pornographic in nature and threatened the nation's health. In a rhetoric determined both by Cold War anxiety over popular morality and by the recent regulations of the film industry (in the Hays, or Production Code, and in the Paramount decision of 1948, to which I move shortly), the committee, relying on literary critical and medical "experts," sought to establish an innocent national readership prone to the dangers of corruption. These dangers the committee con-densed in a delicious list: obscenity, violence, lust, use of narcotics, blas-phemy, vulgarity, pornography, juvenile delinquency, sadism, masoch-ism, perversion, homosexuality, lesbianism, rape, and nymphomania.[21] Of course, these innocent readers presumed by the committee were products of the very industrial organization that engendered the paper-backs, but they nevertheless were thought to require rescue by direct state intervention or industrial self-regulation, as motion picture spectators had been several years earlier, also through both forms: straightforward legal regulation in the form of the Supreme Court's decision in the Paramount case, and indirect self-regulation through the Production Code.

The form of regulation concealed the crisis to be regulated. The committee, unable to attack the books' content directly due to First Amendment protection and debates regarding the difficult legal parameters of obscenity, produced and investigated allegations (not charges) of "block selling" and monopoly against the distributors, the American News Company in particular, of the mass-market paperbacks. As with the Paramount decision four years earlier—which dismantled the film industry's particular form of monopoly called vertical integration, where all facets of the film industry were held by the major studios, including production of films, their distribution, and their exhibition in theaters—the Gathings Committee invoked the nature of autonomous copyright violated by the practice of block-selling. In the Paramount case, the district court held illegal what it called block-booking, the practice of requiring exhibitors to book a group of films at once, thereby likely acquiescing to screen lousy films in order to book a sure hit. The court reasoned that "it adds to the monopoly of a single copyrighted picture that of another copyrighted picture which must be taken and exhibited in order to secure the first."[22] Moreover, "where a high-quality film greatly desired is licensed only if an inferior one is taken, the latter *borrows quality* from the former and strengthens its monopoly by drawing on the other. The practice tends to equalize rather than differentiate the reward for the individual copyright" (emphasis added). Block-booking or block-selling, in other words, violates the boundaries thought to stabilize value, the preservation of quality, and the practice thereby opens the field of cultural production to "inferior" copyrights . . . or perverted and sinful paperbacks. The task of the committee, then, was precisely to define and establish a legal field. It could not level charges per se but could suggest arenas in which current law could be enforced, or in which new laws were necessary to regulate pornography. The committee sought to regulate block- and also blind-selling, a practice involving a distributor selling a group of books without providing to the retailer information regarding their content, especially as some were yet to be written! They therefore meant to effect a shift away from the constraints of obscenity law, with its First Amendment allegiances, the taint of "censorship," and its problematic

focus on content, toward the seemingly more malleable (and entrepre-
neurial) spirit of copyright protection under antimonopoly law. But "content" haunted the proceedings, again, "under the cover." To understand
how, one needs to understand the constraints the committee sought to
avoid: in obscenity law.

Obscenity law, as summarized in the Gathings Committee Report, is
founded upon the impossibility of citation. The more obvious dimension
of this founding paradox is that any selection or quotation found to be
obscene within the meaning of a judicial decision cannot be reproduced
within the report itself: "to include those quotations herein would be to
disseminate obscenity which would therefore result in making this report pornographic" (12). This modest disclaimer (one that has been used
to the present day) is, however, belied by the evolution of obscenity law
from its common law roots in *Regina v. Hicklin* (3 Queens Bench 360
[1868]) to the "modern" rule set down in *United States v. One Book Called
Ulysses* (5 F.Supp. 182; confirmed, 72 F.2d 705 [1933]). In the common
law rule, "the test of obscenity is this, whether the tendency of the matter charged as obscene is to deprave and corrupt those whose minds are
open to such immoral influences, and into whose hands a publication of
this sort may fall" (*Regina v. Hicklin*). The test, according to the Gathings
Committee Report, applied "to the passages of the writing which were
charged as obscene without viewing them in relation to the remainder
of the writing, and without considering the intent with which they were
written" (34). By contrast, the *Ulysses* case, a case based upon the violation
of the Tariff Act, "was an attempt to point out that indictable 'obscenity'
must be 'dirt for dirt's sake,' and not just vulgarity without considering
its relationship to the rest of the text."[23] The court's understanding of
"intent" in *Ulysses* thus led directly to its definition of obscenity, as follows:

> In any case where a book is claimed to be obscene it must first be de-
> termined whether the intent with which it was written was what is
> called, according to the common phrase, pornographic, that is, writ-
> ten for the purpose of exploiting obscenity . . . The meaning of the
> word "obscene" as legally defined by the courts is: tending to stir the
> sex impulses or to lead to sexually impure and lustful thoughts . . .
> Whether a book would tend to excite such impulses and thoughts
> must be tested by the court's opinion as to its effect on a person with
> average sex instincts—who plays in this branch of legal inquiry, the

same role of hypothetical reagent as does the "reasonable man" in the law of torts.

The "modern" or federal rule thus not only produces a new normative sexual legal entity, whose average sex instincts must be established by expert psychological criteria, a way of sneaking psychology in as the regulative discipline of sexuality; it also re-opens obscenity to intent and also to context, two related and notoriously slippery, if not undecidable, analytic domains.

Who identifies an "obscene" passage and how? How is it possible to mark the obscene, the salacious, the vulgar, "dirt for dirt's sake" from the literary as such, especially when the "content," as we have seen, is already an effect of a substitution, where the cover comes to signify, to circulate, to stand in for the whole complex of genre differentiation, marketability, appeal, and encodings of the relation between the subcultural and the so-called mainstream readership, as well as of the relation between the mass readership constituted by a popular form and the standards of high literature, artistic integrity, and the like? To put it less abstractly and yet still in the midst of the Derridean jumble we seem now to have encountered, if the cover signifies "content," and yet we remain in a disjunction between the two; and if genre follows product differentiation, and yet the cover never absolutely marks its boundaries; and if our readers are *both* those, for example, bonding with lesbian "themes" and those pruriently or pornographically consuming them; and if we remain, finally, rather on the fringes of what literary types consider to be a national literary canon (and, to put a final spin on it, because many paperback originals were published pseudonymously many of the books cannot be accessed in terms of intention): if all of these obtain, through what procedures could one possibly and definitively delineate obscenity?

What is at stake here and what the committee's report struggles to contain, to my mind, is the social or legal regulation of metonymy or synecdoche itself, which is another name for the complex of reading as a social activity—the chain of substitutions traced by authorship and address beneath the cover. The report presents, in a remarkable nutshell, an ensemble of excesses produced by this effort at containment. First, it makes visible the contamination of the literary by the judicial and vice versa, resulting in the necessity of jury trials where the judge and jury become not only the "hypothetical reagents" posited in the *Ulysses* opinion, but also "common sense" literary critics, who, in a distinctly Ameri-

can vein, refute the highbrow erudition of "experts." The minority report
of the committee worries about precisely such populist criticism: "It is
not the province of any congressional committee to determine what is
good, bad, or indifferent literature. This carries with it echoes of thought
control" (125). Second, in the report appears the insidious nature of biographical evidence and "representative" positions and politics, when one
opinion favorable to the dissemination of certain novels is refuted by the
allegation that the judge's impartiality is impaired by his ownership of
stock in a publishing company, or where the children of the representa-
tives on the committee become the "average readers" representing the
populace in committee testimony. Third, it foregrounds the incommensurability of capitalist innovation and the regulation of "morality," where
the practices of block-selling are the logical consequences of an industrial expansion which cannot itself be regulated. And finally, it marks
the unstable nature of the signature, measured retrospectively by literary
"integrity" and, as I have suggested parenthetically, by the prominence
of pseudonyms and anonymity in the field of pulp fiction.[24] A potentially
obscene portion of a novel is identified by the literary-critical insight of
a judge who declares that "the filthy, scatological portions are written in
a bluntly different and distinct style from the pretentious metaphysical
reflective manner of writing, otherwise."[25]

One cannot see the law as exterior to the domain it seeks to regulate. The pulp novels in large measure treat the investigative nature of
modern society itself, "thematizing" the encounter between the law and
its subjects across a wide domain of emergent social categories. Such
encounters, in all of their diversity, become *signified* through sexual iconography on their covers, but the committee's focus is not unified by
the singular interest in sexuality; instead, the committee generates a hypothesis through which, in turn, the report generates a stable text, on the
one hand, and a hypostasized readership, on the other. The decidability
of both poles of the author-readership relation rests on the cover. In the
language of the minority report:

> The committee has rightfully observed that the covers of many of
> these volumes are extreme and in bad taste. We agree with that ob-
> servation. There is no doubt that in many instances the covers do not
> reflect the content of the book and are designed to promote sales by
> catering to the sensational. The book, however, must not be confused
> with the cover.

How is it possible to prevent such confusion? It is difficult to find a terminology that adequately characterizes the assumptions on which this hypothesis of separability rests in relation to the audience it presupposes, both within the chokehold of the moral and everyone else outside it, and in relation to the practices of reading it presupposes for this populace. These can only be shorthanded as questions of authorship, genre, and address. The dangers in citing the language of the report are in reproducing a surface/depth model of ideology, which the metaphor of the cover might appear to solicit but instead belies, as well as falling into the psychological or psychoanalytic language which characterizes pathology.[26] On the one hand, the committee activates the fear (which persists now with television regulation or self-regulation) that readers understand these novels, say, about "narcotic abuse," in realist terms as instruction manuals, "how-to" books on how to shoot heroin, smoke pot, or snort cocaine: "[the novels] describe the pleasures of narcotics, how to use them, how to use the needle" (45). So too do they "expand upon homosexuality, and one book advises or supports polygamy, and any number of books deal with lesbianism and nymphomania" (45). Yet, on the other hand, the committee hears and approves testimony which tests the implicit class and gender bases of the hypothesis that those most prone to corruption are women, children, and others disempowered due to their social position outside, for whatever reason, the comfort of the middle-class nuclear family.

If it is the case that the report struggles to contain the signifying capacities of the covers, the extent to which the covers (1) betray the ostensible content, (2) level distinctions between "quality" and "inferior" copyrights, and (3) disrupt socially sanctioned and industrially necessary codings of value (legitimizing perverse and pathological challenges to normative practices), then we can begin to develop a critical rejoinder to the report's stress on the counterhegemonic potential of these novels. The committee is not so much operating within the nexus of "realism" versus "escapism," a binary which has miscalculated the social function of the reading of popular literature (as Modleski and Radway have shown), but more within an anxiety over what is at stake in the visualization of perversion, albeit through highly conventional iconographic repertoires. If the covers are seen to be excessive, they excessively present to sight (something we struggle to name as lurid or salacious) that which cannot be calculated or contained in moral, aesthetic, and political arithmetic which subtends the law. Within the elementary dynamic of capital, that oscillating wave of innovation and cooptation, pulp fiction appears to be a processing, or translating, or "machinic" transformation of a variety of non-normative products of modernity and urbanity, all through the industrial inscription of sex; this transformation is then subsumed into a spectacular stasis, which is tamed through the very category of sexuality, and non-normative sexuality in particular. That is to say, "sexuality" can be understood in this case as a substitution or cover for containment itself, since what is visualized can be dissected, taxonomized, regulated, or policed.

This argument is slightly different from Foucault's argument from *Discipline and Punish* through the three volumes he completed of his *History of Sexuality* project, since I am suggesting here that the undecidable dimensions of authorship and address trouble the condensation of meaning *within* the category of sexuality per se, even if it is understood to be operative within a specific historical moment as discourse. Foucault's vigilance against the liberatory sloganeering that takes place beneath the banner of sexuality needs to be augmented, as I have been trying to demonstrate, by an investigation into the visualization of sexuality as an alibi for the slippages it struggles to contain. The film *Forbidden Love* provides a case study for such an investigation.

Popular Culture as Lesbian History

In the United States, New York City vies with San Francisco as a mythographic mapping of dyke nirvana, homosexual heaven, the capital of the "queer nation." The myth, of course, has a basis in social reality: the postwar expansion of gay culture, the reproduction of New York as a center for intellectual and artistic activity, the incipient demands for "gay rights" in the late 1960s through activist groups with competing ideological demands. This situating of New York is certainly not new or recent; indeed, New York, through Greenwich Village and through its synecdoche, Stonewall, for some years functioned in common sense as the mark of a rupture, the sign of a break, in lesbian and gay history and cultural expression. (The cover of one pulp paperback asks tellingly, "What can Natalie do in Greenwich Village that she can't do at home?"[27]) The contemporary myth dubbed "pre-Stonewall," as Angela Weir and Elizabeth Wilson describe it eloquently and at length, is comprised of mixed horror and nostalgia, a "kitsch dystopia":

On the one hand, we have been inundated with fifties pastiches—from Levi jeans advertisements to films, from sharp haircuts to dark-red lipstick, from pop graphics to golden oldies. The world that is thus recreated is deeply romantic—sexuality is hedged about with prohibitions, passions both personal and political are hidden, secret, threatening. A wonderful style exists to express this, a combination of Paris Left Bank and Greenwich Village, Jean Gabin and Audrey Hepburn, outlawry and bohemianism to set against the uptight heterosexuality of tight-waisted fashions inspired by Christian Dior. On the other hand, we re-create the period of the Cold War, the nuclear threat, McCarthyism, spies, treason, fear, while according to our feminist folk myth, all women were pushed back into the home, all gays were persecuted; there was no chink of radical light at the end of the tunnel.[28]

Elements of this contradictory myth, which in its descriptive points of reference alone limits the "we" it invokes considerably, persist even in historiographic accounts that challenge the conception of the 1950s as a period of seamless conservatism and conformity.

More recently, however, lesbian and gay historians and ethnographers (including D'Emilio, Berubé, and Kennedy and Davis) have emphasized the post–World War II years as creating the possibility for lesbian and gay relationships in embryonic gay communities in large American cities, New York and San Francisco, in particular, but also the cities that now comprise the Rust Belt, including Buffalo, Detroit, and Pittsburgh. That dissent was alive in this period is confirmed by the eruption we call Stonewall, an event that shorthands a number of translations, themselves fabrications, that found contemporary gay and lesbian politics and culture: from shame to pride, from isolation to community, from silence to activism. None of these translations is complete or adequate, yet queer communities are nonetheless steeped in the iconography, the visualization, of this caesura: the signposts of the Village's Gay Street (featured on the cover of Ann Bannon's novel, *Beebo Brinker*) and Christopher Street, images of gay men and lesbians spilling into the streets, butches and femmes huddled over tables in cozy bars, clones cruising, queens dragging, bikes gleaming. The street becomes, in effect, a specific street, the iconography emptied of the dialectic of hiding and disclosure which produced it in the first place.

This iconography, indeed, overwhelms the 1996 film by Nigel Finch,

Stonewall, notable only for its ability *not* to treat any single component of the matrix "Stonewall" in adequate detail but instead simply to invoke the entire ensemble in dreamlike fashion. In the years post-Stonewall, films have recirculated and recreated the energy of that fantastical inaugural moment: of massed gay and lesbian bodies in the streets, of public seduction and exuberant sexuality, of collective, active, and loud demands for survival and well-being, even in the face of the most profound threats to them. Some, including B. Ruby Rich, have called this the "new queer cinema," and others have rightly, I think, been hesitant to celebrate a repertoire of images that are mainly white, highly commodifiable to mainstream audiences, and anchored in rights-based discourses of political activism.[29] This is nonetheless a dominant vision of gay and lesbian metropolitan life, a universalizing image that is all the more easily disseminated through the organs of our relatively recent national lesbian and gay culture industry, not coincidentally based in New York and San Francisco. What I want to emphasize here is not the measurement of these myths against something like "concrete reality," but the forms of historicizing the myths solidify, as well as the sense in which they circulate in order to bestow a form of retrospective (hallucinatory) continuity on contemporary cultural and political struggles which are *not* unified within the iconography of that mythology.

D'Emilio and Freedman are among the historians who characterize the postwar years as creating the possibilities for a new gay subculture, emphasizing the extent to which, during the 1920s and 1930s "the resources for naming homosexual desire slowly expanded."[30] Laying the groundwork for naming both emergent gay identities and erotic experiences in urban centers were massive immigration, including the racial realignments resulting from the post–World War I "great migration, the penetration of psychoanalytic and psychiatric language into popular culture,"[31] and fictional characters in novels such as Radclyffe Hall's *The Well of Loneliness* and in plays such as Edouard Bourdet's *The Captive.* In studies by Carroll Smith-Rosenberg and Esther Newton one cannot but call pioneering, the shifts in the discursive fields through which lesbianism was available for naming and understanding produce historical and generational discontinuities between the models of inversion, the intermediate sex, and the "Mannish Lesbian."[32] These parallel movements, identitarian and erotic, suggest to D'Emilio and Freedman that "truly, World War II was something of a nationwide 'coming out' experience."[33] In referring to "nationwide," they agree that "what appeared as a deviant form of sexual behavior on the fringe of society now seemed to permeate American life," as evidenced by the paperback pulp novels of Ann Bannon and Paula Christian, which "offered easily available images of self-affirming lesbian love."[34] There are a number of conflations here which bear mention, not as reproach but because they demonstrate how the pulps themselves and the popular historiography of which they are a part can be deployed in order to naturalize an equation between contemporary urban gay life and "our history." Here, I want to pause first at the undifferentiated role of Broadway plays, British novels, psychoanalytic theory, and African American music, not to mention the lesbian pulps, in producing a national (read, New York and presumably white) gay culture, as well as the repetition of the idea of "coming out" into the public sphere. Pulp iconography even graces the cover of Sherrie A. Inness's book, *The Lesbian Menace*, a book that seeks to address various elements of this gay culture (significantly *not* lesbian pulps, but Hall's novel, Bourdet's play, women's college fiction, and the like), and although her discussion of "queer geography" makes claims strikingly similar to my own regarding the centrality of urban visions, Inness remains locked resolutely within the "realist/escapist" binary in her readings, leading to a practice of identifying, and lamenting, stereotypes. Her own book cover provides yet another illustration of how the pulps speak their allure, even while the argument would allege otherwise.[35]

How are pulps then used as evidence? In *Intimate Matters*, there appears a still photograph of a pulp cover, *Chris*, wonderfully subtitled "Life in the Limbo of Lesbianism, An Intimate Story of the Third Sex Told with Tenderness and Unblushing Honesty."[36] Passing over the alliterative bravado, knowing allusion to Hirschfeld and the terms of sexology (and earlier conceptions of lesbianism), and the novel's cover art, D'Emilio and Freedman note: "Many of the lesbian pulp novels appealed to male voyeurs as well as to lesbians." D'Emilio had earlier distinguished between regressive and progressive pulps, citing a survey by Barbara Grier from the early lesbian publication of the Daughters of Bilitis, *The Ladder*. D'Emilio asks, "How was one to know that inside the covers of *Guerilla Girls, The Savage Salomé*, and *The Twisted Ones* could be found, according to Grier, 'interesting, sympathetic studies' of lesbian characters?"[37] By 1966, one knew, or at least Barbara Grier was certain: lesbianism, she reported for *The Ladder*, had achieved a "complete integration" into the American mainstream.[38] Grier bases her conclusion on a calculation of the declining number of "lesbian" paperbacks from 1964 to 1966 (161 to 104) and also on her own evaluations of the relatively "sympathetic" nature of the characters within those novels.[39]

While there is no doubt that certain versions of lesbians were circulating widely by 1965, one sees with the efflorescence of pulps (as well as with the 1966 film *Chained Girls*, which I visit in the next chapter) that the "popular" picture of lesbianism that emerged during this period is a significantly domesticated glance backward which desires coherent support for a contemporary emancipatory narrative. The most significant effect of this domestication is that the "public" sphere broadly sketched by commercial iconography is seen as uncontaminated by division, by antagonism, and most of all by the transformations of capitalism during this crucial period, particularly in the industries wherein visualizations of sexuality are produced. Under the "cover," again as thing, as fact of and metaphor for the pulps' circulation, we see the nexus of exchange and the signifier of a differential of sex that continues to haunt regulatory efforts. One can read the uses of the past which rely on these codings of lesbianism's presence as contributing directly to the current reconsolidation of lesbian and gay "identity" as consumer positions. Succumbing to the imperatives of the market and the contours of the science of demography, these identity positions forget their alliances with the most abjected regions of the street, whether understood, as Newton does, as the pathologization of the figure of the butch, or understood as racial conflict coded through the threat of cultural miscegenation, or other figures of sin, criminality, vice, pathology. The 1992 film *Forbidden Love* is exemplary of a "cinematic use of the past" to reconfirm contemporary myths of continuity.[40] Or, as Ruby Rich puts it on the back of the video box, "The film to see for everyone who wants to know where lesbian chic came from."

Forbidden Love: A Diamond in Your Pocket

Within this narrative of progress, films repetitively fabricate a history of isolation and exclusion, marginalization and vulnerability, hidden pleasures and lurking dangers of the twilight and shadows. *Forbidden Love* is one such re-creation, tending to reproduce both poles of the contradictory myth sketched by Weir and Wilson: that is, a cherished, melodramatic, and contradictory preservation of the shadows and twilight of a lesbian past, as well as the public dangers exterior to it, all framed by conceptions of linearity, progress, and liberation. The glances both backward and forward in the film produce a tension of history, since the specificity of the twilight past is universalized to anticipate the coherent and inclusive present, a coherence nonetheless torn asunder, in my view, by the film's attempt to "include" women of color in its present and to banish questions about sex as labor, sex as imbricated with exchange.

Briefly, *Forbidden Love*, subtitled in the pulp tradition *The Unashamed Stories of Lesbian Lives*, is a Canadian National Film Board–financed hybrid documentary organized loosely around the phenomenon of lesbian pulp fiction. The film takes two routes in addressing these novels: it builds its own four-part "forbidden love," girl-meets-girl narrative within the film, the opening and closing segments of which frame the documentary, and it also uses the novels as a starting point for talking-head interviews with older Canadian lesbians who recollect their experiences of the emergent urban lesbian culture in Canadian cities (Vancouver, Toronto, Montreal) during the 1950s. Intercut with the interviews are the requisite personal photographs of the women in their youth, as well as an entire newsreel which purports to disclose the ideological construction of women in the decade: as workers and consumers, in some version of suburban hell, in tension with dominant conceptions of femininity. The combination of these myriad elements makes for an eclectic text.

Through its structure, then, the film gestures toward substantial questions about the function of lesbian popular culture as it is invoked through the lesbian pulp novels both as narrative impetus and as historical phenomenon. The film's initial tracking shot of the novels is followed with stories about the interviewees gleefully picking those novels coded as lesbian (through their cover art and titles) off the shelves of local drugstores. An interview with Ann Bannon follows. Bannon, the leading author of lesbian pulps and often, it seems, burdened with having to represent them all, recounts her own romance with Greenwich Village. Shots of the novels are subsequently intercut to punctuate, to add support for, the memories of the women interviewed; the cuts as well as the fictional chapters, as Linda Dittmar puts it, "recast the passion and thrill of the original reading experience."[41] According to the film in its initial moments, then, the function of the novels is to fabricate, through widely disseminated representations, a collectivity out of isolated individuals whose longings, desires, sexual practices, glances, clothing, bodies, roles, jobs, and/or fantasies incline them toward something that seems odd, queer, homosexual, lesbian, "resistant" to the totalizing burdens of heteronormativity. As Bannon suggests in her filmed interview, the books "reached out and connected [like the telephone] with women who were very isolated and sequestered almost in little towns across the country . . . [this is] the reason why paperback originals which did deal with the lesbian theme became so valuable to so many women."

To recirculate these novels as affirmative celebrations of lesbian identity is again to reduce the complexity of these relations to the register of a known sexuality, to read their own history, in effect, as realist representations of lesbian lives rather than fantasy worlds wherein "home—and indeed everything about everyday life—[is] subordinated to the fierce dictates of sexual desire."[42] They are, after all, novels. What one needs to probe is the "fabulous concreteness," Gramsci's oxymoron, these conceptions assume, whereby the twilight of isolation (represented by myths of Greenwich Village and the street) comes to carry with it resonances of outlawry, rebellion, and ritual excluded from most white middle-class women's lives during the decade of the 1950s. The film thus offers popular cultural nodal points for attaching danger and excitement to a hallucinatory past fraught with contradictions arising from the desire to locate contemporary lesbianism within a sphere of galvanizing liberatory politics and equally rousing consumption, or lesbian chic.

Bannon remembers in the film her first encounter with Greenwich Village life, where she escaped her husband and children in search of fodder for her Gold Medal originals: "It [the Village] mattered to me, and therefore it was imprinted on all of my senses as something to take away with me and keep and use and mine it for my subsequent writing . . . As my grandmother would say, it was like a diamond in your pocket. You carry it forever, and it feeds the stories." The figure is equally apt for characterizing the role of film or the paperbacks themselves: a gleaming, solicitous commodity shaken from its productive constraints or structural determinations, and affectively ensconced as historical memory. Under the covers, the novels fit perfectly in pockets, but, still, what lurks there?

Lesbians Under the Cover(s)

Forbidden Love, I think, borrows the pulp paperback for its own "cover." First, literally: its promotional materials (poster, t-shirt, video box, advertisements) feature a contemporary rendition of a lesbian pulp cover. Featured boldly in the Women Make Movies catalogue, the film has been an aggressively marketed title on their "lesbian" list and has consequently

Figure 18. Borrowing pulp
iconography: the graphic
advertisement for the film
Forbidden Love. Courtesy of
Women Make Movies.

found an audience at festivals, within academia, and also for "home" consumption (a vexing term I take up in the next chapter). The cover, then,
continues to beckon to us at the "point of sale," though now in parasitic
fashion, seizing the cache of lesbian pulp fiction for a largely conventional documentary form. By thus riding the affective and historiographical appeal of lesbian pulp, the film would appear to borrow its quality
for its own purposes. Second, the film borrows its narrative frame from
what it imagines to be a 1950s-era lesbian pulp novel. The narrative's
mainstays—the lesbian "Laura" leaving her now-heterosexual girlfriend
for the city, Laura's encounter with the butch "Mitch" in a bar, romantic
dancing and drinking in Mitch's apartment leading to foreplay, and the
final erotic encounter—partake of the stylized iconography of the 1950s,
described by Weir and Wilson, including a quite Fonz-like moment at
the bar's jukebox.

   This text under the cover of pulp raises, then, a second set of questions
about the role of documentary as historiography, and the relationship of
narrative to historical memory and the role of "evidence" in *Forbidden*

Love. The film's fictional narrative of "forbidden love," subtitled "the *un-ashamed* stories of lesbian lives" (emphasis added), is the most explicit revelation of the film's "take" on the pulp novels and lesbian culture of the 1950s. Through its staging of the narrative, the film corroborates the common sense understanding that we have moved from shame to pride, from isolation to affirmative connection; the visual evidence for these translations comes (pun intended) in the final installment of the narrative: the love scene between Laura and Mitch, when Laura, apparently without shame, declares that she is a lesbian. But the film then disclaims its own role as historiography in a title at its end:

> *Forbidden Love* presents the story of lesbians whose desire for a community led them on a dangerous search for the few public beer parlours or bars that would tolerate openly "queer" women in the 1950s and 1960s. It is not intended to be a survey or overview history of lesbians in Canada; indeed, most lesbians were forced to live intensely private lives, often isolated from one another. This film, like all lesbian and gay histories, is meant to contribute another fragment, another telling, as we break the silence of our lives.

The metaphor of the fragment structures lesbian and gay historiography, within an additive logic whereby any contribution merely augments its predecessors, and the subalterns speak partially, yet truly, to replace the silence, and shame, of hiding. A number of routes of analysis open here: Eve Kosofsky Sedgwick's work on shame in her article, "Queer Performativity: Henry James's *Art of the Novel*," is one road one might follow in unpacking the various affective registers condensed in the concept-affect shame (the coding of the body, the constitutive role of shame in identity formation) which pose challenges to the "(always moralistic) repression hypothesis."[43] Without recharting the specific contours of her argument, I would second her impulse to resist the recoding of Foucault's critique of the repression hypothesis as "subversion," and rather to face the force of that critique in the persistence of the repression hypothesis' persistence and/or its denial. Another route, toward perhaps the same end, involves asking after the exclusions the documentary makes in producing "unashamed" contemporary lesbian identity.

These exclusions involve, above all, race and labor. *Forbidden Love* carefully "includes" two nonwhite talking head interviewees in its bid toward a panorama of lesbian herstory: Amanda White and Nairobi Nelson, Native and Costa Rican–Quebecoise, respectively. Both are framed in significantly different fashion from the white women in the film. Rather than filmed at home, on the couch (with cats, of course), Amanda is set off against a wall of enormous wood sculptures, shot in tight focus to cue her appearance, while Nairobi is interviewed in a dimly lit night-club as visual reminder of her career as a cabaret singer. The film recognizes that the pulp paperbacks do not generally chart a multiracial world, so that when a pulp paperback cover appears with an African American woman on it (*Duet in Darkness*), its iconography prompts a cut from a lingering shot of that cover to Nairobi's interview. It seems reasonable as a visual strategy: African American to Costa Rican-Quebecoise, specificity trammeled under the cover. Nairobi's appearance is also signaled by stills of her band's promotional posters. Since no indigenous equivalents seem to exist, Amanda's appearances are generally cued by mention of the street, since Amanda's story focuses on her experiences where she was torn between Native culture and white culture, experiences that drove her into street life.

The film's specular marking of Nairobi and Amanda functions to parry the challenges the two women provide to the seamless universalism of the film's historical and narrative recreation. They are reminders that the urban lesbian culture of the 1950s and 1960s the film retrieves is not simply white and middle-class—though it appears monotonously so—but instead dependent upon white and middle-class fantasies of danger and outlawry associated with people of color and street life, precisely such as the pulps provide. Yet, within the historiographic logic of the fragment, these are present as corrective, as visual evidence that the film is not itself committing a parallel sin. Amanda's story in particular seems, however, to suggest otherwise: it is she, uniquely, who names the structural support on which the film's version of lesbian history rides, first in the early stages of her recollection, in her first interview. After rejecting the constricting options of indigenous culture to go to the white man's school, she observes in "this" white culture the pressures of patriarchy, the weight of the patronym, and she hopes that with a woman she would find an erotic/emotional relationship untarnished by repressive power. "So I thought," she says. Caught within the interstices of two cultures, or their clashing schemes of value-coding, Amanda finds refuge in street life.

Several interviewees provide colorful and detailed descriptions of lesbian and gay bars in Toronto and Vancouver during the 1950s. Most vivid are their memories of dirt: dirty toilets, cockroaches, cigarettes stubbed out on the floors, and "dirty," "wicked," or "dangerous" neighborhoods, intersections, in which the bars were located. The movement of the film's editing shapes a pattern: Carol Ritchie Mackintosh describes the "beautiful people" of her set, on the beach in whites, with yachting caps, picnics, wine, and "posh Toronto." This interview introduces the second segment of the pulp narrative, set in a lesbian bar, but one that appears cozy, clean, and embracing. After the dramatic installment, Stephanie Ozard recalls both her fear and her elation at finding the bar, the New Fountain, in an area replete with drunks and drug addicts, "really skid row."[44] Amanda finds herself on the bottom rung of this ladder of the lesbian socius: "I knew nothing about skid row. All I knew was that it was home to me, it was just like home. There were Native people around, people were drinking and all of that . . . and I felt comfortable there." Later, she remembers her own *dis*comfort in the lesbian bar, the Vanport, in Vancouver: the women looked like men, and "it was hurtful, too, because everybody was either drunk out of their mind or stoned out of their mind, and to me what I was trying to run away from was exactly this."

In the interviewees' recollections, the geography of the idyllic interior represented in the pulp narrative gives way to a cartography of exclusion, territoriality ("it was like animals, almost, like lions, it was that fierce"), brawls, rigid roles, and policed sociality, unsettlingly aligned with the streets on which the bars were located. Both visually and through the metaphors invoked to describe bar culture, *Forbidden Love* starts to resemble its squalid other, the discourse of self-affirmative discourse veering toward the discourse of medicosocial regulation, and the abject figure of that slippage is now exteriorized in the street embodied by Amanda. But it is again Amanda who reminds us that the street is not only that which marks the dangerous space of the bar, but a site of labor, labor performed predominantly by lesbians: "most of the people working in the street—in drugs, prostitution, dancing—were lesbian women. They wouldn't identify themselves as lesbian, it was an unwritten code." Through Amanda's comments, we are returned to the displacement of the pulp cover, where the predication of identity-formation as represented by the film's understanding of bar culture in the 1950s seems to rely on the exclusion of work that cannot be coded as "lesbian" but is nonetheless fetishized and consumed as outlawry. Rebelling is seen by the film as a way to access or enter a generalized otherness coded simultaneously as racial, affective (in offering excitement, danger), and political.

Lois M. Stuart and Keeley Moll, two of the film's interviewees, offer two poles of this operation's mechanics, positions that indicate the mobile nature of affective coding. On the one hand, Lois understands the heightened and intensified identifications with street life as modes by which lesbians embraced their outcast status, accepting marginalization as strength: "If you're going to live a double life, then live a double life!" Lois carried an eight-inch dagger, strove toward butch splendor, and enjoyed accentuating the contrast in her own leisure/sexual/social life from the normalized femininity and heteronormativity that characterized her working hours. The film relishes her energy, spunk, humor, vigor, and, most of all, her continued engaged politics around the body, retrospectively seen to emanate from her earlier butch stylizations. The closing interview with Lois takes place on the street, not as destitute locale but now as a site for a pro-choice march ("What do we want? Choice. When do we want it? Now."). In voice-over and then in her home, Lois observes, "If you aren't mistresses of your bodies, you're a slave. That's what slavery is . . . I think postmenopausal women should run the world!" Though one might agree heartily with the latter suggestion, one may want also to reject the equation of the politics of choice with the definition of slavery. In fact, while the film does not appear to endorse that equation, it *does* support Lois's assertions of current strength as derived from her past, with a chorus of the other women who translate their past courage into affective support for their contemporary political and personal engagements. Stephanie, now a Metropolitan Community Church minister threatened by arson and the murder of church members as well as the single mother of a strong, antihomophobic daughter, cherishes the memory of the past: "to be what we were, flaunting the law, doing something illicit." Amanda is now off the streets, thanks to a friend who helped her move in new directions: the streets were fine, it seems, for renegade identity-formation, but people, lesbians, ought not to have to *live* there.

In Stephanie's final comments, we find the equation on which the film's history relies: being = doing. In Keeley Moll's closing interview, we hear it become faulty arithmetic, while an even more dangerous calculus of normativity replaces it:

> I think that not being able to move through society as a human being and [as] a person without dignity isn't exciting. I think maybe robbing

a bank is exciting, but not being an outcast because you have preferences that the majority doesn't have. That's not exciting . . . I don't
want to be harmed, I just want to have nice social contacts. I just want
to have fun . . . I don't want to sit at the back of the bus. That sucks.

Keeley is the only interviewee associated with the country, on a pastoral
farm, with a horse, in rural Alberta. This closing segment is shot with
Keeley resting against a post of her isolated cabin, and it is privileged as
one of the film's final words in that it precedes the final installation of the
pulp narrative: the sex scene, followed by morning coffee, and a voice-
over which jubilantly announces Laura's proud realization that she is a
lesbian. Being, therefore, means: to be a lesbian is to mean a politics, a
position toward and in the world. As with the previous installments, the
scene blends from freeze frame into a stylized recreation of a pulp cover,
stressing the *unashamed* (through self-declaration, one supposes) stories
of lesbian love.

And yet this conclusion neither wards off the ambivalence of the film
regarding the delicious dangers of the past (clandestine, exciting dangers
Keeley Moll rejects), nor provides the last word. Kelly Hankin, in a study
of lesbian bar documentaries, suggests that the film's irony embeds a
"desire to maintain the secret space of the bar," as evidenced, too, in the
film's *actual* final scene, after the credits have rolled. As she describes it,

> the viewer is privy to a conversation between [Lois] Stuart and Jeanne
> Healy, both elderly white women living in Toronto. Half-jokingly,
> Healy taunts Stuart: "Lois, with our luck this movie will be a hit and
> [there will] be people lined up outside with baseball bats to get us,"
> to which Stuart gleefully responds, "Won't be anything new for me.
> It'll be just like the old days outside one of the gay bars. They were
> great stuff!"[45]

Is the "Laura" figure, or Lois M. Stuart, or Jeanne Healy, or Keeley
Moll, our Rosa Parks?[46] Has outlawry become entirely divorced from
the real? Have fun in the country and the joy of nice social contacts replaced even the slightest of engagements with those lesbians, working
in an unwritten code, on urban streets? Or are these questions unautho-
rized, improperly addressed to a fragment that disclaims its social force?
If the viewer is to make any sense of what being a lesbian *means*, I think
she has to ask them, even as she is made possible by a signifier caught
within their denial. The questions, as they have appeared throughout this

book, involve the relation of affect to subject predication, the encrypting of value, and the overwhelming mobility of cultural forms specularly and spectacularly condensed in static conceptions of identity.

In the original version of this essay, I concluded with a set of axioms I wanted us to remember as we circulate the things by which we define our shared lesbian lives. I reproduce that set here, but not without a gentle fondness for *Forbidden Love* that perhaps was occluded by my righteous rush toward contextualization. To have inaugurated as the film has done such an important discussion about the lesbian pulps, and to have done so on the National Film Board's (Canadian) nickel, is no small achievement, and we, I, thank Fernie and Weissman for getting this conversation started. Here are the things I wanted to emphasize:

1. That lesbian bar culture has been and is involved in the production of racist enclaves, hallucinations of urban life which depend for their existence on street culture (drinks, drugs, sex work, and pornography), which provide a sense of outlawry, but yet that very culture is frequently denied or disdained by white lesbians seeking "community."

2. That the labor of the streets, particularly sex work, is often performed by lesbians. Lesbian bourgeois culture has hitherto ignored that labor, the predication of these women's sociopolitical subjectivity. We need more work on lesbians who do, and who study, sex work.

3. That the participation in subcultural leisure activities does not guarantee a politics, much less an anti-racist agenda or awareness of the competing determinations of political subjectivity (by which I mean, more simply, other things that determine who we are, what struggles to fight and when to fight them, and how to think about other peoples' struggles).

4. And that when we think that *we* are "odd girls out" on the town, to borrow one of Bannon's titles, we must remap the streets of that town, since it has always belonged to others, both to capital and to struggles we don't necessarily see in our lesbian chic finery.

To remember these things is not, however, to move out from "under cover" into what is right or true; it is simply to be more critically vigilant within contradiction and undecidability. The pulp cover as visual condensation of popular cultural domestication helps us to *forget,* as does a certain form of analogizing gay and lesbian struggles with, say, the history of integration and the civil rights movement. Such analogizing finesses the violent appropriation of an origin as solidarity. Again, more simply, it violently makes the origin, itself mythic, of Rosa Parks's defiance into "our own" history, which it is not, although there may be moments when we can speak of intersections between the civil rights movement and the gay liberation movement. If pulp seems to mark a desire for outlawry more generally, if it seems to privilege a mode of transformation—note, not subversion—of dominant codes, it does not do so by escaping the confines of representation. It does so, instead, only by reworking, within generic *and* industrial constraints, routes of travel within culture.[47] The contemporary recirculation of lesbian pulp, moreover, coexists with other appearances of the lesbian that, in the obverse direction, flee the streets to no less fraught or contested enclosures. I conclude in the next chapter with one such enclosure, if not *the* one: the home, where "things" abound, and where the visualization of lesbian takes place differently, frequently on the small screen. In the home market, things can go straight, to video.

Straight to Video

The foregoing chapters have suggested the need for investigations into specific visualizations of what we condense in the term *lesbian* in order to understand the slippages those visualizations struggle to contain, the limits at which representation functions. The thing and the metaphor of the pulp cover provided an opportunity, in the previous chapter, to reckon with the historical *and* historiographical stakes of such an investigation, disclosing under the pulp cover a dense traffic in sexuality, commodities, exchange value, and regulation. By way of a conclusion to *Lesbian Rule,* I turn in these last few pages to what might be an equivalent at the dawn of the twenty-first century to the pulps of the last mid-century: home video. By "home video" I mean to shorthand the practice of viewing at home texts that come to us via a *range* of sources and formats, such as cable/satellite and pay-per-view television, mail order services (that send in the mail gay-related videotapes to far-flung subscribers), Web-based media, videotapes, laser discs, and DVDs.[1] Like the pulps, each of these forms brings with it a distinct history and a regulatory matrix that cannot quite be apprehended solely through the paradigms of visibility and representation, because they conceal the translations and condensations at work *within* each form. Like the pulps, these formats come on a wing, as they too will peak and yield to other popular forms in time. Indeed, while it may seem odd to title a conclusion, even if playfully, after what may soon be an obsolete format—video—it is in part the goal of these concluding remarks to remind us of the persistence of multiple formats, the extent to which the history of queer media is not a long march of progress or continual improvement, but rather an uneven and multiple shuffle, back to cheap and exploitable retro-formats such as Super-8 and Pixelvision (the Fisher-Price toy used with great effect by Sadie Benning and others) and forward to digital productions such as the "butch buddy" queer festival hit, *By Hook or by Crook* (Harry Dodge and Silas Howard,

2001). I am allowing *video* to stand for all of these formats, all of the obsolete and emergent forms at once, insofar as they oppose themselves to "film."

Home, as in *home video,* is an equally knotty term, and it deserves at least a bit further explanation. In one sense I mean it plainly and literally. In most of the foregoing chapters, I have dealt with films, with the exception of *Forbidden Love,* that circulate in embattled public venues such as queer film festivals and museums. It is quite obviously the case, however, that most queer folks get their media fixes elsewhere: from the occasional gay film to hit the art house, such as *Big Eden* (Thomas Bezucha, 2000), or, alternatively, at home. Television, video/DVD rentals and purchases, mail order services, and the like supply far larger markets than do the venues of public exhibition that offer queer media, and even the documentary form finds more congenial hosts in the home than at museums or festivals.

At the same time, however, I want to invoke through *home* all of its resonances—some positive, some negative, some neither—in queer life: haven, retreat, private realm, scene of violence, space of normativity, mise-en-scène for family, barrier to legal intrusion, romantic refuge, site for political struggle, unaffordable luxury, commodity sphere, house, decorating opportunity, home-shopping, home-bound, home-improvement, whatever. Depending on the resonance, the idea and experience of home video will be different, and necessarily, since the range of texts and contexts for home video is measurably much larger than the available array of texts and contexts in public film culture. As the realm of public media shrinks, I think it's time to take a look at what the idea of home might energize, as well as what it might limit or contain.

I do not, however, mean to align the idea of home with "the private," even or especially *private* without modifier, such as "private domain," "private property," or "private sphere." What follows is not a set of conclusions about the individual, or the family, or the psyche, or emotion, or interpersonal relationships. Neither does it posit a realm of analysis opposed to or distinct from the state, or civil society, or a sphere untrammeled by late capitalism. Finally, it is not a realm of passivity, or pure consumption, or pure spectacle. Instead, I hope to invoke through home some of the limits of the oppositions facilely bandied about between public and private, economy and emotion, activity and consumption, since home video, like Habermas's forty-year-old book, is about *transformations* in the lifeworld, including the realm of media. Tracking these transformations involves being alert to their forms, including what I will call the displaced cartography of documentary.

For example, many of the elements of home video, old and new, betray their commodity status in tactile and sensational ways. They challenge us to rethink the issue of participation in popular culture insofar as they solicit forms of spectatorship, collecting, affect, and commentary that are distinct from those of cinema-going whether at the multiplex or the film festival. The processes of moving film to other formats for home-viewing, for example, may involve translations in optical effects, image resolution, contrast ratio, and audio so extreme as "to produce a product no longer a suitable signifier of the film signified."[2] The dynamics of spectatorship similarly shift in the move from the theatre to the home, as the more televisual "distracted gaze" replaces the rapt gaze produced by and through the cinematic apparatus. Anne Friedberg usefully, I think, distinguishes the mobility inherent in the "distracted gaze" alongside four other factors distinguishing home viewership: the nonprojected nature of the television image, its time-shifting potential (through analog and digital recording devices), its synchronic *and* diachronic choice of viewing options, and its smaller scale.[3] Many of these differences may be equalized as industry relentlessly pursues innovative sites for monstrous expense: larger screens, the replication of theatrical sound, digital filtration, and widescreen formats are becoming standard on high-end home theater systems. Regardless of these innovations, the changes brought in practices of home-viewing, including those transformations wrought by the televisual, appear to be irreversible, no matter how vigorously the industry mimes theatrical norms in its appeals to us at home by offering us director's cuts and commentaries, theatrical trailers, and other memorabilia of the production site.

There are, furthermore, two central contradictions pertaining to the industry's form in which scholars of the emergent cinema(s) and home viewers alike are embedded. The first: contrary to the myth that new technologies and deregulation have allowed independent filmmakers to compete significantly with Hollywood major studios, quite the opposite has taken place. The Hollywood majors, as Janet Wasko puts it, have merged "into large synergistic corporations that control huge chunks of popular cultural production."[4] The publicity surrounding the occasional breakthrough independent film, whether documentary or narrative in form, distracts from awareness of the control exerted by the five or six distribution companies that control nearly 90 percent of domestic theatrical rentals. Just as *reality* in the television industry signaled a genre-busting boon for a moribund production wing, *independent* in film-economic terms signifies the potential for magnified profits based on innovative financing packages and small overall production and post-production budgets. Foreign television rights, for example, can finance post-production costs and then be bundled with domestic pay-television rights, video and DVD releases, and a more standard theatrical distribution deal. More significant, because the idea of an independent production suggests the renegade, the democratic, and the anti-trust all at once (and because the plural form, *independents* is homonym to one of our most cherished ideologemes), it carries with it a kind of ideological force that not only mystifies the conditions of industrial film production, distribution, and exhibition but also affects its presumed content.

This leads to the second significant contradiction: contrary to the myth that new technologies and expanded information systems have produced more diversity in offerings, the proliferation of cultural conduits (more channels, more systems, more formats) has produced a companion effect to the corporate synergistic mergers in form: the synergistic *replication* of cultural contents from one form to another, producing what Wasko, again, calls a kind of "recycled culture" (252). There is no reason, in other words, to suppose that the circuit of innovation and co-optation that defines capitalist cultural production would be interrupted or displaced by the mere multiplication of sites, but there is, I would urge us to acknowledge, therefore much more to track, rendering the task of cultural analysis more overwhelming despite the increasing availability of information.

In moving from the conceptual systems built upon the norms of theatrical exhibition to the increasing practice of home-viewing, then, it is necessary but not sufficient to address these more glaring of the effects of industrial modifications. In addition to these technological and spectatorial mutations are transformations in what we might, following Marcia Landy, call "affectivity," by which she means "a form of labor expended in the consumption of cinematic images, in the enterprise of voluntarily offering up our lives 'as free contributions to capitalist power.'"[5] Landy's term shares with *affective value* (a term I examined at length in the first chapter) a way of understanding how our very attention is commodified in the production of cinematic value, in exchange for which we receive different forms of compensation in terms also of sensation or affect. To put it more concretely, the exchange nexus of cinema is not limited to the moment at which we pay for a ticket for a screening, buy a related tie-in product, or "bring the film home" on videotape. In addition, we offer our sensory/affective constellations to cinema, in return for which we are compensated by thrill, tears, suspense, or contemplative relations. Cinema processes our attention and returns it to us as subjection to the cinematic.

Presumably, the production of affective value or the processes of "affectivity" would shift, mutatis mutandis, in moving from cinema to home, provided that we understand such a movement beyond pat distinctions of public and private, shared and atomized, political and otherwise. The bold challenges in making sense of the translation come instead in the different forms of attention we offer to home viewing, since those forms are commanded by different kinds of texts. Unlike the relatively standardized fare of the popular commercial cinema, that is, we have access to an extraordinary variety of texts that can come to us at home in addition to those popular films in various formats: erotica, hard- and soft-core pornography; straight-to-video productions (such as, for example, an intriguing lesbian detective film called *Lesbionage*); documentary nontheatrical features (such as the inexplicably popular documentary *Moments . . . The Making of* Claire of the Moon); independent features, short films, and experimental works (including animation); "foreign" films, including a proliferation of anime and action films; and, finally, television programs, including music videos and comedy performances. Forms of attention obviously vary, as well, depending upon the genre and format of the text in question, and the mood or interest of the donor of that attention.

For the queer community, home-viewing plays a social role that can be further distinguished in terms of the forms of affectivity it might command. Because gay and lesbian films have historically circulated in festival venues, the home video market makes films in a number of genres much more widely accessible. Many of the feature films that have appeared in festivals without gaining distribution theatrically go straight to video for the queer market. In a list of more than 130 videos for sale by mail, the documentary genre listing includes films such as *Blood Sisters* (Michelle Handelman) on the San Francisco lesbian s/M community, *It's Elementary* (Debra Chasnoff), on teaching lesbian and gay issues in schools, and *Paris Was a Woman* (Andrea Weiss and Greta Schiller), on the artists and intellectuals of the Left Bank.[6] The proliferation of queer work is not simply a concomitant process of democratization, of course.

The videos submit to the logics of the market as quickly as we do, for the counterforce exerted in the exchange that affectivity marks is inescapably bound to the interests of a globalizing and transnational capitalism. Yet, as I have wanted to do in earlier chapters, I want here to linger over the notion of value produced in that exchange. I want to ask ourselves what surplus value is created when a fellow film scholar and gay man whom I adore excitedly shows me Judy Garland outtakes from the "Born in a Trunk" number from *A Star is Born* (George Cukor, 1954) on his new anamorphic-lens projection television? Or when the archivist/video pirate David Johnson, director of the compilation film *Lavender Lens*, passes me a copy of the 1960 Mike Wallace investigative report, *The Homosexuals*, as a kind of pedagogical nostalgia piece? Or when the same person sends me a video called *Chained Girls*, described in one catalog, in its "After Dark Video" section (!), as a "wicked exposé . . . [that] takes a 'factual' slant on gay culture."

In this book I have barely glanced off the surface of how sexuality makes an affective difference, or produces affective value differently. But one conclusion I should like to draw is that we produce commentary differently when the tape, or the pulp novel, is in our hands, certainly as opposed to the kind of commentary possible on the fleeting object that is more properly "cinema." Part of home-viewing is replaying, savoring pieces, reassembling them, collecting them, and speaking back. To continue the parallel to the pulps of the previous chapter, I turn in these last pages to an ethnographic and taxonomic counterpart from 1965 (roughly contemporaneous with the last breaths of the lesbian pulp efflorescence), to this "documentary" film called *Chained Girls*, directed by one George Mawra and apparently starring one June Roberts. To have it in hand is to produce a reading that takes some delight in this outrageous film; to have it at home allows a certain kind of fun.

Chained Girls: The Imprint of Lesbian Titillation

The videotape, *Chained Girls,* has shed its enunciative context: like many other B films, exploitation films, and soft-core porn films, it exists primarily in the limbo of video distribution, neither attached to its initial scene of production nor to any particular audience in its sites of exhibition. Perhaps it is a "lesbian" video? Might it, as such, provide an occasion, as Timothy Murray suggests, for "reflection anew on the 'overaccentuation of visual elements [which provide] imprints of psychic and cultural exile that continually signify *to* particular states of belonging"?[7] If *lesbian* can be understood as a catachresis but as nonetheless a term that bears such an imprint of a "particular state of belonging," then the reading of the catachrestical depends upon these imprints, these traces that reverberate and seize us even as we unlearn them. Through them, we can also track the movement of affective value: that which attaches to the lesbian video, and that which we attach to that name, even if with a tinge of embarrassment.

An exposé, *Chained Girls* aims to expose a problem it will not solve, and it seeks to name a phenomenon it cannot name. A low-budget aesthetic contributes to its hybrid form. It consists of precisely two aural components: a voice-of-God monotonous narration, interspersed with orchestral music composed for the film. There is no dialogue, indeed no synchronous sound. It consists of precisely five visual components: (1) scenes of the streets of New York City; (2) an interior dramatic recreation of a photo shoot at a modeling agency; (3) statistics compiled from medical reports in graphic form (relying frequently upon the typographic thrill of the exclamation mark); (4) a narrative of sorts of a "coming-out" party in a "fashionable part of town"; and (5) a bedroom scene of prostitution virtually indistinguishable, both in terms of mise-en-scène and in the film's editing, from the coming-out party. These aural and visual pieces combine almost willy-nilly, and it is tempting to me to recreate the film in its entirety in order to savor the glorious juxtapositions upon which it makes its putative meaning. I will limit myself, however, to three observations and examples: the combination of the definitional and taxonomic project with the urban landscape and its threats; the dimensions of "coming-out" that emerge in tandem with rites of initiation and cult behavior all tied to specific and detailed class positions; and the stress on sight and proximity as allied with sex and exchange.

The film opens with the first, the combination of the taxonomic project with the landscape. The voice-over asks, "Who and what is a lesbian? Is lesbianism a disease or natural occurrence? Is it reserved for a few or a common happening? How do lesbians live? Are they happy with their lives? And how does society accept them?" As it would scientifically approach the mating habits of water buffalo, the voice-over refuses to answer these questions and instead will "discuss" them. What we *see*, over and again, during this opening delimitation of the question of the lesbian are apartment buildings (shots of midtown New York streets). How do lesbians live? Apparently in apartment buildings.

Cut abruptly to stills of Greece, while the voice-over intones that the name *lesbian* derives from Sappho; we are treated to dramatic readings from her poems, accompanied oddly by a tracking shot of the Brooklyn Bridge. A metaphor for the movement of history, or the relocation of Sapphic sexuality to the situation that is present-day New York, or the only footage left? Now, the taxonomy:

> Medical reports and several well-known authoritative books on the subject tell us that there are all types of lesbians, the masculine stereotype known as the butch or dyke, with many variations: the bull dyke, the stomping butch, and the baby butch. Science tells us that for every type of creature who walks the Earth, there is a counterpart, and so it is also true for the butch. In this case, the feminine counterpart is known as the femme, or doll.

In this snippet one can notice not only the more obvious structuring appeal of scientific discourse, but also the rapture of the taxonomic project itself, whereby the mastery of knowledge becomes an alibi for the lusciousness of description; such rapture will reappear. More apartment buildings, more street scenes in the dark now, of Greenwich Village bars, and then a tight shot of the exception to the general rule of lesbians' discretion: two women kissing in a telephone booth. The film will later stroll away from its "narrative" investigation of a coming-out party to continue the taxonomy associated with the street, and here it offers, too, the only reference to the eponymous chains.

> Lesbians have their variations from one group to another. There are those women who are cultured and refined who sneak away to some dirty bar in order to meet a trampish-looking woman to make love to. Some women break up homes, forsake children, for the love of another woman. Then there are the teenage lesbians, or baby butch. They roam city streets in large gangs assaulting everyone who falls in their path. Some of the weapons they use run the gamut of fists, lead pipes, chains.

The hyperbole, reminiscent of tabloid sensationalism, relies on a particularly pulp scenario: the clandestine, the tramp, grime, broken homes, chains, and gangs. In this case, however, the visual accompaniment is a shot of a woman at a party, "in a fashionable part of town," sitting at a grand piano, smoking a cigarette in a holder—all signifiers of the "cultured" and "refined" environment she might forsake for the street life.

It is in this juxtaposition that the first significant point of my brief reading lies, for a peculiar cartography emerges here that recalls the structural mobility of pulp. The place of the question (the formulation, that is, of lesbian as social problem) is precisely in the desire to see what is hidden under the cover of social respectability, including the titillating figure of the "trampish" woman having sex with another woman. But the place of this desire is the form of the representation as such: the documentary film, with its respectable invocation of science, medicine, and statistics. In other words, the making-visible of lesbian requires a position which is untenable precisely because the phenomenon or the problem is itself hiding. As the voice-over instructs us, "Even when they think and live like men, lesbians for the most part generally enjoy the chic look of womanhood." Allying lesbianism with the street, with urban spaces and their capacity to enclose lurking dangers (our pulp iconography of twilight, shadows, clandestine kisses stolen in telephone booths), produces a fantasy of a guarantee, a visual scene laid in front of a camera positioned elsewhere; the framing of the question is thus dependent upon an interior (chic femininity, a signifier of class-inflected, white, normative gendered and sexualized positions) which is haunted by that which lies outside of it, indeed is virtually indistinguishable from it. The street, not just any street but the streets of Greenwich Village, becomes precisely an effect of a displaced cartography drawn elsewhere, namely in the language of popular psychology and popularized medicine, sanctioned by normative and classy femininity. The inside thus appears to become the outside, not in order to resist the construction of lesbian as nature, as Biddy Martin's crystalline discussion of Joan Nestle's work reveals,[8] but instead as an effect of a visualization of lesbianism the film's own discourses cannot quite manage. This displacement of the inquiring lens produces, in turn, an instability in the film's delineation of these privileged class positions and normative gendered positions, an instability I think one can explore through the second of the concerns I suggested above: the idea of "coming-out." The term's contemporary usage, as we shall see, is quite different from the gloss provided by *Chained Girls*.

Coming-Out

In its social history and its permutations for queer culture, the idea of coming-out (even in the Pocket Books advertisement that appears as epigraph for the preceding chapter) is saturated with the idea of the

debut. And the debut itself marks a trajectory, a movement of innovation and authentication, the (re)coding of value and the necessity of
its transformation. As an exclusionary practice of the upper classes in
Anglo America, coming-out is the value-matrix for what Gayle Rubin has
importantly called the "traffic in women,"[9] the mechanism by which a
woman becomes eligible for social/sexual union with a male counterpart of her class. Where she had no (use, capital, reproductive) value
as a daughter, she acquires (exchange) value as a commodity, potential
wife/mother. In America, this value-coding is staged at a party with attendant private functions, in England at court. What is accorded value
is therefore not any positive attribute of "woman" as debutante—that is,
no specific attribute of femininity such as beauty, grace, dress, or charm,
although all become proxies for capital value—but instead the perpetuation of class distinction itself, staged for men. (The compulsion to see
this as regulated by the phallus as general *subjective* equivalent is a move
Rubin carefully avoids.) The Pocket Books advertisement seizes on the
capital logic inherent in the mode of transformation: the commodity's
value at its debut is only assessed by and within the general equivalent of
exchange (the universal symbol excluded from the commodity function):
a quarter "leaps" to a dollar in retrospective fashion to stage the paperback's worth for the consumer. *Chained Girls* similarly inflects the *social*
dimensions of the debut in its gloss on what coming-out means in the
ostensible lesbian community it explores. That inflection restores some
of the social connotations I have just sketched that the phrase appears to
have shed in connection with queer culture.

Chained Girls initially defines *coming-out* among a host of terms that
form a lesbian's "own special vocabulary." "Coming-out," the voice-over
intones as we cruise the streets of the Village, "indicates a lesbian's sexual
debut." The "coming-out party" that occupies that latter half of the film,
for well over forty minutes, emphasizes the ritualistic dimensions of
this subcultural appropriation of the debut. We cut to the interior to witness, as the voice-over explains it, the film's dyke dressing the femme
for her special moment, a highly choreographed process of preparation.
"At the conference table" (a strangely corporate and institutional name
for what appears to be a dining table), the film's dykes draw straws in
order to plan the femme's rite of initiation (which is, in fact, gang rape,
a point to which we will return). Ritualistic courting, coupling, violence,
and mating occur within the privacy of this fashionable part of town,

free from the social constraints of secrecy the film has sought to present visually through the streets. Within the sphere of class respectability, within the lush interiors of an uptown apartment, the film, in other words, presents its spectators with bizarre mating rituals, cult violence, drinking and smoking, perversion unimaginable, all of which become, then, simultaneously projected by the voice-over onto the street in the hyperbolic form of "baby butch gangs" assaulting "everyone who falls in their path."

The film thus becomes obsessed, through the figure of "coming out," with its counterpart, the "lesbian within," the extent to which, incredibly, "quite often, the boundaries of female homosexuality are so vague that women slip into lesbianism without realizing they're lesbians." Unlike Adrienne Rich's desire to grant women and lesbians fluidity in the name of a continuum, the film's desire is much more explicitly anthropological: to grant lesbians structural specificity which gives the lie to their omnipresence, even at the expense of preserving a stable boundary between cultured and refined women and the "tramps" they apparently seek out. If they (the lesbians) are here (in the sanctity of an urban refuge, in the space of the film's own enunciation), *Chained Girls* seems to say, and if they (the lesbians) are not us (since we are straight men), and if we are here (the paradox cannot be denied), they must be there (on the street, at least metaphorically, or isolated as another tribe, another race, another cult, masquerading as us).

The figure of coming-out manages this instability that lies at the core of any anthropological or ethnographic project. The effect of representing the "coming-out party" is to translate, backward, the contemporary identity-driven connotations of coming-out as revelation, disclosure, and truth back into ritual, the social coding of value within an enclosed milieu documented and studied as other. In *Chained Girls,* coming-out is, finally, the staging of a femme's value for dykes, whereby a femme becomes eligible for exchange among dykes (who are, the voice-over tells us, "naturally prone to jealousy and possessiveness"). The femme becomes a commodity which solicits the worst affective dimensions of capitalist circulation (jealousy, possessiveness) but which nonetheless mimics the sense of coming-out in the restricted sense intelligible through class logic.

How, one might wonder, has the contemporary, queer connotation of *coming-out* overtaken the ritualistic and social value-coding of the class-specific debut? Where along the way did the phrase shed these dimensions? The film, in effect, narrates the same impossibility about which Judith Butler inquires in a frequently cited passage from "Imitation and Gender Insubordination."

> What or who is it that is "out," made manifest and fully disclosed, when and if I reveal myself as lesbian? What is it that is now known, anything? What remains permanently concealed by the very linguistic act that offers us the promise of a transparent revelation of sexuality? Can sexuality even remain sexuality once it submits to a criterion of transparency and disclosure, or does it perhaps cease to be sexuality precisely when the semblance of full explicitness is achieved?[10]

Where Butler asks questions (the implied answers to which might appear upside-down on the bottom of the page as "nothing, nothing, everything, no/yes, it ceases"), the film provides explicit answers. "What or who is it that is 'out,' made manifest and fully disclosed?" Dykes and femmes, about whom we have learned through the confident taxonomies of documentation, who engage in predatory and ritualistic sexual activities upon coming-out understood as an *event* and not a discourse of revelation. "What is it that is now known, anything?" Value is now on the move; transformation is in full swing. And "can sexuality even remain sexuality once it submits to a criterion of transparency and disclosure?" Transparency and disclosure belong to the enunciative domain of the subject, defining an object that is destined to remain something other than sexuality in its difference.

Butler's set of questions perhaps deflects from our own ability to answer the construction of coming-out presented to us by the film, precisely because they flee from the force of the phrase's resonance as class-specific social ritual elsewhere, its *hesitancy* to signify the very fullness of being and transparent revelation accorded it in contemporary queer usage and in Butler's critical text. In fact, Butler later offers the strong conviction that this "deferral of the signified," the very suspension of the phrase at the level of the signifier is "*to be valued,* a site for the production of values."[11] If the idea of the debut is dependent on the circulation of the commodity within a form of equivalence (money), a slightly different way of asking the question appears. What different form of equivalence could possibly regulate the circulation of the queer debutante? Into what does she "come out" and under what predication of value? How, in other words, does the scene of coming-out produce value otherwise?

The ritual registers of coming-out that are attached to its class-specific form are, in fact, generalized in its contemporary usage to the sense of coming out into *publicness* or a public purview: "to come into public view or notice, as from concealment," as the OED notes. If the signified is suspended, we have nonetheless to deal with the residue shimmering behind the signifier: the translocation from the privatized interior into the public marketplace, the movement from sexual immaturity to commodity-status, the marking of the individual within larger social structures or units. Although one may come out into particular enclosures of publicness (to one's colleagues in the workplace, to one's teammates, or to the teachers or caregivers of one's children), the public into which one might come out is immeasurable, at once mute and saturated with regulatory discourses. Insofar as it is an act one chooses to initiate or complete, the individual experience of coming-out is thus frequently located in microalignments, slight shifts in social relations, though these may be violent or embracing; in order that these microalignments signify, they are accompanied precisely by ritual and celebration. And insofar as one might not come out through a declaration of one's identity, one might be far more likely to experience coming-out as an effect of being "outed," whether through gait, gesture, clothing, or other, frequently visible, sign of one's putative lesbianism.

Publicness, sociality, and shifting political relations lie at the center of coming-out as an event, even if what is disclosed is to remain permanently unclear through the deferral of the signified. The lesbian debut may disclose or produce affective value; what remains to be understood is how that very nexus of sexuality and exchange ritualized in the significance of coming-out might produce value, and toward what ends. In *Chained Girls*, what appears to be a rather direct translation of the coming-out rituals of the American upper classes onto its dykes and femmes preserves intact the scene of exploitation, degradation, and abjection that inhere in the production of woman as sexualized commodity. Lesbian makes no difference at all. To probe further at our own translation of some of the questions surrounding coming-out (What value is produced at the scene of a "femme" debut?), let us look more closely at how sex and exchange join together in *Chained Girls*.

Exchange and Sight

The film places a particular emphasis on sight and proximity as a means for expressing what becomes a sex/exchange analogy. In the (again, very long) coming-out party sequence, the voice-over narrates the bull dyke's conquest of the young debutante. At this point and no other point in the film, the gender slips: "In this case the dyke would support *his* femme. In a more literal sense of the word, the femme would become the mistress of the dyke" (emphasis added). We know, or, better, we have learned from a previous commentary that dykes easily become femmes and vice versa, and this mobility (gendered, sexualized, and now economic) proves just too much for the film possibly to contain. It leaps, therefore, to a whole new topic: "A strange occurrence happens when a lesbian has to turn to prostitution in order to keep her female lover." Visually, it is within the same room of the coming-out party that we see a lesbian prostitute (one of the same actresses who had been one of the party femmes), receiving $150 from a man who is willing "to pay an additional $50 to be with a lesbian." The logic of the exchange that we learn is worth citing at length.

> The men were highly stimulated to think that they were able to draw a response from a woman who was known to be indifferent to men. In prostituting herself to finance her woman lover, the lesbian finds it ironic that it's a man's money that's paying for her pleasure with a woman. Men unknowingly sometimes use lesbians as procurers for them, and in many cases, the lesbian usually samples the girls before she turns them over to a man. It is not uncommon for a lesbian to do what she hates most: prostitute herself to a man. It is also not uncommon for a prostitute to turn, in moments of extreme loneliness and despair, to the warm, soft arms of another woman.

As the john and the prostitute finish kissing on the bed, the lesbian/femme-cum-prostitute joins another lesbian's warm, soft arms to re-enter the coming-out party.

Despite a few glitches in the rest of the film, *Chained Girls* generally manages to adhere to the strictures of continuity editing, keeping the spectator clearly oriented in space and time, with the glaring exception of the prostitution sequence. It is as if the film, in this sequence alone, must obey another set of conventions which suspend the force of continuity's requirements. I am inclined to call these conventions *pop lesbianism,* the product of a certain value-coding through the popularized discourses of medicine and psychology. What is at stake here is understanding popularization not as a bastardized or impure version of a pristine original discourse, since even *Chained Girls* is sympathetic to lesbians through its frequent invocations of "Dr. Freud," who contends through this voice-

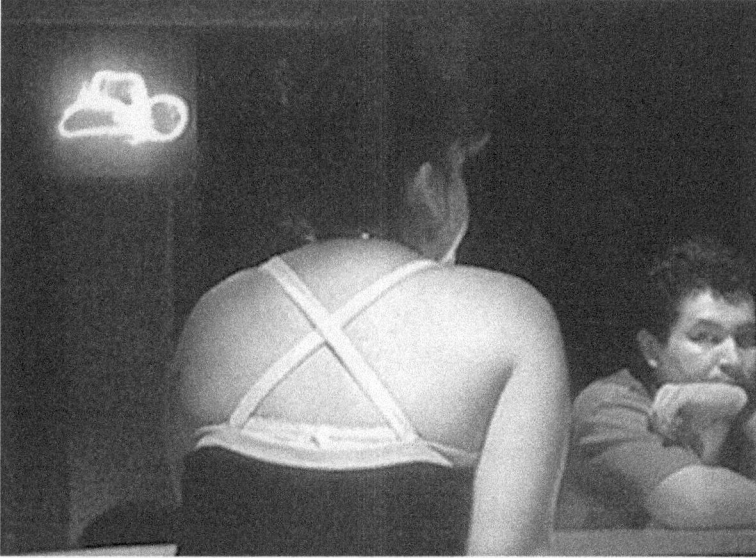

Figure 19. *Performing the Border,* directed by Ursula Biemann. Courtesy of Women Make Movies.

over's channeling that lesbians are not only "ignored by the law, but also by society." Popularization involves a series of condensations, translations, anchorings of meaning around distinctions of sex, sexuality, gender, and exchange which cannot be entirely managed by the ad hoc assumption of authority upon which it depends. Through the discourses of ethnography, pop psychology, and sociology, *lesbian* is a signifier inserted into a chain that produces necessarily contradictory effects, not the least of which is that lesbianism can fascinate both as a realm of woman-loving and identification, as well as an object for heterosexual men. That the economic traffic in lesbians can be made to mirror heterosexual prostitution (as it is in *Playboy,* which began its circulation in 1953) does not limit thereby the extent to which *lesbian* is simultaneously encircled by domains of homosociality which interrupt that mirroring gaze.[12]

The narration I cited above, combined with the visual displacement from the coming-out party to the prostitution scene and back again makes available the gaps in both the homophobic containment of normative sexuality as well as the gaps in progressive liberatory narratives of sexual emancipation. It does so in the language of the popular, as it encodes "the public" in the specific sense in which it emerges through the

Figure 20. *The Basement Girl,* directed by Midi Onodera. Courtesy of Women Make Movies.

language of coming-out: attaching to a cityscape of anonymity, circulation, isolation, trade, prey, exchange. Like the mobility of pulp, *Chained Girls* offers us a scenario in which the femme becomes the dyke becomes the prostitute becomes the petit bourgeois pimp (a predator "sampling" the goods), savoring the "irony" whereby she profits now from male heterosexual desire for sexual mastery over her abjection. Where else can these encodings function but on the street, broadly taken as the mise-en-scène for category violation? Even in the gang rape I mentioned earlier that is the debutante's "initiation," the reverse shots of the predatory and violent dykes (who, in terms of the explicit "action," essentially leer at the debutante while clawing at her underwear) abandon all pretense toward realism, shot as they are against a backdrop in close-up rather than in the room where the action is said to occur. There is both heightened movement *and* rhetoric in these sequences (orgiastic, if not orgasmic) that cannot, I think, be drowned out either by the assertions of affirmation or the dismissals of denigration condensed in the misnomer "sexuality."

And there, perhaps, I find an answer to my questions earlier. Does "sexuality" somehow cease to be sexuality when processed through the transparency and revelation figured through "coming-out"? Yes: if that figure is conceived as a signifier bound to a plentiful and self-evident signified. But if the signified is permanently deferred, it is also endlessly elaborated, and those elaborations, I have been arguing, hold the key precisely to the *value* of that deferral.

There are other, of course, questions that remain, the generation of which will have to await other publics, other gestures of coming-out, other readings. There are other films to watch, ways of blurring the lines between creative and critical work. In closing *Lesbian Rule*, I would urge you to seek out the work of those makers who continue to challenge us toward new permutations of what *lesbian* might name, if it continues to do so. Among those whose work touches me are Leah Gilliam, Ursula Biemann, Sadie Benning, Barbara Hammer, Su Friedrich, Nisha Ganatra, Pratibha Parmar, Rosa von Praunheim, Isaac Julien, Mike Hoolboom, Marga Gomez, and Stanley Kwan.

Introduction

1 Judith Mayne, *Framed: Lesbians, Feminists, and Media Culture* (Minneapolis: University of Minnesota Press, 2000), xviii.

2 See Marcia Landy and Amy Villarejo, *Queen Christina* (London: BFI Publishing, 1995).

3 Denise Riley, *Am I That Name? Feminism and the Category of Woman in History* (Minneapolis: University of Minnesota Press, 1988); and Judith Butler, *Gender Trouble* (London: Routledge, 1989).

4 See Lisa Duggan, *Sapphic Slashers: Sex, Violence and American Modernity* (Durham, N.C.: Duke University Press, 2000).

5 Eric Clarke examines the various routes through which commodification functions to integrate excluded groups into "publicness" or "publicity," in his *Virtuous Vice: Homoeroticism and the Public Sphere* (Durham, N.C.: Duke University Press, 2000).

6 For a more extended discussion of my sense of Foucault's *History of Sexuality* project and its importance for queer theory, see my "Queer Film and Performance, In Theory," *GLQ* 7, 2 (2001): 313–33.

7 Biddy Martin, "Sexualities Without Genders and Other Queer Utopias," in her collection, *Femininity Played Straight: The Significance of Being Lesbian* (London: Routledge, 1996), 93.

8 Peggy Phelan, "Dying Man with a Movie Camera. *Silverlake Life: The View From Here*," *GLQ: A Journal of Lesbian and Gay Studies* 2, 4 (1995): 390–91.

9 Here it may be useful to distinguish between my project and that of another writer interested in lesbian identities through a Marxist grid: Rosemary Hennessey's *Profit and Pleasure: Sexual Identities in Late Capitalism* (New York: Routledge, 2001). Hennessey is impatient with the extent to which queer theory influenced by poststructuralism deploys a diminished understanding of sociality, and of capitalist exploitation more particularly. As corrective, she wants to develop a critical practice of "making visible," of rendering clearly the relationships between contemporary lesbianisms, their cultural products, and the reality of the social structures "they are shaped by

and help support" (9). The rhetoric of vision sustains her project throughout, in metaphors of lenses, double vision, losing sight, making visible, and the like, and she seems confident that such "making visible" can be done most fruitfully through the sober invocations of class and the insertion of those subjectivities debased by the largely middle-class triumphs of lesbians' visibility, invoking among others "manual workers, sex workers, unemployed and imprisoned" gays and queers (140–41). She contends, in other words, that one has direct access to social contradiction through ideology critique, and that the materiality of desire can become a ground for radical politics.

There are two substantive grounds on which our approaches diverge. First, I insist that the process of "making visible" simultaneously conceals even as it may prove heuristically revelatory. Because the rest of *Lesbian Rule* is dedicated to the task of probing that process, I will not dwell on it here. The second ground of our divergence lies in our respective understandings of cinema. Hennessey follows Masud Zavarzadeh's practice of reading commercial narrative films' "tales," those cognitive maps or ideological syntaxes that are lodged within social codes through which spectators learn to make sense of films: "the dominant tale of a film is its most obvious reading" (145). For Zavarzadeh and by extension for Hennessey, then, the most useful approach to narrative cinema lies not with its formal dimensions but with the tale and its alternatives, those other possible readings or tellings whose contestatory potential the tale attempts to suppress but cannot. As a protocol for reading, then, the cultural critic would produce the most obvious reading of a film's *narrative*, would locate that narrative within a historical and social context through language that is itself presumed to be transparent, and would then disclose the extent to which the film is complicit with dominant ideology, or, to allow for the more complicated assertion, with the various symbolic demands of postmodern patriarchy.

I am sympathetic to the challenge to formalism Zavarzadeh and Hennessey develop. I have sometimes taught with Zavarzadeh's book, *Seeing Films Politically* (Albany: State University of New York Press, 1991). In teaching it, however, I have discovered that the method he proffers for reading "for the tale" yields four unpleasant effects. Following Zavarzadeh, my students demonstrated that (1) the lack of attention to formal elements—such as a film's particular narrative sequences, images, or structured gazes—tends to flatten films into sociological documents that are "really" about their own conditions of emergence; (2) by withholding any description of *how* a critic locates or systematizes elements in a film in order to derive its tale, the critic mystifies his/her own protocols of and investment in reading; (3) by assuming that the description of context is transparent, indeed having the status of facts, the critic becomes not a reader of the film but a weak student of history;

and (4) the invocation of such facts forestalls rather than heightens critical engagement with the ethicopolitical consequences of their invocation.

Lesbian Rule simply complicates these matters by analyzing films in which the tale and the presentation of it would seem to be inseparable: documentary films are "really about" what they are really about. My own readings, however, suggest that as with narrative films, documentaries emerge from specific locations and discourses. They rely on their own codes (formal, stylistic) and conventions (in terms of narration, or how they tell the stories they choose to tell). Rather than assume that the language of context will adequately and exhaustively disclose the films' interests, as Zavarzadeh and Hennessey do, I work backward, assuming that films teach us as much about their interests as they do about the film itself, about the visual field, about our perceptual habits and potential dislocations of them.

10 Diana McLellan, *The Girls: Sappho Goes to Hollywood* (New York: St. Martin's Press, 2000).

11 A departure from popular narrative cinema for me. See Marcia Landy and Amy Villarejo, *Queen Christina* (London: BFI Publishing, 1995); and *Keyframes: Popular Cinema and Cultural Studies,* edited by Matthew Tinkcom and Amy Villarejo (New York: Routledge, 2001).

12 Michael Renov explores these dimensions of documentary cinema in "Toward a Poetics of Documentary," in *Theorizing Documentary,* edited by Michael Renov (New York: Routledge, 1993), 12–36.

13 Such are the stakes of Terry Castle's reading of Garbo in *The Apparitional Lesbian: Female Sexuality and Modern Culture* (New York: Columbia University Press, 1993). Her conviction is tautologically founded on her own conviction.

> That the meaning of *lesbian* is in practice more stable and accessible than some of its would-be deconstructors would allow can be demonstrated, I think, by the following somewhat comic example. In my opening paragraph, I refer to Greta Garbo as a lesbian, despite the fact, as some readers will know, she occasionally had affairs with men as well as women. Why not refer to her, more properly, as a bisexual? Because I think it more *meaningful* to refer to her as a lesbian. And I am not the only person to think so. When asked by an orchestra manager in 1938 about his purported affair with the Swedish actress, the conductor Leopold Stokowski responded, "Jerry, have you ever made love to a lesbian? It's wunnnderful . . . !" (15)

Castle then cites Norman Lebrecht's book, *The Maestro Myth: Great Conductors in Pursuit of Power* (New York: Birch Lane, 1991), in support of Stokowski's sexual relationship with Garbo as well as a competing account offered by Stokowski's biographer to Lebrecht. Despite the fact that Castle's support for her own contention that it is more meaningful to refer to Garbo as a lesbian comes in this anecdote about Garbo's *heterosexual* relationships, there is ample biographical evidence from Garbo's side to contradict this story of a romance between them, as well. See, chronologically, John Bainbridge, *Garbo* (Garden City, N.J.: Doubleday, 1955), 193–202; Norman Zierold, *Garbo* (New York: Stein and Day, 1969), 107–11; and Barry Paris, *Garbo* (New York: Knopf, 1994), 349–55. These three versions of "Garbo" emphasize, as Castle does not, how significant Garbo's time with Stokowski was *not* for evidence of her sexual identity (bisexual or lesbian) but for her flight from the press, her desire to be left alone. *Alone* comes to mark, paradoxically, a number of different relationships to gender, to the family, and to the film industry, relationships that sought to bind Garbo's sexual identity throughout her life. In the crevices of these biographical accounts of Garbo's several months with Stokowski in Ravello, there are therefore a number of riveting details about something we could take seriously in terms of Garbo's life and its significance, even if Castle sees them as comic elsewhere. This is not to correct Castle with the facts, but to suggest that for Garbo, sexual identity is measured less through a choice of descriptors, bisexual or lesbian, for an affair that lasted a few months than through a set of determinations that are familial, historical, industrial, personal. As with the appropriation of Hepburn's name by the Philadelphia bar, Castle asserts Garbo's identity as a lesbian in order to secure her own, at the cost of neglecting a life and image that continues to circulate under the sign of "Garbo." I suppose a poststructuralist, would-be deconstructor would point that out.

14 Roland Barthes, *Camera Lucida: Reflections on Photography*, translated by Richard Howard (New York: Hill and Wang, 1981), 6.

15 Linda Williams, "Mirrors Without Memories: Truth, History, and the New Documentary," in *Film Quarterly, Forty Years: A Selection*, edited by Brian Henderson and Ann Martin with Lee Amazonas (Berkeley and Los Angeles: University of California Press, 1999), 316.

16 Roland Barthes, "The Shock-Photo," in *The Eiffel Tower and Other Mythologies*, translated by Richard Howard (Berkeley and Los Angeles: University of California Press, 1997), 71.

17 Judith Butler, *Gender Trouble: Feminism and the Subversion of Identity* (New York: Routledge, 1990).

18 Gilles Deleuze, *Cinema 1: The Movement-Image* (Minneapolis: University of Minnesota Press, 1986). On melodrama, see *Imitations of Life: A Reader on Film and Television Melodrama*, edited by Marcia Landy (Detroit, Mich.: Wayne State University Press, 1991).

19 See *Lesbians and Psychoanalysis: Revolutions in Theory and Practice*, edited by Judith M. Glassgold and Suzanne Iasenza (New York: Free Press, 1995); and

That Obscure Subject of Desire: Freud's Female Homosexual Revisited, edited by Ronnie C. Lesser and Erica Schoenberg (New York: Routledge, 1999).

20 Hortense Spillers, "'All The Things You Could Be By Now, If Sigmund Freud's Wife Was Your Mother': Psychoanalysis and Race," in *boundary 2* 23, 3 (1995): 87–8.

21 Eve Kosofsky Sedgwick, "How to Bring Your Kids Up Gay," in *Tendencies,* edited by Eve Kosofsky Sedgwick (Durham, N.C.: Duke University Press, 1993). Whether past studies of the prevalence of suicidal thoughts or acts in gay versus straight teens are confirmed by new studies, the knowledge of despair, whatever its numerical or statistical frequency, prompts much queer reflection.

22 Paul Gilroy, *Against Race: Imagining Political Culture Beyond the Color Line* (Cambridge: Harvard University Press/Belknap Press, 2000).

23 I am extremely grateful to one of my anonymous readers for putting the contradiction into these terms.

24 *New York Times,* 23 September 1999.

25 *Bay Area Reporter,* 18 February 1999.

26 Jacques Derrida, *Of Hospitality, Anne Dufourmantelle Invites Jacques Derrida to Respond,* translated by Rachel Bowlby (Stanford, Calif.: Stanford University Press, 2000), 14.

27 Danae Clark, "Commodity Lesbianism," in *The Lesbian, Gay, Bisexual Studies Reader,* edited by Henry Abelove, Michèle Aina Barale, and David M. Halperin (New York: Routledge, 1993), 186–201.

1. Lesbian Rule

1 Gayatri Chakravorty Spivak, "More on Power/Knowledge," in her *Outside in the Teaching Machine* (New York: Routledge, 1993), 28. Judith Butler has similarly commented in enormously useful ways on Foucault's nominalism in *Excitable Speech: A Politics of the Performative* (New York: Routledge, 1997), especially 35–36.

2 Ibid.

3 Gayatri Spivak, "Who Claims Alterity?" in *Remaking History,* edited by Barbara Kruger and Phil Mariani (Seattle, Wash.: Day Press, 1989), 270.

4 Gayatri Spivak, "Feminism and Deconstruction, Again: Negotiations," in *Outside in the Teaching Machine,* 132.

5 Gayatri Spivak, "Scattered Speculations on the Question of Value," in her *In Other Worlds: Essays in Cultural Politics* (New York: Methuen, 1987), 154–175. Hereafter all references to the essay will appear parenthetically and refer to this text.

6 Gayatri Spivak, "Poststructuralism, Marginality, Postcoloniality, and Value,"

in *Literary Theory Today*, edited by Peter Collier and Helga Geyer-Ryan (Ithaca, N.Y.: Cornell University Press, 1990), 227.

7 Miranda Joseph, *Against the Romance of Community* (Minneapolis: University of Minnesota Press, 2002), 32.

8 William Pietz, "The Problem of the Fetish, I," *Res* 9 (1985), 5. Hereafter all citations of this essay will appear parenthetically and refer to this text.

9 Karl Marx, *Capital*, vol. 1, translated by Ben Fowkes (New York: Random House, 1977), 169.

10 William Pietz, "Fetishism and Materialism: The Limits of Theory in Marx," in *Fetishism as Cultural Discourse*, edited by Emily Apter and William Pietz (Ithaca, N.Y.: Cornell University Press, 1993), 121. Hereafter citations to Pietz's essay will appear parenthetically and refer to this text.

11 Pietz approvingly cites Robert Meister's book, *Political Identity: Thinking Through Marx* (Cambridge, Mass.: Basil Blackwell, 1990), as an example of what a Marxian project entails. In Meister's understanding, "Marx thought that the intrinsic problems in formulating the best available theories must also be problems about the role of theory in completing the social reality it depicts" (23). Meister's conception of critical analysis is powerful, but his sexism is more so, since his practice of reading requires damning a feminist "they" who are incapable of serious critique. Pietz does not attend to this dimension of Meister's thought.

12 Jacques Derrida, *Glas*, translated by John P. Leavey Jr. and Richard Rand (Lincoln: University of Nebraska Press, 1986), 210.

13 Lorraine Gamman and Merja Makinen, *Female Fetishism: A New Look* (London: Lawrence and Wishart, 1994).

14 Teresa de Lauretis, *The Practice of Love: Lesbian Sexuality and Perverse Desire* (Bloomington: Indiana University Press, 1994), xiii. De Lauretis chides Jacqueline Rose for obscuring the distinction between lesbians and straight women in her discussions of female desire, a fair charge but hardly one meriting the complete omission of substantive reference to Rose's *Sexuality and the Field of Vision* (London: Verso, 1986), a book that proposed this "negative" reading of Freud almost ten years earlier.

15 Michel Foucault, *The History of Sexuality*, vol. 1, *An Introduction*, translated by Robert Hurley (New York: Random House, 1980), 101.

16 In her footnote on page 217, de Lauretis cites Goux in the context of a dismissal of readings of Lacan that link desire inextricably to the phallus, that emphasize the inability of the woman to desire and therefore see her only as an object of exchange, a commodity. De Lauretis is critical of Goux's concept of excess (*jouissance*); she reads his ultimate characterization of the phallus as "the hyperbolic hypothesis of an absolute mediation with nothing to mediate" (217) as optimistic, throwing master signifiers as chips into a "writing game." De Lauretis insists that the game has high stakes in the terms and

conditions of the mediation, "who does it and for whom." I am interested precisely in those stakes here.

17 Elizabeth Grosz, "Lesbian Fetishism?" in Apter and Pietz, *Fetishism as Cultural Discourse*, 101.

18 Sigmund Freud, "Splitting of the Ego in the Process of Defence," *Standard Edition* 23 (1938): 277, cited in Grosz, "Lesbian Fetishism?" 109.

19 E. L. McCallum has examined in synthetic fashion fetish-discourses as they pertain to feminist and lesbian criticism in *Object Lessons: How to Do Things With Fetishism* (Albany, N.Y.: State University of New York Press, 1999).

2. Droits de Regards/Right of Inspection

1 Jacques Derrida, *Right of Inspection*, translated by David Wills. Photographs by Marie-Françoise Plissart. (New York: The Monacelli Press, 1998). A shorter version appeared in *Art & Text* 32 (1989), with far fewer photographs and a different translation of Derrida's text by Wills. All references in this chapter are to the Monacelli edition.

2 Judith Butler, *Bodies That Matter: On the Discursive Limits of "Sex"* (New York: Routledge, 1993), x.

3 Butler, *Gender Trouble*, xxvii.

4 Adrienne Rich, editor's letter, *Sinister Wisdom* 21 (1982): 120.

5 See, for example, Peter Brunette and David Wills, *Screen/Play: Derrida and Film Theory* (Princeton, N.J.: Princeton University Press, 1989).

6 Jacques Derrida, "What is a 'Relevant' Translation?" *Critical Inquiry* 27 (winter 2001): 178.

7 Gayatri Chakravorty Spivak, *A Critique of Postcolonial Reason: Toward a History of the Vanishing Present* (Cambridge, Mass.: Harvard University Press, 1999), 426. In nominating the periodization between, on the one hand, a phase in which Derrida sought to guard the question of the origin (making indeterminate any answer to questions of origin) and, on the other, a phase begun in the mid-seventies as "affirmative" (Spivak attributes the word to Derrida himself), Spivak explains that Derrida's more recent work takes up his persistent concern with radical alterity as an affirmative call, or appeal to the wholly other.

> The affirmative call or appeal to the wholly other presumably addressed whatever may be prior to the trace of the other-than-origin instituting the origin; most often through the new concept-metaphor of "the experience of the impossible." If radical alterity was earlier conceived of as a methodologically necessary presupposition that is effaced in being named, now the category of presupposition is deliberately blurred and made more vulnerable as "experience."

8 Even at the most basic level of citation, *Right of Inspection* confounds translation. Derrida's commentary is placed after 103 pages of photographs (101 in the French edition), but there are no page numbers throughout the book. David Wills's translation is placed alongside photographs of the original French pages, themselves numbered in Roman, but the translations do not necessarily correspond precisely to the French pagination. I have opted, with awareness of the provisional and pragmatic nature of the gesture, to indicate the "French" page number for citations. Thus, the "linguistic frontier" appears on xxvii.

9 Many of us have been steeped in "like a language" riddles through Lacan's observation that the unconscious is structured like a language, or in the psychoanalytically driven work on cinema that tends to make reference to cinematic language. Derrida's conjuration or conjugation of an elusive photogrammar tests the limits of something like the language of photography, as we might talk about the language of psychoanalysis, insofar as he *uses* that language in such a way that suspends a decision about whether it is concept or metaphor. He also confounds the distinction between the imaginary and symbolic, since his topographical sense of the photographic refuses the priority of primary process(es) or scene(s), yet his interest, along with Freud and Lacan's, involves the *function* of the imaginary, the *place* of fantasy. See J. Laplace and J. B. Pontalis, *The Language of Psychoanalysis,* translated by Donald Nicholson-Smith (New York: Norton, 1973); Jacques Lacan, *The Four Fundamental Concepts of Psycho-Analysis,* edited by Jacques-Alain Miller, translated by Alan Sheridan (New York: Norton, 1978), 20.

10 "Tampering with" comes from a citation from Mallarmé (referred to but not cited in *Right of Inspection*), "verse had been tampered with" (*on a touché au vers*), that Derrida tampers with in order to talk about tampering with sexual difference (x, xi).

11 Wills, "Translator's Preface," in *Right of Inspection,* 105.

12 Derrida, *Right of Inspection,* ii.

13 Jacques Lacan, "The Symbolic Order," in *The Seminar of Jacques Lacan, Book I, Freud's Papers on Technique, 1953–1954,* edited by Jacque-Alain Miller, translated with notes by John Forrester (New York: Norton, 1988), 220.

14 Lacan, "What Is a Picture?" in *Four Fundamental Concepts,* 106.

15 Derrida, *Right of Inspection,* xxiii.

16 Ibid., xi.

17 Ibid., xxiv.

18 Ibid., xxv.

19 Lacan, "The Symbolic Order," 221.

20 Derrida, *Right of Inspection,* xxxiii.

21 Ibid., xxxv.

22 Ibid., xxxvi. These are the essay's last or final words.

23 See ibid., x.

24 Rodger Streitmatter, *Unspeakable: The Rise of the Gay and Lesbian Press in America* (Boston: Faber and Faber, 1995).

3. Archiving the Diaspora: A Lesbian Impression

1 The phrase *point of view,* though commonplace in the study of cinema, is particularly loaded in relation to Ottinger, who has used it to describe the project of her three-part documentary, *China–die Kunste–der Alltag:* "visual discourse . . . about exoticism as a question of point of view," cited in Therese Grisham, "An Interview with Ulrike Ottinger," *Wide Angle* 14, 2 (April 1992): 32. Recent discussions of Ottinger's ethnographic documentaries focus, as I suggest, on the dynamics of an exoticist point of view and its value for inquiry into globality. For a comprehensive bibliography of Ottinger criticism through 1992, including the largely negative commentary in the German journal *frauen und film,* see Katie Trumpener's excellent article, *"Johanna d'Arc of Mongolia* in the Mirror of *Dorian Gray:* Ethnographic Recordings and the Aesthetics of the Market in the Recent Films of Ulrike Ottinger," *New German Critique: An Interdisciplinary Journal of German Studies* 60 (fall 1993): n.3. More recently, the following texts have undertaken to address Ottinger's work: Kristen Whissel, "Racialized Spectacle, Exchange Relations, and the Western in *Johanna d'Arc of Mongolia,*" *Screen* 37, 1 (spring 1996): 41–67; Kay Armitage, "Ethnography and Its Discontents: Ulrike Ottinger's *Taiga,*" *Arachne: An Interdisciplinary Journal of the Humanities* 3, 2 (1996): 31–47; Temby Caprio, "Ulrike Ottinger's *Ticket of No Return:* Drinking, the Masquerade and Subverting Gender Norms," *Arachne: An Interdisciplinary Journal of the Humanities* 3, 2 (1996): 97–115; Shanta Rao, "Ethno-Documentary Discourse and Cultural Otherness in Ulrike Ottinger's *Johanna d'Arc of Mongolia,*" in *Other Germanies: Questioning Identity in Women's Literature and Art,* edited by Karen Jankowsky and Carla Love (Albany: State University of New York Press, 1997), 147–64; Nora Alter, "Ottinger's Benjamin: *Countdown's* Alternative Take on Unification," *Germanic Review* 73, 1 (winter 1998): 50–69; Nora Alter, "Triangulating Performances: Looking After Genre, After Feature," in *Triangulated Visions: Women in Recent German Cinema,* edited by Ingeborg Majer O'Sickey and Ingeborg von Zadow (Albany: State University of New York Press, 1998), 11–27; Julia Knight, "Observing Rituals: Ulrike Ottinger's *Johanna d'Arc of Mongolia,*" in the same volume, 103–15; Kaja Silverman, "Narcissism: The Impossible Love," in the same volume, 139–52; and Alice A. Kuzniar, *The Queer German Cinema* (Stanford, Calif.: Stanford University Press, 2000), 139–56.

2 Miriam Hansen, "Visual Pleasure, Fetishism and the Problem of Feminine/ Feminist Discourse: Ulrike Ottinger's *Ticket of No Return*," *New German Critique* 31 (winter 1984): 108.

3 As Sabine Hake notes, in the version of her essay in *Gender and German Cinema*, vol. 1, *Feminist Interventions*, edited by Sandra Frieden, Richard W. McCormick, Vibeke R. Petersen, and Laura Melissa Vogelsang (Providence: Berg Publishers, 1993), 182.

4 Taken up more recently by Kaja Silverman in "Narcissism: The Impossible Love." Mayne's term is "marginality of lesbianism" (*The Woman at the Keyhole: Feminism and Women's Cinema*, 154).

5 Grisham, "Interview," 31.

6 A preliminary insufficiency involves the listing of those who were branded as social outsiders in Nazi Germany: Jews, Communists, "Gypsies," foreign workers, prostitutes, criminals, homosexuals, the homeless, Seventh Day Adventists, the unemployed, and the chronically ill. When I began to research this chapter, I reacted especially palpably to the often-used triadic shorthand of "Jews, Gypsies, and homosexuals" to denote the combination of anti-Semitism, eugenic programs, and arbitrary persecution that characterized the Third Reich. This triad and the even briefer shorthand "Jews" tend to eclipse the specificity of persecution each group and each individual faced and thereby obscure even further the tasks of critical understanding. What undergirded my discomfort was the stronger sense that "homosexuals" lay claim constantly to this history under the sign of the pink triangle (arguably now in the process of being replaced by the mundane rainbow) but without undertaking the analysis of this history in relation to identity politics. This chapter became an attempt, therefore, to work at an alignment between this revised list: German, Jewish, lesbian, feminist, Shanghai.

7 Marcia Landy, *The Cinematic Uses of the Past* (Minneapolis: University of Minnesota Press, 1996).

8 See www.nysca.org.

9 Patricia R. Zimmermann, *States of Emergency: Documentaries, Wars, Democracies* (Minneapolis: University of Minnesota Press, 1999), xv.

10 The National Association of Media Arts Centers (NAMAC) recently sponsored a digital "salon" devoted precisely to this recalibration, stressing the challenges posed to existing organs of distribution by digital media. See www.namac.org.

11 Patricia White et al., "Queer Publicity: A Dossier on Lesbian and Gay Film Festivals," *GLQ* 5, 1 (1999): 73–78.

12 Vanessa Domico, marketing director, Women Make Movies, interview 5 March 2001. Domico estimates that more than 80 percent of Women Make Movies's total gross income derives from sales and rentals.

13 This argument is implicit in B. Ruby Rich's coining of the term "new queer

cinema," a phrase that deliberately invokes the New American Cinema of the 1970s. The films of Shirley Clarke, Richard Leacock, and Jonas Mekas, to name but three, combined in astonishing and surprising ways in terms of genre and form, yet shared enough common ground to inaugurate a short-lived "movement." Neither did the new queer films and videos Rich encountered in 1992 "share a single aesthetic vocabulary or strategy or concern" (163), and Rich's attribution of a common style, "Homo Pomo," to these films is no more audacious than any number of critical gestures of the decade finding "postmodernism" or "performativity" wherever they looked. Pratibha Parmar's rejoinder to Rich nonetheless raises crucial questions about the effects of attributing to a wildly differentiated body of work a single aesthetic. Particularly regarding access for lesbians and people of color to festival program slots, the present chapter is in solidarity with Parmar's brief comments, as well as with Rich's efforts toward such access. And as a footnote to a footnote, it is not a coincidence that the New York State Council on the Arts provided Ruby Rich with her training in independent film. (B. Ruby Rich, "Homo Pomo: The New Queer Cinema," in *Women and Film: A Sight and Sound Reader,* edited by Pam Cook and Philip Dodd [Philadelphia, Pa.: Temple University Press, 1993], 164–74; and Pratibha Parmar, "Queer Questions: A Response to B. Ruby Rich," in the same volume, 174–75).

14 See Douglas Gomery, *Shared Pleasures: A History of Movie Presentation in the United States* (Madison: University of Wisconsin Press, 1992), 93–102, 193–195.

15 Although a reader of a previous draft of this chapter thought my attention to the film's length extraneous, it remains important to stress the frequency with which the length of Ottinger's films is mentioned in the critical literature and by audiences. I take it as a real challenge to write on a film of this length and density.

16 I would for this reason take issue with Kuzniar's recent efforts to make the term *queer* manage the tensions others have found powerful in Ottinger's work, particularly in *Dorian Gray im Spiegel der Boulevardpresse/Dorian Gray in the Mirror of the Yellow Press* (1984).

17 Roy Grundmann and Judith Schulevitz, "Minorities and the Majority: An Interview with Ulrike Ottinger," *Cineaste* 18, 3 (1991): 16. The phrase is obviously a loaded one to which I shall return.

18 See Grisham, "Interview," 26. Grundmann and Schulevitz's interview is cited (incorrectly in the endnotes) by Alter in her otherwise careful analysis of the significance of Walter Benjamin's writings for Ottinger's film *Countdown* ("Ottinger's Benjamin"). I make reference to Alter's analysis later in my brief mention of that film. Alter has also commented on Ottinger's remarks about nomadism in Grisham's interview in her contribution to the volume *Triangulated Visions.* In the latter essay, Alter finesses questions

about Ottinger's point of view and ethical stance through the language of transcendence and hybridization; ibid.

19 Promotional material on *Exile Shanghai* courtesy of Atara Releasing.

20 I borrow the term from Jacques Derrida, "Archive Fever: A Freudian Impression," *Diacritics* 25, 2 (summer 1995): 52; later *Archive Fever: A Freudian Impression*, translated by Eric Prenowitz (Chicago: University of Chicago Press, 1995). All further citations will refer to the original essay published in *Diacritics*.

21 Sir Victor Sassoon reputedly was turned away by one of Shanghai's fanciest nightclubs, as well, but revenged that outrage "by building Shanghai's first air-conditioned nightclub on Bubbling Well Road, located close to not only the nightclub that had rejected him but the ultra-snobbish British Country Club, which had long refused admittance to Jews. The nightclub was called Ciro's, but wags dubbed it 'Sassoon's sing-song house'" (Stella Dong, *Shanghai, 1842–1949: The Rise and Fall of a Decadent City* [New York: HarperCollins, 2000], 222).

22 The authoritative history remains David Kranzler's *Japanese, Nazis, and Jews: The Jewish Refugee Community of Shanghai, 1938–1945* (Hoboken, N.J.: KTAV Publishing, 1988). Others have written more anecdotal histories, including the more recent *Escape to Shanghai: A Jewish Community in China* by James R. Ross (New York: Free Press, 1994) and Dong's "biography of Shanghai," *Shanghai, 1842–1949: The Rise and Fall of a Decadent City*. Invaluable to the discussion of aid, particularly the role of the American Joint Distribution Committee, are the documents by its wartime Shanghai administrator, Laura Margolis, and her assistant, Manuel Siegel, housed in the archives of the AJDC in New York. Also useful are the many shorter articles, memoirs, clippings, and reports amassed by survivors and others who were associated with the Shanghai community, many of which are cited in Kranzler and Ross. The refugee memoirs are not in wide distribution, with the exception of Ernest G. Heppner, *Shanghai Refuge: A Memoir of the World War II Jewish Ghetto* (Lincoln: University of Nebraska Press, 1995). He cites Rena Krasno's *Strangers Always* (Berkeley, Calif.: Pacific View Press, 1992), which is out of print and much more difficult to find.

23 "Half Day Tour, 'The Hongkou Ghetto,' with Mrs. Flora Amiel," www. chinajewish.org/flora.html.

24 Carol Giacomo (Reuters), "Hillary Visits Synagogue," *ABC News World*, 1 July 1999.

25 Jacques Lacan, "The Freudian Thing," *Écrits: A Selection*, translated by Alan Sheridan (New York: Norton, 1977), 118.

26 Yosef Hayim Yerushalmi, *Freud's Moses: Judaism Terminable and Interminable* (New Haven, Conn.: Yale University Press, 1991), xvii.

27 The resonance of *ash* makes imperative the connection to Jacques Derrida,

Cinders, translated and edited by Ned Lukacher (Lincoln: University of Nebraska Press, 1991).

28 The term *Heime* was used by the Shanghai refugees to describe the refugee camps established by the relief organizations from the beginning of 1938. The reference, as Kranzler suggests, was most frequently an ironic one, as the refugees' experience of the camps was "to become the antithesis of a 'home'" (*Japanese, Nazis, and Jews,* 92).

29 Ross, *Escape to Shanghai,* 125. Note: Members of the Mir and other yeshivas have since argued that not only were the German and Austrian Jews less worthy of rescue, but also that their assimilation caused the Holocaust by bringing forth the wrath of God. See Yecheskel Leitner, *Operation Torah Rescue: The Escape of the Mirrer Yeshiva from War-Torn Poland to Shanghai, China* (Jerusalem and New York: Feldheim, 1987).

30 Primo Levi, *Survival in Auschwitz: The Nazi Assault on Humanity* (New York: Collier Books, 1961), 36; Saul Friedlander, *Memory, History and the Extermination of the Jews of Europe* (Bloomington: Indiana University Press, 1993). Note: there is no umlaut in Friedlander's name in the publication data for this book, but one is used in the subsequent reference.

31 Saul Friedländer, *Nazi Germany and the Jews,* vol. 1, *The Years of Persecution* (New York: HarperCollins, 1997), 5.

32 Giorgio Agamben, *Remnants of Auschwitz: The Witness and the Archive,* translated by Daniel Heller-Roazen (New York: Zone Books, 1999), 13. Elsewhere Agamben groups the concentration camp, "a zone of indifference between public and private as well as the hidden matrix of the political space in which we live," with a set of other phenomena that are not usually considered political: the natural life of human beings, the state of exception, the refugee, language, and the "sphere of gesture or pure means," to which I turn below (Giorgio Agamben, *Means Without End: Notes on Politics,* translated by Vincenzo Binetti and Cesare Casarino [Minneapolis: University of Minnesota Press, 2000]), ix–x).

33 *After* is not, therefore, restricted to a linear chronological meaning. A significant element of Agamben's recent arguments, in fact, involves the attempt to risk thought and practices anti-teleologically, without "ends." As I understand his argument, "remnant" is but one name for an "irreducible disjunction" (*Remnants,* 159), an aporia of testimony and of messianic time (163) within which subjectivity resides and without which there is no possibility of witness. Dominick LaCapra stresses a similar point regarding the title of his book, *History and Memory After Auschwitz* (Ithaca, N.Y.: Cornell University Press, 1998), 6.

34 Derrida, "Archive Fever," 50.

35 Derrida, *Right of Inspection,* vii.

36 See Nichols, "The Voice of Documentary."

37 Grundmann and Shulevitz, "Interview," 40.

38 Ross, *Escape to Shanghai*, 209.

39 Alter, "Ottinger's Benjamin," 53.

40 Ottinger, too, would appear to harbor a certain will to untranslatability, as Will remarked of Derrida. Her title *Johanna d'arc of Mongolia*, insofar as it incorporates at least three languages, is but a literal example.

4. Absolut Queer: Cuba and Its Spectators

1   In *Improper Conduct*, the writer Guillermo Cabrera Infante tells an apocryphal story linking post-revolution Cuba to Shanghai: "[Cuban leaders] were all obsessed with homosexuality when visiting Communist bloc countries. Ramiro Valdes, Minister of the Interior, went to China and asked to meet the Mayor of Shanghai. Why did Valdes want to meet him? Shanghai had always had a large homosexual population, dating back to Imperial China. It had very free morals, it was the capital of Westernized China, as opposed to Peking, the cloistered capital. So he met the Mayor of Shanghai and asked how they had solved their homosexual problem. The mayor replied through an interpreter, 'There are no homosexuals here.' 'You no longer have a homosexual problem here?' 'No, we took advantage of a traditional holiday where homosexuals gathered in a park in Shanghai on the banks of a river. Party officials went there carrying clubs to eliminate the problem once and for all.' They clubbed them and threw them in the water. The bodies were carried downstream as a grim warning! It was the end of homosexuality in Shanghai." The story provides a glimpse of the difficulty in dealing with *Improper Conduct*: one is tempted to argue with the story itself (the Whangpu River flows into the harbor, and Ramiro Valdes was demoted in 1985) rather than understanding how it functions rhetorically to produce the phantasm of such a holiday alongside the disdain for such "solutions."

2   For an appreciative overview of the film, see Paul Julian Smith, "Blood of a Poet," *Sight and Sound* (June 2001): 30–31.

3   B. Ruby Rich, "Collision, Catastrophe, Celebration: The Relationship between Gay and Lesbian Film Festivals and Their Publics," in Patricia White et al., "Queer Publicity," 84.

4   Eileen R. Meehan, "Why We Don't Count: The Commodity Audience," in *Logics of Television*, edited by Patricia Mellencamp (Bloomington: Indiana University Press, 1990), 117–37.

5   Nestor Almendros and Orlando Jimenez-Leal, "Improper Conduct," *American Film* 9, 10 (September 1984): 18.

6   Ibid.

7   Ibid., 71.

8   There are few book-length studies on the issue. An early text is Allen Young,

Gays Under the Cuban Revolution (San Francisco: Grey Fox Press, 1981). More recent is Ian Lumsden, *Machos, Maricones and Gays: Cuba and Homosexuality* (Philadelphia, Pa.: Temple University Press, 1996).

9 Although I wish I had coined the term, I did not. It is taken from the front page of the *New York Times Magazine* (25 March 2001), wherein Philip Weiss's article on the director of *Before Night Falls* appears, "Julian Schnabel's Lust for Life." The term appears beneath the cover photo of Schnabel and would therefore seem to describe him.

10 Judith Mayne, *Framed: Lesbians, Feminists, and Media Culture* (Minneapolis: University of Minnesota Press, 2000), 59.

11 Almendros and Leal, "Improper Conduct," 18.

12 Lumsden cites Young's conclusion that the UMAP camps laid emphasis primarily on hard labor (Young, *Gays Under the Cuban Revolution,* 26). Almendros and Leal explicitly expand the UMAP to encompass subsequent names for repression, so as to extend the force of the Nazi comparisons: "Our narration establishes that although UMAP camps were disbanded in 1969 after four years of existence (not just two years, as Ms. Rich asserts) because of protests from outside and inside Cuba (by people like Franqui, who had problems of his own later on), new camps under different names were soon created; this occurred after the Congress of Education and Culture of 1971" (Almendros and Leal, "Improper Conduct," 70).

13 The phrase was coined by Raymond Williams.

14 www.ins.usdoj.gov/graphics/services/asylum/ric/documentation/cub99001.htm.

15 Ibid.

16 By comparison, the rate of infection in Los Angeles County, with a population slightly smaller than that of Cuba, is roughly ten times as high. See Jon Hillson, "The Sexual Politics of Reinaldo Arenas: Fact, Fiction and the Real Record of the Cuban Revolution," (www.SeeingRed.com, 2001).

17 Ibid., 5.

18 See Lauren Berlant and Michael Warner, "Sex in Public," *Critical Inquiry* 24 (1998): 558–64.

19 The list of accoutrements echoes an oral history description of queens preparing for carnival before the revolution: "They prepared carefully for these days. They bought wigs, high-heeled shoes, evening bags, fans, earrings, necklaces and the costumes they made—many of them—were lovely."(*Reyita: The Life of a Black Cuban Woman in the Twentieth Century,* by María de los Reyes Castilla Bueno, as told to her daughter Daisy Ruiera Castillo [Durham, N.C.: Duke University Press, 2000], 75.)

20 Personal conversation with Margaret Gilpin, 1997.

21 Personal conversation with Margaret Gilpin, 1997.

22 Personal conversation with Margaret Gilpin, 1997.

23 *Propaganda:* 1. (More fully, *Congregation* or *College of the Propaganda*). A committee of cardinals of the Roman Catholic Church having the care and oversight of foreign missions, founded in 1622 by Pope Gregory XV (*OED*).

5. Forbidden Love: Pulp as Lesbian History

This chapter originally appeared in *Out Takes: Essays on Queer Theory and Film*, edited by Ellis Hanson (Durham, N.C.: Duke University Press, 1999), and it is reprinted here with minor changes owing to recent work on lesbian pulps and a virtual conversation with Ann Bannon, who generously read and commented on the first version.

1 See Christopher Nealon, "Invert-History: The Ambivalence of Lesbian Pulp Fiction," *New Literary History* 31, 4 (autumn 2000): 745–64.

2 Susan Stewart's brief and brilliant discussion of the book collection in *On Longing: Narratives of the Miniature, the Gigantic, the Souvenir, the Collection* (Durham, N.C.: Duke University Press, 1983), touches on this transformation: "In the realm of market competition," Stewart writes, "speed is the auxiliary to consumption, and the rapid production and consumption of books, their capacity for obsolescence in material form, necessarily seems to transform their content" (33). Such transformation can obviously be hastened: in the introduction to a 1993 exhibit of the pulps at the Lesbian Herstory Archives, we learn that: "Although tame by today's standards of lesbian literature and erotica, these volumes were so threatening that women hid them, burnt them and threw them out" (cited in Nealon, "Invert-History," 748).

3 Antonio Gramsci, *Selections from the Prison Notebooks*, edited by Quintin Hoare and Geoffrey Nowell-Smith (New York: International Publishers, 1971), 324.

4 Stuart Hall, "Gramsci and Us," in his *The Hard Road to Renewal: Thatcherism and the Crisis of the Left* (London: Verso, 1988), 161.

5 See Marcia Landy, *Film, Politics and Gramsci* (Minneapolis: University of Minnesota Press, 1994).

6 Gramsci, *Selections*, 295.

7 Eve Kosofsky Sedgwick and Adam Frank, in a long footnote to their introductory essay to the volume *Shame and Its Sisters*, edited by Eve Kosofsky Sedgwick and Adam Frank (Durham, N.C.: Duke University Press, 1995), attribute the binary question, "is [a given cultural manifestation or text] subversive or hegemonic?" to certain misreadings of Foucault. While I share their impatience with the mantra-status of this question in reductive cultural study, it seems important to note how Gramsci's affiliation with the immensely tangled but nonetheless significant idea of hegemony becomes effaced through contemporary intellectual history. It is not so much to resuscitate Gramsci as to bring the many strands with which hegemony is im-

bricated in Gramsci's work (including the distinction between the state and civil society, the function of the intellectual, the mobile nature of cultural forms) to bear on questions of cultural analysis that is at stake in my reading of these texts, even while that reading is also informed by attention to Foucault's work. Elsewhere in this chapter my own understanding of the affect shame is indebted to Sedgwick and Frank's comments and to Sedgwick's work more generally. Finally, Carol Stabile has similarly attributed to Gramsci faults that more properly lie with his readers, such as John Fiske, in her article "Resistance, Recuperation, and Reflexivity: The Limits of a Paradigm," *Critical Studies in Mass Communication* 12 (1995): 403–22.

8 Antonio Gramsci, *Selections from the Cultural Writings*, edited by David Forgacs and Geoffrey Nowell-Smith, translated by William Boelhower (Cambridge: Harvard University Press, 1985), 350.

9 Jaye Zimet's book of lesbian pulp cover art, *Strange Sisters: The Art of Lesbian Pulp Fiction, 1949–1969*, with a foreword by Ann Bannon (New York: Viking, 1999), undoubtedly boosted interest in lesbian pulps, enough to inspire spin-offs such as refrigerator magnets and postcards, and perhaps the lesbian pulp address book published by Chronicle Books and attributed to Susan Stryker (San Francisco: 2000). My thanks to Bruce Levitt for the gift of the latter.

10 Janice Radway, *Reading the Romance: Women, Patriarchy and Popular Literature* (Chapel Hill: University of North Carolina Press, 1984), 27. My debts to Radway's study are inestimable.

11 Cited in Thomas L. Bonn, *Under Cover: An Illustrated History of American Mass Market Paperbacks* (New York: Penguin, 1982), 36–40. Bonn's history is as fine as Geoffrey O'Brien's *Hardboiled America: The Lurid Years of Paperbacks* (New York: Van Nostrand Reinhold, 1981) and Lee Server's *Over My Dead Body, The Sensational Age of the American Paperback: 1945–1955* (San Francisco: Chronicle Books, 1994).

12 The size of mass-market paperbacks remains to this day precisely the same, and varied only during the Second World War, when the books were reoriented (wider than they were high) and slightly enlarged, in order to fit military uniform (fatigue) pockets.

13 Karl Marx, *Capital, A Critique of Political Economy*, vol. 2, translated by David Fernback (New York: Penguin, 1978), 326–33.

14 Ibid., 303.

15 O'Brien, *Hardboiled America*, 47.

16 Ann Bannon, personal correspondence, 2000.

17 See Karal Ann Marling, *As Seen on TV: The Visual Culture of Everyday Life in the 1950s* (Cambridge: Harvard University Press, 1994), especially p. 40. Marling's dizzying and extremely fun discussion of Mamie Eisenhower and popular fashion emphasizes the significance of color as "a symbol of the

shock of the new," and color palettes as sites for displacing the rigidity of sexual coding of pinks and blues in an emergent generational divide and battle during the decade.

18 O'Brien, *Hardboiled America*, 38.

19 Cited in Jeannette Walls, *Dish: The Inside Story on the World of Gossip* (New York: Avon Books, 2000), 11.

20 A history of the very thing that gives pulp its name, paper, would yield no doubt significant ties to questions of colonialism. I leave that task aside here.

21 House, *Report of the Select Committee on Current Pornographic Materials*, 82nd Congress, 31 December 1952 (Washington, D.C.: Government Printing Office, 1952), 12. Hereafter, all citations to the report will appear parenthetically and refer to this text.

22 *United States v. Paramount Pictures, Inc.*, 334 U.S. 131 (1948), 22.

23 *United States v.* Ulysses, cited in Gathings report.

24 The pseudonym "Vin Packer" provides a rich example through which to probe the relations among genre, intent, and a tremulous understanding of identity. Packer, the author of a significant number of lesbian pulps, was one of Marijane Meaker's pseudonyms. "Most of my work was written under the pseudonym Vin Packer, and many were paperback originals. Packer became a writer of suspense eventually, solely because I'd heard that the *New York Times*' mystery columnist, Anthony Boucher, would review paperbacks." Meaker's more famous alter ego, M. E. Kerr (herself primarily a writer of adolescent fiction), authored these lines on Packer and this description of her initial adventures in naming in her richly titled book, *Me Me Me Me Me: Not a Novel by M. E. Kerr* (New York: Harper and Row, 1983):

> Once I received a letter from a kid doing a paper on M. E. Kerr. "Why did you decide to name your pen?" he asked me . . . I think I was drawn to the idea that I could create this separate entity for myself, and write about people I knew without them ever knowing who was telling their secrets. Since nearly all of my pseudonyms were male, I must have also felt that a female wouldn't be taken seriously.

Kerr's book is thus a memoir by a fictional novelist recounting to her adolescent readership the resemblances between her "own" life and the lives of her characters, many of them based on Meaker's own experiences. I should add that I myself seem to have been drawn into a vortex of Meaker's pseudonymous lives: M. E. Kerr was one of my favorite novelists in adolescence (I'm *just* the right age for her books); I now live a stone's throw from her hometown in upstate New York (which provides the mise-en-scène for many of her novels); for this project I discovered and devoured the novels of Vin Packer; and I am a bit of *both* main characters in the book she calls her favorite, *Shockproof Sidney Skate*.

25 *United States v.* Ulysses, cited in Gathings Report, 8.

26 There is nothing in the Gathings Committee Report of the specificity regarding readers or their textual interests or uses gracing Tania Modleski's or
Janice Radway's accounts of popular literature and its readers, though Modleski seizes on the metaphor of the cover in her introduction to the by-now
canonical *Loving with a Vengeance: Mass-Produced Fantasies for Women* (New
York: Methuen, 1984).

> It is an important part of my project to show that the so-called masoch-
> ism which pervades these texts [Harlequin romances, gothic novels, and
> soap operas] is a "cover" for anxieties, desires and wishes which if openly
> expressed would challenge the psychological and social order of things.
> For that very reason, of course, they must be kept hidden; the texts, after
> arousing them, must, in Jameson's formula, work to neutralize them. (30)

Modleski, following Jameson, seems here to invoke only the metaphor and
not its material referent, and it is for this reason, as it is but less so for Radway, that psychological and psychoanalytic modes of the analysis of these
novels as texts and as function become enticing. Troubling these modes is
the instability we have charted at both ends of the subject-object relation of
the categories which underpin them: namely, the categories of normative
and pathologized sexual practices and gender.

27 A. Martin Zweiback, "Me, Natalie" (New York: Columbia Broadcasting System, 1969).

28 Angela Weir and Elizabeth Wilson, "The Greyhound Bus Station in the Evo-
lution of Lesbian Popular Culture," in *New Lesbian Criticism: Literary and
Cultural Readings*, edited by Sally Munt (New York: Columbia University
Press, 1992), 97.

29 Rich, "Homo Pomo," 164–73; Parmar, "Queer Questions," 174–75.

30 John D'Emilio and Estelle Freedman, *Intimate Matters: A History of Sexuality
in America* (New York: Harper and Row, 1988), 288.

31 Ibid. In an early article on the gay and lesbian subculture of the Harlem
Renaissance, Eric Garber very briefly chronicles the blues's expression of
homosexuality, following a mimetic model whereby "the blues reflected a
culture that accepted sexuality, including homosexual behavior and identities, as a natural part of life" (Garber, "A Spectacle in Color: The Lesbian
and Gay Subculture of Jazz Age Harlem," in *Hidden from History: Reclaiming
the Gay and Lesbian Past*, edited by Martin Duberman, Martha Vicinus, and
George Chauncey Jr. [New York: Meridian/Penguin, 1990], 320). In striking
similarity to the parallel construction of *Forbidden Love* (interviews interwoven with a dramatized story of hidden history), Inge Blackman's film *B.D.
Women* (1994) also explores the blues in relation to black lesbian history. The
tape is distributed by Women Make Movies.

32 Carroll Smith-Rosenberg, "Discourses of Sexuality and Subjectivity: The New Woman, 1870–1936," and Esther Newton, "The Mythic Mannish Lesbian: Radclyffe Hall and the New Woman," both in Duberman, Vicinus, and Chauncey Jr., *Hidden From History*. See also Esther Newton, *Margaret Mead Made Me Gay* (Durham, N.C.: Duke University Press, 2000).

33 D'Emilio and Freedman, *Intimate Matters*, 289.

34 Ibid.

35 Sherrie A. Inness, *The Lesbian Menace: Ideology, Identity, and the Representation of Lesbian Life* (Amherst: University of Massachusetts Press, 1997).

36 D'Emilio and Freedman, *Intimate Matters*, photograph #57.

37 John D'Emilio, *Sexual Politics, Sexual Communities: The Making of a Homosexual Minority in the United States, 1940–1970* (Chicago: University of Chicago Press, 1983), 135.

38 Ibid., 137.

39 Barbara Grier [Gene Damon], *Lesbiana: Book Reviews from* The Ladder (Tallahassee, Fla.: Naiad Press, 1975), 8. Grier is the founder and editor-in-chief of Naiad Press, which has republished a number of "golden oldie" lesbian pulps, including *Chris* (though with a strikingly banal floral cover) and Ann Bannon's *Beebo* series. Grier has almost single-handedly kept this literature alive and is the major publisher of lesbian literature in the United States. As the book reviewer (publisher, founder) of the *Ladder,* she also had an enormous impact on the reception of the books published during "the golden age of the lesbian paperback" (as noted on the copyright of the republished *Chris* by Naiad in 1988). Her assessments of sympathy levels in the *Ladder,* however, do not always correspond to lesbian popular opinion and are interesting precisely for that reason. Of the play, *The Killing of Sister George,* she wrote: "Reactions are very mixed to the play; some see it as very unsympathetic. I find it very warm, human and poignant and recommend it highly to everyone" (11). Lillian Faderman, whose award-winning social history of lesbianism was deemed popular enough to be converted from the Columbia University Press hardcover edition to a Penguin paperback, adjudicates similarly between positive and negative visions of lesbians in pulp novels in a brief discussion in *Odd Girls and Twilight Lovers: A History of Lesbian Life in Twentieth-Century America* (New York: Penguin, 1992), especially pages 146–48.

40 The phrase is Marcia Landy's, from her book *The Cinematic Uses of the Past* (Minneapolis: University of Minnesota Press, 1996).

41 Linda Dittmar, "Of Hags and Crones: Reclaiming Lesbian Desire for the Trouble Zone of Aging," in *Between the Sheets, In the Streets: Queer, Lesbian, Gay Documentary,* edited by Chris Holmlund and Cynthia Fuchs (Minneapolis: University of Minnesota Press, 1997), 85.

42 Weir and Wilson, "Greyhound Bus Station," 95.

43 Eve Kosofsky Sedgwick, "Queer Performativity: Henry James' *Art of the Novel*," *GLQ* 1 (1993): 1–16; 14.

44 The origins of this term, a variant of skid road, reveal a pulp connection. *Skid road:* "A track made of logs laid transversely about five feet apart that is used to haul logs to a loading platform or to a mill" (*American Heritage Dictionary*, 2d coll. ed.). The "squalid district inhabited by derelicts and vagrants" presumably surrounded such a road.

45 Kelly Hankin, "The Girls in the Back Room" (Ph.D. diss., University of Rochester, 1999).

46 Or perhaps Ellen DeGeneres is or wants to be: Ellen invoked Parks, in much the same spirit as does Keeley Moll, in her interview with Diana Sawyer on *20/20*, broadcast 25 April 1997. Judith Butler offers Parks as an example of performative force, a reiteration of conventional formulae in nonconventional ways, in *Excitable Speech: A Politics of the Performative* (New York: Routledge, 1997), 147.

47 I would advance a similar argument concerning the popularity of mystery or detective novels among lesbians (many of which feature female detectives, and some of which feature lesbian detectives, such as those penned by former pulp author Katharine V. Forrest): that as a middle-class lesbian presence within a certain public sphere takes hold, we translate the unease associated with the status quo (sometimes coded as privilege) into imagined encounters with the streets and with the law. The terrain of such an encounter is expanding to include lesbian detective films, such as the low-budget pulp video, *Lesbionage*, which takes the blackmail of an African American lesbian congresswoman (played by Jewel Gomez) as its premise. Thirty-five years measure the distance between *Lesbionage* and its precursor film about homosexuality and blackmail, *Victim* (Basil Dearden, 1961). Pulp might thus be understood as taking the pulse of the movement of lesbian publicity, or publicness, and its avenues of consumption.

Conclusion

1 The modifier *home* can be put to the same redefinition as is necessary for *video*, since viewing of such works can happen in an endless variety of actual places. See Anna McCarthy, *Ambient Television* (Durham, N.C.: Duke University Press, 2001).

2 Charles Shiro Tashiro, "Videophilia: What Happens When You Wait for It on Video," in *Film Quarterly, Forty Years: A Selection*, edited by Brian Henderson and Ann Martin (Berkeley and Los Angeles: University of California Press, 1999), 358.

3 Anne Friedberg, *Window Shopping: Cinema and the Postmodern* (Berkeley and Los Angeles: University of California Press, 1993), 136–37.

4 Janet Wasko, *Hollywood in the Information Age* (Austin: University of Texas Press, 1994), 249.

5 Marcia Landy, *The Folklore of Consensus: Theatricality in the Italian Cinema, 1930–1943* (Albany: State University of New York Press, 1998), xii.

6 These titles are available through the mail from Giovanni's Room, a queer bookstore in Philadelphia; their lesbian list includes 132 titles. Wolfe Video and Naiad Press (discussed in the previous chapter) are also major distributors of queer video to the home market.

7 Timothy Murray, *Like a Film: Ideological Fantasy on Screen, Camera, and Canvas* (New York: Routledge, 1993), 18–19.

8 Biddy Martin, "Sexual Practice and Changing Lesbian Identities," in her volume *Femininity Played Straight: The Significance of Being Lesbian* (New York: Routledge, 1996), 115.

9 Gayle Rubin, "The Traffic in Women: Notes on the 'Political Economy' of Sex," in *Toward an Anthropology of Women*, edited by Rayna R. Reiter (New York: Monthly Review Press, 1975).

10 Judith Butler, "Imitation and Gender Insubordination," in *The Lesbian and Gay Studies Reader*, edited by Henry Abelove, Michèle Aina Barale, and David M. Halperin (New York: Routledge, 1993), 309.

11 Ibid.

12 Linda Ruth Williams makes a similar argument regarding lesbianism and the complexity of female response to straight-to-video erotic thrillers in "Sisters Under the Skin: Video and Blockbuster Erotic Thrillers," in *Women and Film: A Sight and Sound Reader*, edited by Pam Cook and Philip Dodd (Philadelphia, Penn.: Temple University Press, 1993), 105–14.

Amy Villarejo is Associate Professor in the Department
of Theatre, Film, and Dance and the Feminist, Gender,
and Sexuality Studies Program at Cornell University.
She coauthored (with Marcia Landy) *Queen Christina*
(1995) and coedited (with Matthew Tinkcom) *Keyframes:
Popular Cinema and Cultural Studies* (2001).

Library of Congress Cataloging-in-Publication Data
Villarejo, Amy.
Lesbian rule : cultural criticism and the value of desire /
Amy Villarejo.
p. cm. — (Next wave)
Includes index.
ISBN 0-8223-3155-1 (cloth : alk. paper)
ISBN 0-8223-3192-6 (pbk. : alk. paper)
1. Lesbianism—Philosophy.   2. Lesbians—Identity.
3. Lesbian feminist theory.   4. Marxist criticism.
5. Culture—Semiotic models.   I. Title.   II. Series.
HQ75.5.V55   2003
306.76′63′01—dc21   2003005955